A Tree is Lighted

by
ELLEN DAVIES-RODGERS

With Illustrations

Published by
The Plantation Press
Brunswick
Memphis, Tennessee 38134

©Copyright 1984
by
E. Davies-Rodgers

All Rights Reserved.
Printed in the United States of America

Library of Congress
Catalog Card Number: 84-90673

Third Edition

Manufactured by
Brandau, Craig, Dickerson Co.
Nashville, Tennessee

Illustrations

Christmas Tree, Davies Plantation
   by Britt Woodward 1983

Gillie Mertis Davies 1891

Frances Ina Stewart Davies 1891

Hillman Philip Rodgers 1932

Frances Ellen Davies Rodgers 1932

Twenty Fifth Wedding Anniversary
  (Cutting Cake at Reception,
    Davies Manor) 1957

Twenty Fifth Wedding Anniversary
  (On Steps, Davies Manor) 1957

Davies Manor (Snow) 1961

Davies Plantation Christmas Tree
  (The Oaks in background) 1961

Lighted Living Tree
  (Plantation Family Picture,
    Press Scimitar) 12/12/1961

Lighting the Tree 1983
    Jerry Winstead

Dedicated
to
Elba
In Loving Memory
and
In Affectionate Honor
to
Alfred

Christmas Tree

"I'll find me a spruce
in the cold white wood
with wide green boughs
and a snowy hood.

I'll pin on a star
with five gold spurs
to mark my spruce
from the pines and firs.

I'll make me a score
of suet balls
to tie to my spruce
when the cold dusk falls,

And I'll hear next day
from the sheltering trees
the Christmas carols
of the chickadees."

Aileen Fisher
"Treasury of Christmas Stories"

Christmas Tree, 1983
The Oaks, Davies Plantation
Photography by Britt Woodward

"Everywhere, everywhere, Christmas tonight!
Christmas in lands of the fir-tree and pine,
Christmas in lands of the palm-tree and vine;
Christmas where snow-peaks stand solemn and white,
Christmas where corn-fields lie sunny and bright."

A Christmas Carol, Stanza 1
Phillips Brooks
(1835-1893)

A Tree is Lighted

To the woods of Davies Plantation Mose Fraser, Lawrence Herron and Richard Stevens, loyal, faithful helpers went with spades in hand. Their mission had been thoroughly prescribed. Their task was to carefully dig a well-shaped small native, red cedar tree and encase the roots with a ball of dirt in a burlap sack.

The four-foot tree was brought to the house, placed in a large metal tub, set in the parlor and decorated. Strings of popcorn and cranberries and cherished antique ornaments were used to adorn this symbol of Christmas cheer.

Little did anyone foresee the new role of the small tree as a significant annual reminder of the Advent season. Nor was it prophesied that the tree would find a conspicuous place in the Yule time history of the Plantation and of the surrounding community of Brunswick, Shelby County, Tennessee. No one at the time conceived the pending heritage of the small tree.

The Christmas season of 1933 had come to a close and Epiphany had arrived. Decorations were removed from the tree. It was carried by the same three helpers to the wooded, spacious yard in front of the home, "The Oaks". There a hole of appropriate size was dug. The tree was carefully lifted from the tub and planted in its new environment surrounded by other trees, giant oaks—white, red, post—tall cedars, persimmon, hickory and magnolia. There the small tree made its new place of abode having experienced a festive first Christmas.

The tree grew to be thickly fronded—tall and stately.

Strings of outdoor lights were purchased each year as additional strings were needed. After twenty years the tree had grown so tall that the service of an electrician was necessary to install the decorations. The event could no longer be accomplished by family and plantation help. The project had outgrown the amateurs! B. H. Priddy, expert electrician and friend, took over the project, with pride, and created a beautiful Christmas tree. For several years there had been an expressed desire to crown the tree with a star! However, this had not been done.

Because of the timeliness of the record printed in a local newspaper of the marriage of Gillie Mertis Davies and Frances Ina Stewart on June 15, 1891 a copy of the account is inserted here:

> "On Monday evening last at 4 p.m. Mr. Gillie M. Davies and Miss Ina Stewart were united in the holy bonds of wedlock at the home of the bride, the Rev. J. D. Hunter officiating. An hour before the ceremony the guests began to assemble, and in a short time standing room was at a premium, and many were unable to gain admittance to witness the ceremony. The parlors were richly decorated and tastefully festooned with evergreens and lovely June roses. Mr. Davies has been for several years one of our most prominent and successful business men, and stands without reproach in the community. Miss Ina is known to all, having been raised in our town. She has been one of the leaders in society here ever since she was grown, and one of the handsomest and most highly accomplished young ladies in our midst. They have been known to be lovers for some time, and being so suitably mated they have pleased their friends in suiting themselves. Immediately after the ceremony an elegant repast was served, and

Frances Ina Stewart Davies
1891

Gillie Mertis Davies
1891

toasts were numerous by the many friends of the happy couple."

On Thanksgiving Day 1958, Frances Ina Stewart (Mrs. Gillie M.) Davies, died. The Commercial Appeal, November 28, 1958 printed the following account under the caption:

"Mrs. G. M. Davies Dies at Age 95. Services Will Be Tomorrow At Plantation Home. Resident of Brunswick." "Mrs. Gillie M. Davies, a member of one of Shelby County's oldest and most widely known families, died at 2:34 yesterday afternoon at her home on Davies Plantation in Brunswick, She was 95. Services will be at 10:30 tomorrow morning at the home with Dr. Donald Henning, Rector of Calvary Episcopal Church, and the Right Rev. Theodore Barth, Bishop of the Episcopal Diocese of Tennessee, officiating. Burial will be in Pleasant Hill Cemetery at Brunswick with National Funeral Home in charge. Mrs. Davies had lived in Brunswick all her life and died in the home she had occupied since she was a bride. Mr. Davies, a farmer and merchant, died in 1933. She, her daughter and son-in-law, Mr. and Mrs. Hillman P. Rodgers lived together. Mrs. Davies was the daughter of James Rufus Stewart and Ellen Jane Thomas Stewart. For four years after her marriage in 1891, she and Mr. Davies lived in historic Davies Manor. In 1895 the young couple built their own home, taking the plantation commissary as a start. It was put on rollers and pulled a half-mile by oxen and the home was built around it. Mrs. Davies had a lively interest in American history and was an organizing member of the Zachariah Davies Chapter of the Daughters of the American Revolution. Within the past year she had become a member of the

Frances Ellen Davies Rodgers
1932

Hillman Philip Rodgers
1932

Davies Manor
1961

Daughters of the American Colonists. She could trace her ancestry to several of the oldest families of North Carolina and Virginia. At 95 she maintained an acute interest in things and people around her, especially young people. But she was five years short of her goal of living a century. She was stricken with pneumonia on March 5 and had been in failing health since then. Mrs. Davies was also a charter member of the Brunswick Garden Club and an honorary member of the women's auxiliary of the Brunswick and Morning Sun Cumberland Presbyterian Churches. In addition to her own daughter, Mrs. Rodgers, she had reared five foster children, the late William Saxton Gandy and his four daughters. They made their home with her. They are Miss Sarah B Gandy, Miss Frances Gandy and Miss Elba Gandy of Davies Plantation and Mrs. Burnell Dwight Hardee of Gueydan, La. The family asks that no flowers be sent. Those wishing to make memorial gifts may send them to the memorial fund of the Zachariah Davies Chapter of the DAR or the Pleasant Hill Cemetery Chapel Fund."

As the time of this great grief was so close to the Christmas season consideration was given to the thought of not decorating the tree that year. The question, "Shall the Tree Be Lighted," was discussed by the family with the decision that she would not want the tradition of twenty-five years to be broken. So, it was decided to place a large star, electrically lighted, on top of the tree in memory of her, co-founder of "The Oaks" in 1895. By the gentleman electrician the star lighting was most effectively accomplished.

That year a contest of Christmas tree lighting was promoted in Shelby County. Word got around about the tree at Davies Plantation with its star on top! One night

Twenty-fifth Wedding Anniversary Reception
Davies Manor
December 21, 1957

On the steps, Davies Manor

Ina Marie Hardee wearing dress and hat worn by her mother, Mary Gandy Hardee in the wedding of Miss Davies and Mr. Rodgers. Ina Marie Hardee married Farrell J. Woods on September 6, 1969. They are the parents of Peter Woods (7), Sara Woods (6) and Seth Woods (3).

Lighting the Tree, 1983
Jerry Winstead

Through the years numerous pictures of the Tree have been made. A number of articles concerning the Tree have been written. Among these accounts one of the most covering appeared in the Memphis Press-Scimitar in December 1961. The article was written by Katheryne E. (Mrs. L. E.) Dickey, Garden Editor. The well written story is carried in this account and a copy of the picture which accompanied the article is also included.

"Press-Scimitar Garden News, December 21, 1961

"LIGHTED LIVING TREE AT BRUNSWICK CAN BE SEEN FOR MILES AROUND

"In a setting of hollies, red cedars and tall oak trees, there stands a magnificent specimen juniper tree in the front yard of the Georgian Colonial home of Mr. and Mrs. Hillman P. Rodgers of Davies Plantation Road at Brunswick, Tennessee.

"This particular juniper (red cedar) is a very special tree. Twenty-eight years ago today, December 21, it was dug from the woods of the 2000-acre plantation and brought into the house to have the honor of being "the first Christmas Tree" of Mr. and Mrs. Rodgers, who were celebrating their first wedding anniversary.

"The little four-foot tree, after spending the Christmas season in a tub in the parlor and decorated with cranberries, popcorn and ornaments, was planted in the yard where it stands today as a living symbol of the "Spirit of Christmas." It brings happy memories of each passing year.

"This living tree is beautifully shaped with its branches hugging the ground. The tree is decorated each year with hundreds of lights in many colors. It makes a living outdoor picture

Ellen Davies-Rodgers, Elba Gandy, Michael Coleman, Mose Frazer, Hillman Philip Rodgers, Dickie Land, "Sir Top", the Family Dog
(Plantation Family Picture, Press-Scimitar, 12/21/61)

and a contribution to the little community of Brunswick, where it can be seen from miles away. Those driving thru the plantation, on the long meandering road leading from the Old Stage Coach Road (Hwy. 64), will pass historic Davies Manor, where lights will flood the two-story plantation house. There are large plantings of heavily fruited pyracanthas with deep red berries. The lighting will have special significance this year at the 150-year old home on Christmas Eve, as it commemorates the birth of Mrs. Rodgers' father, the late Gillie Mertis Davies. It was in this house that the late Mr. Davies was born on Christmas Day 1861. Only a half a mile on, you come to the "lighted tree", where you have a closer view of its stately beauty. It is seemingly nestled among the trees from a distance, yet it stands majestically alone, and towers above many others.

"On Christmas Eve, the old plantation bell, as it has for these many years, will ring out a "Merry Christmas" to the families on the plantation, calling them to gather around the brightly lighted Christmas tree on the front lawn to receive Christmas gifts and baskets from "Miss Ellen and Mr. Hill" as they are known to them. The Tree is now more than 50 feet tall.

"This native tree has been cared for over the years, by heavy mulching of the oak leaves that fall around it. It is one of the best evergreen trees for both a hedge and as a specimen, but unless there is space it must be controlled, because of its matured size.

"Lights on the Davies Plantation will be turned on at sunset and will burn until 10 o'clock each night during the Christmas season. The

Davies Plantation Christmas Tree
1961
(The Oaks in background)
Photography by Nadia

family invites you to drive thru the plantation entering Davies Plantation Road from Highway 64 or from Brunswick Road.

"Mr. and Mrs. Rodgers have four foster daughters, Misses Sarah B, Frances and Elba Gandy of Brunswick and Memphis and Mrs. Burnell Dwight Hardee of Gueydan, La. Mrs. Hardee with her husband and four children, Ina, 10, Dwight, 8, Richard, 4, and Larry, 2, will come from Gueydan to spend the holidays at Davies Plantation, to enjoy the living Christmas Tree that has meant so much to them every year."

The Commercial Appeal in December 1983 carried a picture of Mr. Winstead, Mr. Walls and the hydraulic bucket and the Tree.

It is difficult indeed to conclude a sketch of this type concerning a subject of such interest and magnitude—a living Tree which in fifty years has become a symbol of the Spirit of Christmas to many people. There are many passages in literature which give significance to trees and their contributions to mankind.

From the Holy Bible these passages are quoted:

Genesis 2:9 "And out of the ground made the Lord God to grow every tree that is pleasant to the sight, and good for food; the tree of life also in the midst of the garden, and the tree of knowledge of good and evil."

Psalms 1:3 "And he shall be like a tree planted by the rivers of water, that bringeth forth his fruit in his season; his leaf also shall not wither; and whatsoever he doeth shall prosper."

Psalms 104:16 "The trees of the Lord are full of sap; the cedars of Lebanon which he hath planted."

Revelation 22:2 "In the midst of the street of it, and on either side of the river was there the tree of life, which bare twelve manner of fruits, and yielded her fruit every month: and the leaves of the tree were for the healing of the nations."

The beautiful folk-song, "O Christmas Tree" (O Tannenbaum) first appeared in Germany in 1799. The melody was used for a song in Latin, "Lawiger Horatius." In America the tune is best known as "Maryland My Maryland." The song remains a great favorite with the German people. The words have been translated from German to an English version by Ruth Heller.

"O Christmas Tree, O Christmas tree
O tree of green unchanging
Your boughs so green in summer time,
Do brave the snow of winter time.
O Christmas tree, O Christmas tree,
O tree of green unchanging.

'O Christmas tree, O Christmas tree,
You set my heart a-swinging
Like little stars your candles bright
Send to the world a wonderous light.
Send to the world a wonderous light.

'O Christmas tree, O Christmas tree
You come from God eternal
A symbol of the Lord of Love
Whom, God to man sent from above.
Whom, God to man sent from above.

'O Christmas tree, O Christmas tree
You speak of God unchanging
You tell us all to faithful be,
And trust in God eternally.
O Christmas tree, O Christmas tree,
You speak of God, unchanging."

*So, take the message
and may it be
 Filled with Christmas
joy to thee!*

"For somehow, not only at Christmas,
    but all the long year through,
The joy that you give to others
    is the joy that comes back to you."
John Greenleaf Whittier

"And Plant your Christmas trees about
All decked with colors gay,
That strangers may the spirit feel,
Who pass along the way."
Agnes Davenport Bond

"Our souls are like the sparrows
    Imprisoned in the clay;
    Bless Him who came to give them
    wings,
Upon a Christmas Day."
A Jewish Legend: The Clay Sparrows,
Stanza 10

BOOKS WRITTEN BY
ELLEN DAVIES-RODGERS

THE ROMANCE OF THE EPISCOPAL CHURCH IN WEST TENNESSEE, 1964 ($12.00)

THE HOLY INNOCENTS, 1966 ($12.00)

EDUCATION—THEN, NOW AND YON, 1971 ($5.00)

THE GREAT BOOK, CALVARY PROTESTANT EPISCOPAL CHURCH, 1832-1972, MEMPHIS, TENNESSEE 1973 ($30.00)

HEIRS THROUGH HOPE. The Episcopal Diocese of West Tennessee 1983 ($30.00)

A TREE IS LIGHTED, 1984 ($10.00)

HISTORY OF SHELBY CHAPTER, NS., SONS OF THE AMERICAN REVOLUTION, BRUNSWICK, TENNESSEE, 1988 ($10.00)

ON WINGS OF FAITH, 1989 ($15.00)

ALONG THE OLD STAGE-COACH ROAD, MORNING SUN AND BRUNSWICK, SHELBY COUNTY, TENNESSEE, 1990 ($30.00)

THE PLANTATION PRESS
DAVIES PLANTATION ROAD
(BRUNSWICK)
MEMPHIS, TENNESSEE 38134

AMERICAN GRAIN TRIMMERS INCORPORATED
309-310 Board of Trade Building
Duluth 2, Minnesota

Robert P. Fisher

GABRIEL AERO-MARINE INSTRUMENTS LTD
351 St. Paul West
MONTREAL, P. Q.
AND AT
HALIFAX & SYDNEY, N. S.
ST. JOHN, N. B.

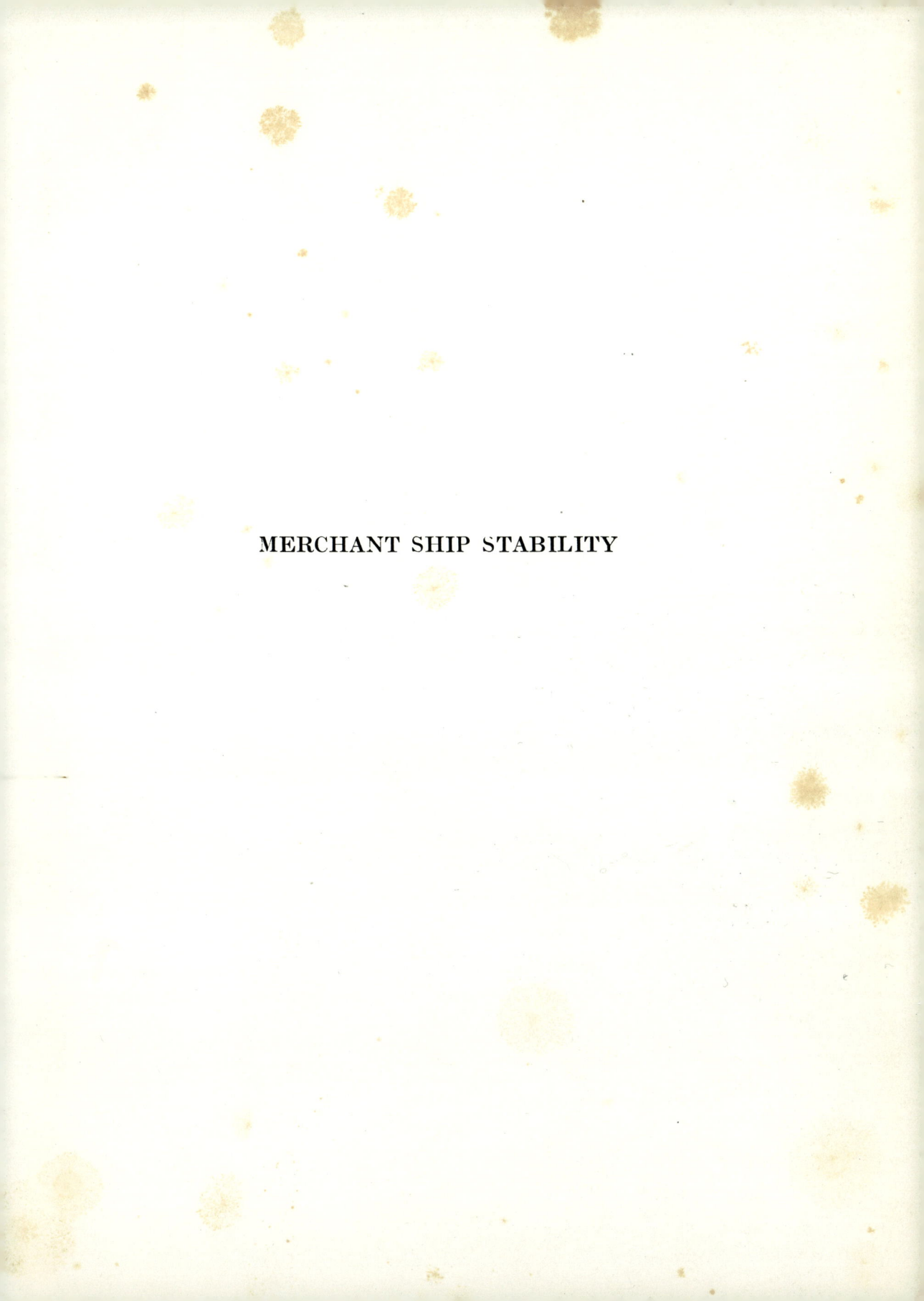

MERCHANT SHIP STABILITY

MERCHANT SHIP STABILITY

A companion to "Merchant Ship Construction"

BY

H. J. PURSEY

EXTRA MASTER

*Lecturer to the Department of Navigation
University College, Southampton*

GLASGOW
BROWN, SON & FERGUSON, Ltd., NAUTICAL PUBLISHERS
52 DARNLEY STREET

Copyright in all countries signatory to the Berne Convention.
All rights reserved.

First Edition 1945
Second Edition 1954
Reprinted - 1957

© 1960 BROWN SON & FERGUSON, LTD., GLASGOW, S.I.
Made and Printed in Great Britain

INTRODUCTION.

THE stability of ships is not a matter for Naval Architects only. Their work is completed once a vessel has been built and thereafter her stability comes under the care of her Master and Officers. Unfortunately, quite a number of the latter have the idea that a properly designed ship cannot come to much harm unless she is allowed to become unstable; in which case, as they think, she is bound to capsize. The fact that these ideas are wrong merely serves to illustrate how important it is that seamen should have a thorough knowledge of the underlying principles of stability. Ignorance of the subject has, undoubtedly, caused the loss of more than one ship and damage to many others.

Young Officers often ask why they are expected to study the stability of box-shapes for ordinary grade Certificates of Competency. Many seamen can tell stories of ships that looked like boxes and behaved like swine; but why study them? The answer is that the behaviour of box-shapes is very closely allied to that of ship shapes. If we can understand the behaviour of the former, and the reasons for it, it is easy to follow that of the latter. Since the mathematics of ship shapes is rather difficult for the average ship's officer, he is thus enabled to understand things which he could not otherwise follow.

What of the applied mathematics necessary for the study of the stability of box-shapes? These are not always easy for Officers. The second and third chapters of this book have been especially written to cover such mensuration and mechanics as are required for an understanding of the chapters which follow. They have been made as simple and as clear as possible, so that the student who reads them carefully, before beginning to study stability proper, should save himself many troubles later on.

The main body of the book is designed to cover the theory of the subject up to, and including, the standard required for a Master's Certificate. This has been carefully linked-up with the practice, since the connection between the two is one of the most common stumbling blocks for ship's officers. A separate chapter is devoted to the rolling of ships in order that those who are interested may be able to gather some knowledge of this important subject. The construction and uses of stability curves and scales, which are described in chapter fifteen, are very important in practice: also, candidates for Certificates should remember that they are expected to understand these and to be able to answer questions about them, if asked. Finally, a summary of abbreviations, formulae and definitions is included, since a quick reference is often useful.

The Author has given particular attention to those matters which are commonly misunderstood, or not appreciated, by ship's Officers and hopes that this book will help to make the subject more understandable for those who read it.

H. J. P.

UNIVERSITY COLLEGE,
   SOUTHAMPTON, 1945.

CONTENTS.

CHAPTER 1.—SOME GENERAL INFORMATION.

	PAGE
Water	1
Density	1
Specific Gravity	1
Increase of pressure with depth	1
The Law of Archimedes	2
Why a ship floats	4
Floating bodies and the density of water	4
Ship dimensions	4
Decks	5
Ship tonnages	5
Grain and bale measurement	5
Displacement and deadweight	5
Draft	6
Freeboard	6
The effect of density on the draft of ships	6
Loadlines	7

CHAPTER 2.—AREAS AND VOLUMES.

Areas of common plane figures	9
Surface areas and volumes	9
Areas of waterplanes and other ship-sections	10
The Trapezoidal Rule	11
Simpson's Rules	12
The "Five-Eight Rule"	14
Sharp ended waterplanes	14
Volumes of ship shapes	14
Coefficients of fineness	15
Wetted surface	16

CHAPTER 3.—FORCES AND MOMENTS.

Force	18
Resultant forces	18
Moments	19
Properties of a moment	20
Combinations of Moments	20
Centre of gravity	21
Effect on centre of gravity of added weights	24
Effect on centre of gravity of removing weights	25
Effect on centre of gravity of shifting weights	26
Inertia	26
Moment of inertia and radius of gyration	26
Moment of inertia of a body about its centre line	28
Moment of inertia of a waterplane about its centre line	28
Equilibrium	29

vii

CONTENTS

CHAPTER 4.—CENTRE OF GRAVITY OF SHIPS.

	PAGE
Centre of gravity of a ship—G	30
KG	30
Light KG	30
Shift of G	30
KG for any condition of loading	31
Real and virtual centres of gravity	32
Effect of tanks on G	33

CHAPTER 5.—CENTRES OF BUOYANCY AND FLOTATION.

Centre of Buoyancy—B	35
KB	35
Centre of Flotation—F	35
Shift of B	36
Horizontal and vertical components of the shift of B	37

CHAPTER 6.—THE RIGHTING LEVER AND METACENTRE.

Equilibrium of ships	39
The righting lever—GZ	41
The metacentre—M	41
Metacentric height—GM	41
Stable, unstable and neutral equilibrium	42
Longitudinal metacentric height—GM_L	42

CHAPTER 7.—TRANSVERSE STATICAL STABILITY.

Moment of statical stability	43
Relation between GM and GZ	43
Initial stability and range of stability	43
Factors affecting statical stability	44
Stiff and tender ships	46
Angle of loll, or list	46
The effect of free surface of liquids	46

CHAPTER 8.—TRANSVERSE STATICAL STABILITY—FORMULAE AND PROOFS.

Calculation of a ship's stability	48
KB	48
The Inclining Experiment	48
Calculation of BM for box shapes	50
Calculation of BM for all shapes	52
Approximate formula for BM	52
Statical stability at small angles of heel	53
Statical stability at any angle of heel	53
GZ by the "Wall Sided Formula"	54
Angle of loll	55
The effect of free surface of liquids	56

CHAPTER 9.—TRANSVERSE STATICAL STABILITY IN PRACTICE.

Placing of weights	60
The effect of "winging out" weights	61
Ships in Ballast	61
Stiff ships	61

CONTENTS

	PAGE
Tender ships ..	62
Unstable ships ..	62
Deck Cargoes..	64
Timber deck cargoes ..	64
Free liquid in tanks ..	65
Free surface effect in oil-tankers	66

CHAPTER 10.—DYNAMICAL STABILITY.

Definition	67
Work	67
Dynamical stability	67
Dynamical stability from a curve of statical stability	67
Calculation of dynamical stability	68
Moseley's Formula	69
Notes	70

CHAPTER 11.—LONGITUDINAL STABILITY.

Recapitulation	71
Trim	71
Inch trim moment	71
Tons per inch immersion	72
Change of draft due to change of trim	72
Change of mean draft due to change of trim	72
The effect of shifting a weight	73
The effect of adding a weight at the centre of flotation.	74
The effect of adding a weight away from the centre of flotation ..	75
Loading weights to obtain a desired trim	75
The effect of removing weights	75
The effect of bilging a compartment	76

CHAPTER 12.—LONGITUDINAL STABILITY—FORMULAE AND PROOFS.

Longitudinal metacentric height—GM_L ..	77
Calculation of BM_L ..	77
Ton per inch immersion—T.P.I.	78
Inch trim moment—I.T.M.	79
Approximate formulae for I.T.M.	80
Change of draft due to change of trim	80
Change of trim due to weights shifted ..	80
Change of draft through loading weights at the centre of flotation	82
Moderate weights loaded off the centre of flotation	82
Large weights loaded off the centre of flotation ..	82
A rough approximation	83
Loading a weight to produce a desired trim	83
Position to load a weight so as not to change the draft aft	84
Increase of draft due to bilging a compartment	85

CHAPTER 13.—ROLLING.

The formation of waves	86
The Trochoidal Theory	86
The true period of waves	87
The apparent period of waves ..	87
The period of a ship ..	87

CONTENTS

	PAGE
Synchronism ..	87
Unresisted rolling	88
Resistances to rolling ..	88
The effects of bilge keels	89
Cures for heavy rolling	89

CHAPTER 14.—MISCELLANEOUS MATTERS.

Drydocking ..	90
Grounding	92
The effect of density on stability	92
The effect of density on the draft of ships	92
Derivation of the fresh water allowance	93
Reserve buoyancy	93
Continuous watertight longitudinal bulkheads	93
Non-continuous longitudinal bulkheads ..	94
Bulkhead subdivision and sheer	94
Pressure on bulkheads	95
The effect of water in sounding pipes, etc.	95

CHAPTER 15.—STABILITY CURVES AND SCALES.

Information supplied to ships	96
Curves of displacement, etc.	96
Use of the curves	98
The deadweight scale ..	98
Use of the deadweight scale	98
Curves of statical stability	99
Cross curves ..	100
Effect of height of G	102
The metacentric diagram	102
Worked Examples	104
Problems and Answers	122
Summary	147
Displacement Curves and Deadweight Scale	Insert in back of book

MERCHANT SHIP STABILITY.

CHAPTER I.

SOME GENERAL INFORMATION.

Water.—The following quantities are usually taken for purposes of stability, unless otherwise stated:—

	Fresh water.	Salt water.
Density	1,000	1,025
Specific Gravity	1·000	1·025
Weight per cubic foot	62·5 lbs.	64 lbs.
Gallons per cubic foot	6·25	6·25
Weight per gallon	10·0 lbs.	10·25 lbs.
Cubic feet per ton	36	35

Density.—This is usually defined as "mass per unit volume". For stability purposes, it can be regarded as the weight in ounces of one cubic foot of a substance.

Specific Gravity.—This is the ratio between the density of a substance and the density of fresh water.

$$\text{Specific gravity of a substance} = \frac{\text{density of the substance}}{\text{density of fresh water}}$$

Since the density of fresh water is 1,000, this becomes:—

$$\text{Specific gravity of a substance} = \frac{\text{density of the substance}}{1,000}$$

Thus, if one cubic foot of steel weighs 7,820 ounces, its density will be 7,820 and its specific gravity 7·820.

Increase of Pressure with Depth.—The pressure on an object which is placed under water is equal to the weight of the column of water above it.

Consider Fig. 1, which represents a column of sea water having an area of one square foot. Let A, B, C, D, E and F be points one foot apart vertically. The volume of water above B is one cubic foot; above C, two cubic feet; above D, three cubic feet; and so on. Sea water weighs approximately 64 lbs. per cubic foot, so the weight above B will be 64 lbs.; above C, twice 64 lbs.; above D, three times 64 lbs; and so on. We can see from this that if point A is at the sea surface, the pressure per square foot at a depth of, say, AF, will be $AF \times 64$ lbs.

FIG. 1

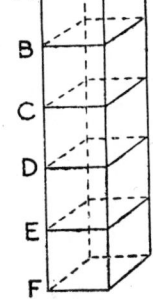

From the above, it is obvious that the pressure at any depth, in pounds per square foot, is equal to 64 times the depth in feet. Since water exerts pressure equally in all directions, this pressure will be the same horizontally, vertically, or obliquely. We can say, then, that if a horizontal surface of area A square feet is placed at a depth of D feet below the surface, then:

$$\text{Pressure per square foot} = 64D \text{ lbs.}$$
$$\text{Total pressure on the area} = 64AD \text{ lbs.}$$

The Law of Archimedes.—A body immersed in a liquid appears to suffer a loss in weight equal to the weight of liquid which it displaces. From this, we conclude that a floating body displaces its own weight of water. This can be shewn as follows:—

A block of iron, one cubic foot in size and of density 8,000, weighs 8,000 ounces in air. If it is placed in fresh water, it displaces one cubic foot of the water and this weighs 1,000 ounces. By the Law of Archimedes, the block will appear to suffer a loss in weight of 1,000 ounces, so that its weight under water will be 7,000 ounces. (Fig. 2A).

Let the block now be taken out of the water and made into a hollow sealed box, having a volume of two cubic feet. If this box is thrown back into the water, it will now displace two cubic feet and will appear to lose 2,000 ounces. Since its weight in air was 8,000 ounces, its weight under water will be 6,000 ounces. (Fig 2B.)

The box can be made larger and larger and each time its size is increased by one cubic foot, its weight under water will decrease by a further 2,000 ounces. When its volume becomes eight cubic feet, its loss in weight will be 8,000 ounces, the same as its weight in air. It will now appear to have no weight under water and in theory will remain in any position in which it is placed, so long as it is beneath the surface. (Fig 2c).

Suppose that the process is carried still further and that the volume of the box is increased to ten cubic feet. If it is pressed down under the water, it will displace 10,000 ounces, whilst its actual weight is only 8,000 ounces. Consequently, it tries to move upwards with a force of 2,000 ounces and will not stay below the surface, unless held down. (Fig 2D).

Let the box in the last example be placed so that it is half in and half out of the water. It now displaces only 5,000 ounces of water, so will try to sink downwards with a force of 3,000 ounces. (Fig. 2E).

The box in the last two cases cannot freely remain in either of the positions mentioned. It must rise or sink, until the loss in weight due to the displaced water is equal to the weight of the box—that is, it must displace 8,000 ounces of water. It thus becomes a floating body, with eight cubic feet of its volume submerged. (Fig 2F).

SOME GENERAL INFORMATION

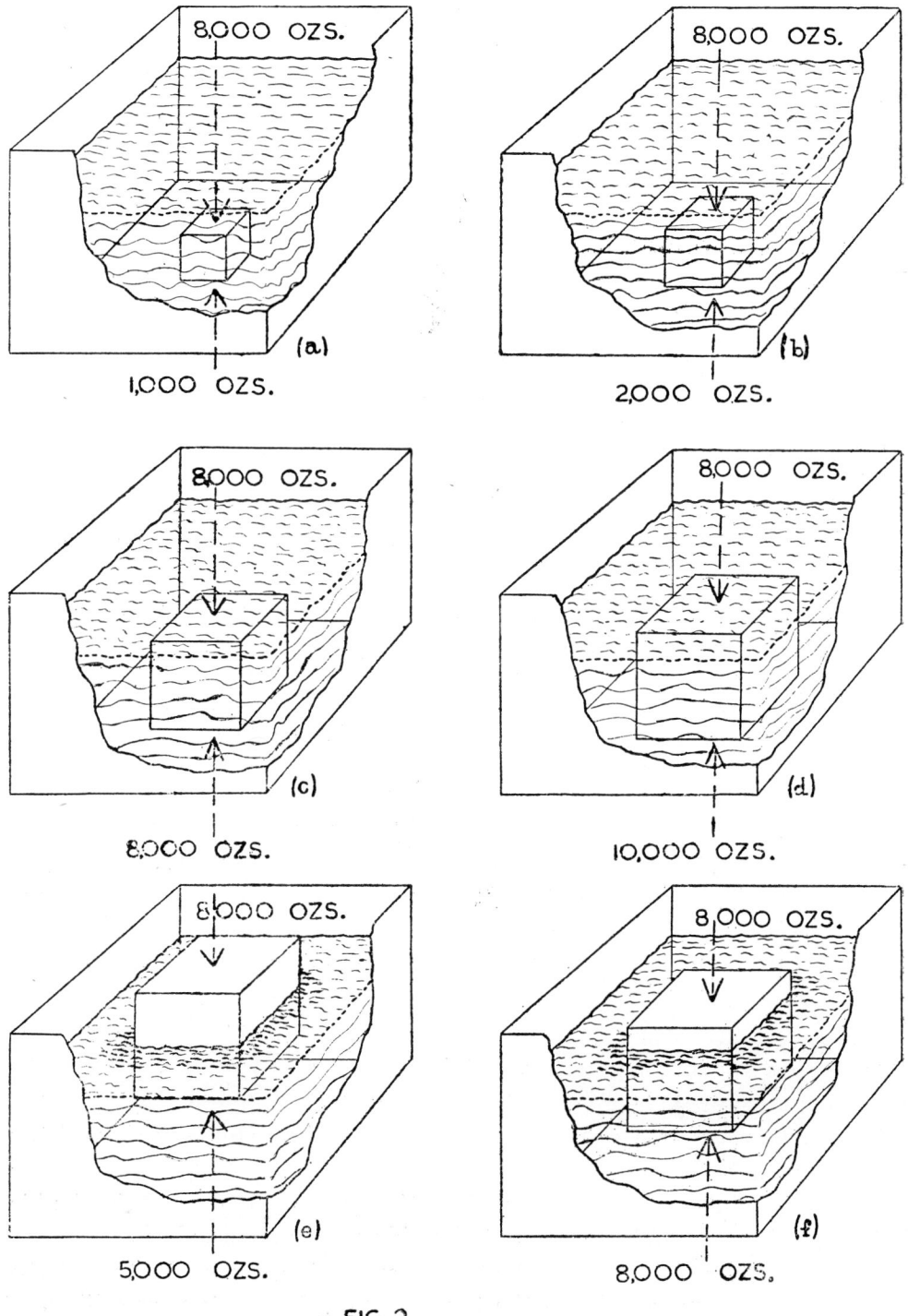

FIG. 2

Application to Ships.—A ship may be regarded as a closed iron box, so that two conclusions can be drawn from a study of the last section:—

(*a*) So long as the weight of the ship does not exceed the weight of its own volume of water, it will float.

(*b*) The draft at which it floats will be such that the weight of water displaced will be equal to the weight of the ship.

Floating Bodies and the Density of Water.—Weight is equal to volume multiplied by density and therefore volume is equal to weight divided by density. In the case of a floating body:—

$$\text{Volume of water displaced} = \frac{\text{Weight of water displaced}}{\text{Density of the water}}$$

The volume of water displaced is equal to the underwater volume of the body and since a floating body displaces its own weight of water, weight of the body can be substituted for weight of water displaced.

$$\text{Underwater volume} = \frac{\text{Weight of the body in ounces}}{\text{Density of the water}}$$

If the weight of the body remains the same, it can be seen that the underwater volume must vary inversely as the density of the water. In other words, if the density of the water changes:—

$$\frac{\text{New volume displaced}}{\text{Old volume displaced}} \quad \frac{\text{Old density}}{\text{New density}}$$

Ship Dimensions.—The following are the principal dimensions used in measuring ships.

Lloyd's Length is the length of the ship, measured from the fore side of the stem to the after side of the stern post at the summer load line. In ships with cruiser sterns, it is taken as 96 per cent of the length overal provided that this is not less than the above.

Moulded Breadth is the greatest breadth of the ship, measured from side to side outside the frames, but inside the shell plating.

Moulded Depth is measured vertically at the middle length of the ship, from the top of the keel to the top of the beams at the side of the uppermost continuous deck

The Framing Depth is measured vertically from the top of the double bottom to the top of the beams at the side of the lowest deck.

Depth of Hold is measured at the centre line, from the top of the beams at the tonnage deck to the top of the double bottom or ceiling.

SOME GENERAL INFORMATION

Decks.—The Freeboard Deck is the uppermost complete deck, having permanent means of closing all openings in its weather portion.

The Tonnage Deck is the upper deck in single decked ships and the second deck from below in all others.

Ship Tonnages.—These are not measures of weight, but of space, the word "ton" being used to indicate 100 cubic feet. For instance, if the gross tonnage of a ship is 5,000 tons, this does not mean that she weighs that amount, but that certain spaces in her measure 500,000 cubic feet.

Under Deck Tonnage is the volume of the ship below the tonnage deck. It does not include the cellular double bottom, unless this is used for cargo, stores, or fuel.

Gross Tonnage is under deck tonnage, plus spaces in the hull above the tonnage deck. It also includes permanently enclosed superstructures, with some exceptions, and any deck cargo that is on board.

Nett Tonnage is found by deducting certain percentages of the non-earning spaces in the ship (e.g. Engine rooms, crew spaces, etc.) from the gross tonnage.

Grain and Bale Measurement.—These terms are often found on the plans of ships and refer to the volume of the holds, etc.

Grain Measurement is the space in a compartment taken right out to the ship's side. In other words, it is the amount of space which would be available for a bulk cargo such as grain.

Bale Measurement is the space in a compartment measured to the inside of the spar ceiling, or, if this is not fitted, to the inside of the frames. It is the space which would be available for bales and similar cargoes.

Displacement.—Is the actual weight of the ship and all aboard her at any particular time. Since a floating body displaces its own weight of water, this means that displacement is equal to the weight of water displaced by the ship.

Light Displacement is that of the ship when she is at her designed light draft. It consists of the weight of the hull, machinery, spare parts and water in the boilers.

Loaded Displacement is that of a ship when she is floating at her summer draft.

Deadweight.—This is the weight of cargo, stores, bunkers, etc., on board a ship. In other words, it is the difference between the light displacement and the displacement at any particular draft. When we say that a ship is of so many tons deadweight, we usually mean that the difference between her light and loaded displacement is so many tons.

Draft.—This is the depth of the bottom of the ship's keel below the surface of the water. It is measured forward and aft at the extreme ends of the ship. When the drafts at each end are the same, the ship is said to be on an even keel. When they differ, the ship is said to be trimmed by the head, or by the stern, according to which is the greater of the two drafts.

Mean Draft is the mean of the drafts forward and aft.

Freeboard.—Statutory Freeboard is the distance from the deck line to the centre of the plimsoll mark. The term "Freeboard" is often taken to mean the distance from the deck-line to the water.

The Effect of Density on Draft.—We have already seen that the volume displaced by a floating body varies inversely as the density of the water. In the case of *box-shaped ships*, the volume displaced is equal to the product of length, breadth and draft; so we can say:—

$$\frac{\text{New volume displaced}}{\text{Old volume displaced}} = \frac{\text{Old density}}{\text{New density}}$$

$$\frac{\text{Length} \times \text{Breadth} \times \text{New Draft}}{\text{Length} \times \text{Breadth} \times \text{Old Draft}} = \frac{\text{Old density}}{\text{New density}}$$

$$\frac{\text{New Draft}}{\text{Old Draft}} = \frac{\text{Old density}}{\text{New density}}$$

Ship-shapes also increase their draft when the density of the water decreases and vice versa. The above does not hold good for them, however, as the change is not in proportion. The calculation of the change of draft for a change of density is, in this case, rather complicated and so a "fresh water allowance" is given to ships when they are assigned their load lines. This allowance is approximately the amount by which the ship will decrease her draft, on going from fresh water to salt water.

The ordinary load lines show the draft at which a ship can safely remain at sea. In the smooth water of a harbour or river, it would be quite safe to load her a little below these marks, provided that she rises to them when or before she reaches the open sea. A ship loading in a harbour of fresh water could submerge her load lines by the amount of her fresh water allowance, since she would rise to her proper load line on reaching salt water.

Ships often load in dock water which is brackish—that is, which has a density of more than 1,000 and less than 1,025. In this case, the amount by which the salt water load lines can be submerged is found from the fresh water allowance by simple proportion.

Let x equal the amount by which the load line can be submerged in water of density, D. Let F equal the fresh water allowance.

A change of density from 1,000 to 1,025 will produce a change of draft of F inches.

SOME GENERAL INFORMATION

A change of density from D to 1,025 will produce a change of draft of x inches.

We can assume, for practical purposes, that the change of draft is proportional to the change of density. Hence:—

$$\frac{x}{F} = \frac{1025 - D}{1025 - 1000}$$

$$x = \frac{F(1025 - D)}{25}$$

Note that where, as in this case, we are dealing with *change* of draft and density, these are directly proportional. In box shapes, when we are dealing with *actual* draft and density, they are inversely proportional.

Ordinary Load Lines.—The load lines and deck line must be painted in white or yellow on a dark background, or in black on a light background.

The deck line is placed amidships and is twelve inches long and one inch wide. Its upper edge marks the level at which the top of the freeboard deck, if continued outward, would cut the outside of the shell plating.

A load line disc, commonly called "the plimsoll mark", is placed below the deck line. The distance from the upper edge of the deck line to the centre of the disc is the statutory summer freeboard. Twenty-one inches forward of the disc are placed the load lines, which mark the drafts to which the ship may be loaded when at sea and in certain zones. All lines are one inch thick and their upper edges mark the level to which they refer. The following are the marks required for steam-ships:—

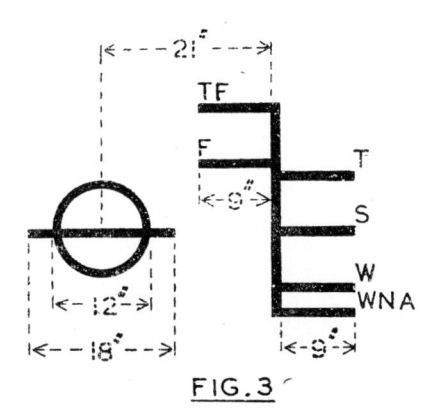

FIG. 3

S—the "summer load line"—is level with the centre of the disc.

W—the "winter load line"—is placed below the summer load line at a distance of $\frac{1}{4}''$ for every foot of summer draft.

T—the "tropical load line"—is placed above the summer load line at a distance of $\frac{1}{4}''$ per foot of summer draft.

WNA—the "winter North Atlantic load line". This is only marked on ships of under 330 feet in length, on all oil tankers and on certain special types of ships, including those marked with timber load lines. The allowance for oil tankers is one inch below the winter load line for every hundred feet of length. For the other types mentioned, it is two inches below the winter line, irrespective of the ship's length.

B

F—The "fresh water (summer) load line"—indicates the draft to which the ship can be loaded in fresh water, if she is to rise to her summer load line at sea. It is found by the formula $\frac{\triangle}{40T}$ where $\triangle$ equals the displacement at summer draft and *T* is the "tons per inch immersion" at that draft.

TF—The "tropical fresh water load line"—is the fresh water line to which the ship can be loaded, in order that she may come to her tropical mark when she reaches the sea. It is found as for *F*, but is measured above the tropical line.

Timber Load Lines.—These are marked-in abaft the load line disc. They show the drafts to which a ship so marked may load when carrying a deck cargo of timber, provided that the cargo is stowed according to special rules and to a certain minimum height.

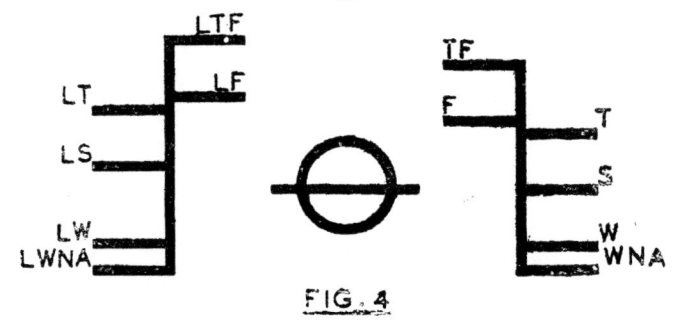

FIG. 4

LS—The "summer timber load line"—This is a little above the ordinary summer line. The distance is such that if a ship, loaded according to the regulations, lost her deck cargo, she would come back approximately to her ordinary summer load line.

LT—The "tropical timber load line"—is placed above the summer timber load line, at a distance of $\frac{1}{4}''$ per foot of summer draft.

LW—The "winter timber load line"—is placed below the summer timber line at a distance equal to $\frac{1}{3}''$ per foot of summer draft.

LWNA—The "winter North Atlantic timber load line"—is placed level with the ordinary *WNA* line.

LF—The "fresh water timber load line"—found by allowing the fresh water allowance above the *LS* line.

LTF—The "tropical fresh water timber load line"—found as above, but measured from the *LT* line.

CHAPTER II.

AREAS AND VOLUMES.

Areas of Plane Figures.—The areas of certain common plane figures are often used in stability calculations.

Square.—Where a is the length of each side:—
$$\text{Area} = a^2$$

Rectangle.—Where a and b are the lengths of the sides:—
$$\text{Area} = a \times b$$

Triangle.—Where a, b and c are the lengths of the respective sides; h the perpendicular height; and ϕ the angle between a and b:—
$$\text{Area} = \frac{bh}{2}$$
$$\text{Area} = \frac{ab \times \sin \phi}{2}$$
$$\text{Area} = \sqrt{s(s-a)(s-b)(s-c)}$$
where $s = \tfrac{1}{2}(a+b+c)$

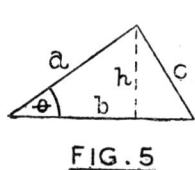

FIG. 5

Trapezoid.—This is a four-sided figure, having two of its sides parallel. Where a and b are the lengths of the parallel sides, and h the perpendicular distance between them:—
$$\text{Area} = \frac{h}{2}(a+b)$$

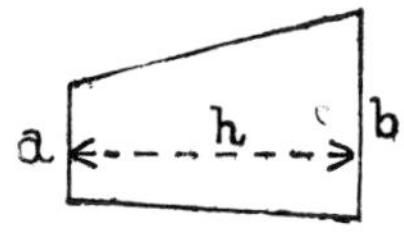

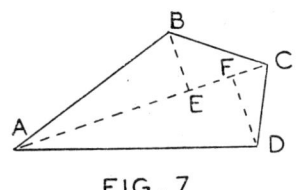

FIG. 6

Trapezium.—Is a four-sided figure, having none of its sides parallel. To find its area, draw a diagonal, AC. Drop the perpendiculars BE and DF on to AC and then find the sum of the areas of the triangles so formed.

FIG. 7

Circle.—Where r is the radius; and where π is equal to $3 \cdot 1416$, or approximately $\tfrac{22}{7}$:—
$$\text{Area} = \pi r^2$$
$$\text{Circumference} = 2\pi r$$

Surface Areas and Volumes.—The following are often useful:—

Cube.—Where a is the length of each edge:—
$$\text{Surface area} = 6a^2$$
$$\text{Volume} = a^3$$

Box-shapes.—Where a, b and l are the lengths of the edges:—
$$\text{Surface area} = 2(al + bl + ab)$$
$$\text{Volume} = abl$$

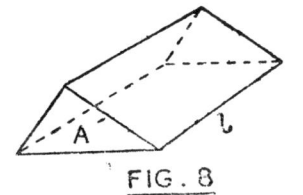

Wedges and prisms.—Where A is the area of either end and l the length:—
$$\text{Volume} = Al$$

FIG. 8

Sphere.—Where r is the radius:—
$$\text{Surface area} = 4\pi r^2$$
$$\text{Volume} = \frac{4\pi r^3}{3}$$

Hollow Sphere.—Where r is the internal radius and R the external radius:—
$$\text{Volume of material} = \frac{4\pi R^3}{3} - \frac{4\pi r^3}{3}$$
$$= \frac{4\pi}{3}(R^3 - r^3)$$

Cylinder.—Where r is the radius and l the length:—
$$\text{Surface area} = 2\pi r(r + l)$$
$$\text{Volume} = \pi r^2 l$$

Hollow round section.—Where R is the external radius, r the internal radius and l the length:—
$$\text{Area of cross section} = \pi R^2 - \pi r^2$$
$$= \pi(R + r)(R - r)$$
$$\text{Volume of material} = \pi l(R + r)(R - r)$$

Areas of Waterplanes and Other Ship-Sections.—These cannot usually be found with any degree of accuracy by simple mensuration, but must be calculated by the "Trapezoidal Rule", or by "Simpson's Rules".

The trapezoidal rule is used largely on the Continent and in the United States of America. When this method is used, the area is divided up into a number of trapezoids and the sum of their areas is found. The area obtained by this method is usually a little too small and it requires very nice judgement to get reasonably accurate results.

Simpson's rules are used largely in this country. They are based on the assumption that the edges of ship-sections and waterplanes are parabolic curves. Although this is not strictly the case, the rules give very accurate results if they are properly used.

AREAS AND VOLUMES

The preliminary steps in calculating the area of a waterplane or section are the same for either of the methods mentioned above. A number of equidistant points are taken along the centre line and perpendiculars are dropped from these points to meet the curved sides. The lengths of these perpendiculars are measured and also the distance between them. The perpendiculars are called "Ordinates" and the distance between them, the "Common Interval". The latter is usually denoted in formulae as "h".

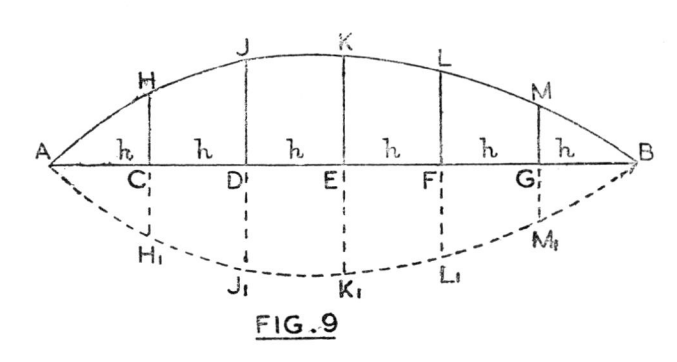

Figure 9 represents a waterplane. In this case, the centre line (AB) is divided into six parts, each having a length of h (the common interval). The ordinates are HH_1, JJ_1, KK_1, etc. A and B are also ordinates, although in this case they have no length.

It will be noticed that half of the figure has been drawn in plain lines and half in dotted lines. This is done because, when the rules are demonstrated, it is easier to prove them for half of the waterplane, although they hold good for either the half or the whole of it. The perpendicular distances shown in the plain lines (CH, DJ, EK, etc.) for the half-waterplane are usually called "Half Ordinates", in order to distinguish them.

The half ordinates, put through the rules, give the area of the half-waterplane; the ordinates will give the area of the whole waterplane, when put through the same rules.

The Trapezoidal Rule.—Suppose that we wish to find the area of the half-waterplane shewn in figure 10. Draw the half-ordinates, v, w, x and y, and let the common interval between them be h. Let the ends of the area be assumed to have a small length of u and z, respectively.

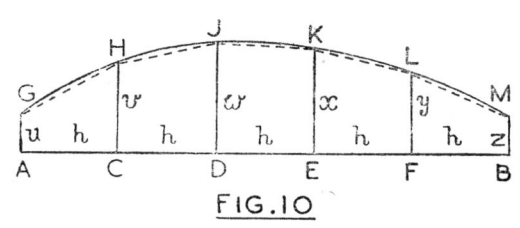

If we now join G, H, K, L and M by straight lines (shown dotted in the figure), the area within them will be very nearly equal to that of the waterplane. The amount of error will depend on the spacing of the half-ordinates and on the curvature of the side. Thus, if we find and add together the respective areas of the trapezoids $ACHG$, $CDJH$, - - - - $FBML$, we shall have a close approximation to the area of the waterplane.

$$\text{Area of trapezoid } ACHG = \frac{h}{2}(u+v)$$

$$\text{,, \quad ,, \quad } CDJH = \frac{h}{2}(v+w)$$

$$\text{,, \quad ,, \quad } DEKJ = \frac{h}{2}(w+x)$$

$$\text{,, \quad ,, \quad } EFLK = \frac{h}{2}(x+y)$$

$$\text{,, \quad ,, \quad } FBML = \frac{h}{2}(y+z)$$

$$\text{Total area} = \frac{h}{2}(u+v) + \frac{h}{2}(v+w) + \frac{h}{2}(w+x) + \frac{h}{2}(x+y) + \frac{h}{2}(y+z)$$

$$= \frac{h}{2}(u+2v+2w+2x+2y+z)$$

$$= h\left(\frac{u+z}{2} + v + w + x + y\right)$$

The rule is, therefore, that *the area is equal to half the sum of the ends, plus the sum of all the other ordinates, all multiplied by the common interval.*

Simpson's First Rule.—In its simplest form, this rule can be stated:— The area between any three consecutive ordinates is equal to the sum of the end ordinates, plus four times the middle ordinate, all multiplied by one third of the common interval.

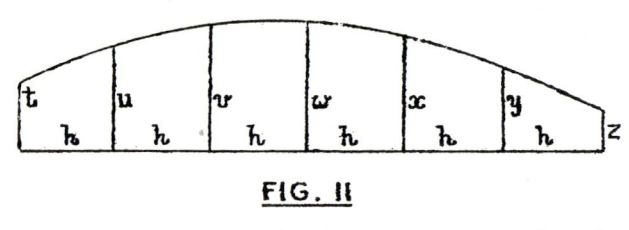

Consider in Fig. 11 the area contained between the half-ordinates t and v. If the common interval is h, this area equals:—

$$\frac{h}{3}(t + 4u + v)$$

FIG. 11

The total area of the half-waterplane can be obtained by finding, in the same way, the areas between v and x, and x and z, and taking the sum of the three.

$$\text{Area between } t \text{ and } v = \frac{h}{3}(t + 4u + v)$$

$$\text{,, \quad ,, \quad } v \text{ and } x = \frac{h}{3}(v + 4w + x)$$

$$\text{,, \quad ,, \quad } x \text{ and } z = \frac{h}{3}(x + 4y + z)$$

$$\text{Total area} = \frac{h}{3}(t + 4u + v) + \frac{h}{3}(v + 4w + x) + \frac{h}{3}(x + 4y + z)$$

$$= \frac{h}{3}(t + 4u + 2v + 4w + 2x + 4y + z)$$

AREAS AND VOLUMES

The numbers by which the successive half ordinates, or ordinates, are multiplied (in this case 1,4,2,4,2,4, - - - - 1) are called "Simpson's Multipliers".

From the above, we can see two things about this rule—

(a) *It can be used when, and only when, an odd number of ordinates are taken.*

(b) *The area is found by multiplying successive ordinates, including the ends, by the multipliers 1, 4, 2, 4, - - - - - 1, adding the results together, and then multiplying by one-third of the common interval.*

Simpson's Second Rule.—The area between any four consecutive ordinates is equal to the sum of the end ordinates, plus three times each of the middle ordinates, all multiplied by three-eighths of the common interval.

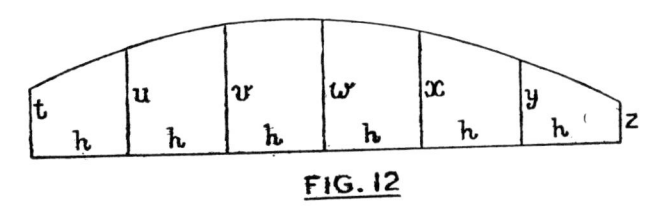

FIG. 12

Consider in Fig. 12, the area between the half-ordinates t and w. If the common interval is h, this area is equal to:—

$$\frac{3}{8}h \ (t + 3u + 3v + w)$$

The area between w and z can be found in the same way and added to the above, to give the total area of the half-waterplane.

$$\text{Area between } t \text{ and } w = \frac{3}{8}h \ (t + 3u + 3v + w)$$

$$\text{,, ,, } w \text{ and } z = \frac{3}{8}h \ (w + 3x + 3y + z)$$

$$\text{Total area} = \frac{3}{8}h \ (t + 3u + 3v + 2w + 3x + 3y + z)$$

The conclusions we can draw for this rule are:—

(a) *The Rule can be used when, and only when, the number of ordinates is four, or four plus some multiple of three (e.g., 4, 7, 10, 13, 16, etc.).*

(b) *The area is found by multiplying successive ordinates, including the ends, by the multipliers 1, 3, 3, 2, 3, 3, 2, - - - 1, adding the results together, and then multiplying by three-eighths of the common interval.*

The "Five-Eight Rule".—This is sometimes used to find the area between two consecutive ordinates. We must know the length of one other ordinate, next to the area which we wish to measure.

The rule is that *the area is equal to five times one end ordinate, plus eight times the other, minus the known external ordinate (in that order), all multiplied by one-twelfth of the common interval.*

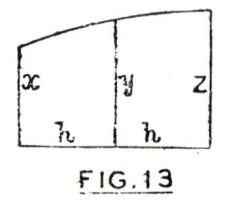

Suppose that we wish to find the area between x and y in Fig. 13. z is the external ordinate and h the common interval.

Then the area $= \dfrac{h}{12} (5x + 8y - z)$

FIG. 13

Similarly, the area between y and z would be equal to:—

$$\dfrac{h}{12} (5z + 8y - x)$$

Sharp-ended Waterplanes.—In the above rules, the ends of the waterplanes have been considered as squared-off, but if they are pointed, the rules still apply. The end ordinates are then taken as **0**, but are put through the multipliers in the ordinary way.

Unsuitable Numbers of Ordinates.—It sometimes happens that a number of ordinates must be used, which will not respond to any of the above rules. In this case, the area is found in two parts, which are later added together.

For example, if there were eighteen ordinates, neither of Simpson's Rules would give the area directly. We could in this case find the area within the first nine ordinates by the First Rule, then add to it the area within the remaining ten (remember that the ninth ordinate would be taken twice) found by the Second Rule. Alternatively, we could find the area between the first seventeen ordinates by the First Rule and that between the remaining two ordinates by the Five-Eight Rule, later adding them together.

Volumes of Ship Shapes.—The ship is divided up into a number of equally spaced sections, the area of each of which is found by Simpson's Rules. The volume is found by putting these areas through the rules in the same way as ordinary ordinates. The sections may be either vertical or horizontal, as convenient. When great accuracy is required, the volume is often worked out by both methods, one being used to check the other.

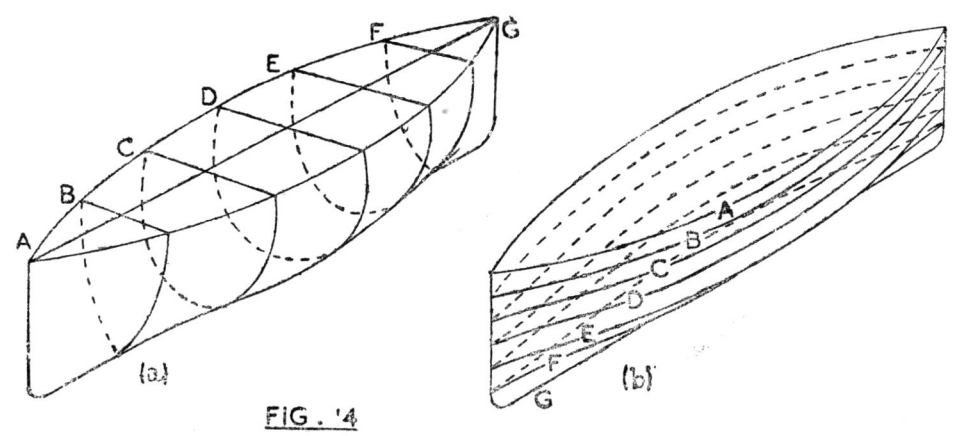

FIG. 14

Fig. 14a shows how the calculation may be done by using the vertical sections B, C, D, E and F. The area of each section is found by the Rules in the ordinary way and the volume can then be calculated by Simpson's First Rule, thus:—

$$\text{Volume} = \frac{h}{3}(A + 4B + 2C + 4D + 2E + 4F + G)$$

Fig. 14b shows how the same volume could be found by using horizontal sections. Where A is the deck area, K the area at the keel, and B, C, D, E and F, the areas of intermediate sections:—

$$\text{Volume} = \frac{h}{3}(A + 4B + 2C + 4D + 2E + 4F + G)$$

Coefficient of Fineness of the Midships Section.—This is the ratio between the actual underwater area of a midships section and that of a rectangle of the same depth and width. In Fig. 15, which represents such a section, the coefficient would be:—

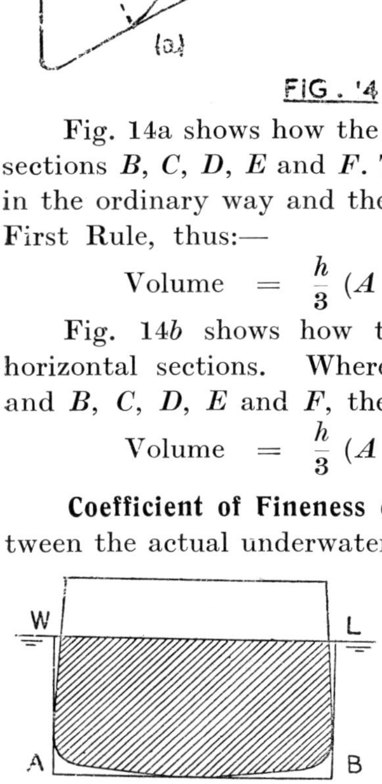

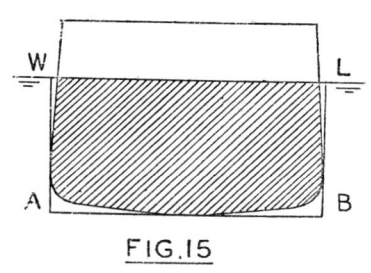

$$\frac{\text{Shaded Area}}{\text{Area of } ABWL}$$

FIG. 15

The average value of this coefficient is 0·9 for merchant ships.

Coefficient of Fineness of a Waterplane.—This is the ratio between the area of the waterplane and that of a rectangle of the same length and breadth. In Fig. 16 the coefficient of fineness of the waterplane shewn is:—

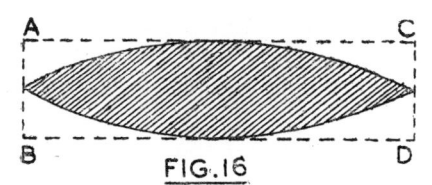

$$\frac{\text{Shaded Area}}{\text{Area of } ABCD}$$

FIG. 16

The average value of this coefficient in merchant ships is usually between 0·75 and 0·8.

Block Coefficient of Fineness of Displacement.—This is usually referred to by seamen as the "Coefficient of Fineness". It is the ratio between the underwater volume of the ship and that of a box-shape, having the same length, breadth and mean draft. In Fig. 17 the shaded volume

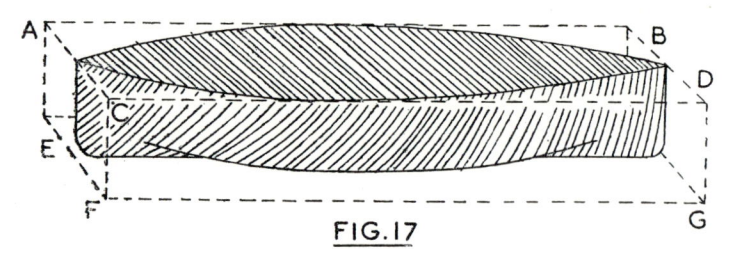

FIG. 17

represents the underwater part of a ship and the dotted lines, the box-shape mentioned above. The coefficient is then:—

$$\frac{\text{Shaded Volume}}{\text{Volume of } ABCDEFG}$$

The average value in merchant ships for this coefficient is between 0·6 and 0·8.

Prismatic Coefficient of Fineness of Displacement.—This is the ratio between the underwater volume of the ship and that of a prism having the same length as the ship and the same cross-section as her midships section. In Fig 18., the shaded area represents the underwater part of the

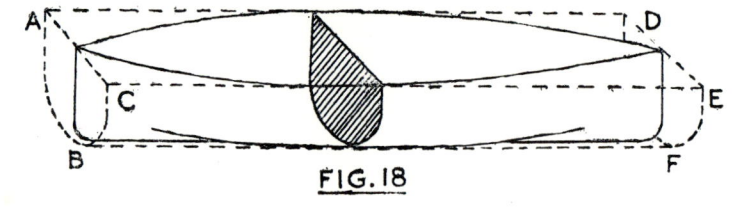

FIG. 18

midships section; the plain lines, the underwater part of the hull; and the dotted lines, the prism described. The prismatic coefficient of fineness of displacement is then:—

$$\frac{\text{Underwater volume of the ship}}{\text{Volume of the prism } ABCDEF}$$

Wetted Surface.—This is the surface area of the underwater part of the ship's hull. It is of great importance to Naval Architects, since it is one of the factors which resist the movement of the ship through the water.

It is almost impossible to calculate the area of wetted surface accurately although it can be found very closely by taking the underwater girths of

AREAS AND VOLUMES

the ship at regular intervals and then putting the "ordinates" so found through Simpson's Rules. More often, it is found by approximate formulae.

$$\text{Wetted surface} = L\ \{1.7d + (C \times B)\}$$

Where L = Length of the ship.
d = Mean draft.
B = Breadth of the ship.
C = Block coefficient of fineness of displacement.

CHAPTER III.

FORCES AND MOMENTS.

The stability of ships depends entirely on forces and moments, so that to understand the subject properly, it is necessary to have a general knowledge of such matters.

Force.—This is any push or pull exerted on a body. When a force is being considered, three things must be taken into account:—

    1. The amount of force applied.
    2. The point at which it is considered to be applied.
    3. The direction in which it acts.

A force pushing in one direction has the same effect as an equal force pulling on the opposite side. A point always tries to move directly away from a force pushing at it, or directly towards a force pulling on it. In Fig. 19 the force x, pushing on the point A, has exactly the same effect as an equal force pulling in the direction y. The point will try to move in the direction Ay.

Resultant Forces.—Any number of forces may act on one point and their combined effect will be the same as that of a single force acting in one particular direction. This imaginary force is called the "resultant force".

If two forces act in one straight line and in the same direction on one point, the resultant force is equal to the sum of the forces and acts in the same direction. In Fig. 20 the forces x and y produce the resultant force R, which is equal to $(x+y)$, which acts in the same direction and which tries to move the point in the direction z.

If two forces act in opposite directions on one point, the resultant force will be equal to the difference of the forces and its direction will be the same as that of the greater of the two. In Fig. 21, x represents the greater of two forces, x and y, acting in opposite directions on the point A. The resultant force will be $(x-y)$, will act in the direction xA and will try to move the point in the direction z.

FORCES AND MOMENTS

When two forces act at an angle to each other, the resultant will depend on the amount and direction of the forces causing it. The resultant is found by using the "Parallelogram of Forces", the principle of which can be seen from Fig. 22. Let x and y be two forces acting on a point A. Let the amounts of the forces be represented by the lengths of AB and AC, respectively. Draw CD parallel to AB and BD parallel to AC. The diagonal AD will represent the amount and direction of the resultant R.

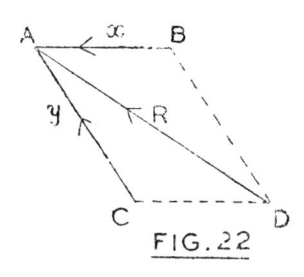

We sometimes find one force pushing and the other pulling on a point at angles to each other. In such a case, one of the forces must be treated as a push or a pull in the opposite direction, so that both are regarded as pushing, or both pulling. This is allowable, since, as we have seen, a push in one direction is equivalent to an equal pull on the opposite side. Suppose force x to be pulling and force y to be pushing on the point A, as in figure 23. Force x can be transformed into force z, exerting a push equal to x on the opposite side of A. The parallelogram can then be completed, and the resultant force, R, found in the same way as in the last example.

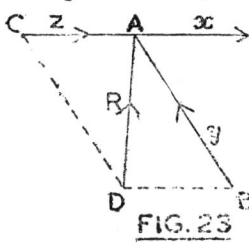

If measurements are not sufficiently accurate, the resultant can be calculated from the parallelogram by trigonometry.

Moment.—When a body is free to turn about some point and a force is applied to it at some other point, the body will usually try to revolve. Such an attempt on the part of a force to turn a body is called "Moment". Its effect will depend on two things:—

(*a*) The amount of the force.

(*b*) The length of the lever on which the force acts: that is, the perpendicular distance between the direction of the force and the point about which the body can rotate.

Suppose that the body shewn in Fig. 24 is free to rotate about the point C, and that a force, x, is applied at the point A. Then the moment trying to turn the body about C is the effect of the force x, acting on the lever BC.

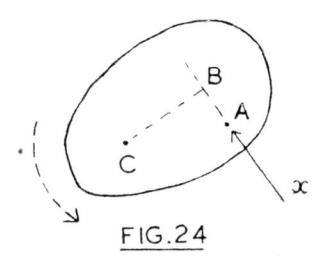

When a lever is used to lift a weight, the "lifting power" depends on the length of the lever and on the amount of force applied to it. If either of these is increased, the lifting power is also increased and vice versa—in other words, the power of a lever is the product of the force and the leverage. Moment is a form of leverage, so we can measure it in a similar way:—

Moment = Force × length of lever.

Various quantities are used to measure moments. Very often the force is expressed in pounds, the length of the lever in feet and the moment in "Foot-Pounds". In ship-stability, where the forces are large, the force is usually measured in tons, the lever in feet and the moment in "Foot-Tons."

Properties of a Moment.—Moments can be taken about an imaginary turning point, or about one side of an area, even though the body is not actually free to turn about that point or side. In other words, we could say that if the body were free to turn about a certain point or side, the moment would be so much. Consider a force of x tons, applied at a point P, in a direction perpendicular to the surface of the area $KLMN$. If we assume that the area were free to turn about the point C, the moment is $x \times PC$ foot-tons. If we assume that the area can turn about the side KN, the moment about this side is $x \times PB$ foot-tons, where PB is the perpendicular distance from P to KN. Similarly, the moment about KL would be $x \times PE$ foot-tons.

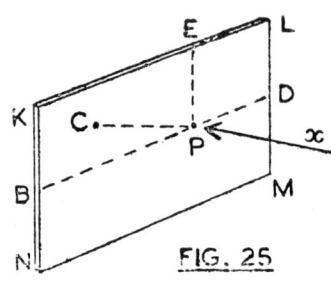

This property of moments is very important in ship-stability, as we shall see later.

Combinations of Moments.—When several moments are considered to act on one point or on one side of an area, their effects may be combined and considered as that of a single moment. This resultant moment must, of course, be regarded as if it were produced by a different force and/or lever. For this purpose, we take the sum of moments which act in one direction, or the difference of moments which act in opposite directions. This is best seen from examples:—

Consider two men working at a capstan. Let them push with forces of x and y pounds respectively, on the capstan bars AC and BC, as in Fig. 26. Then the moment produced by the first man to turn the capstan about its centre, C, is $x \times AC$ foot-pounds. That produced by the second man is $y \times BC$ foot-pounds. Since they are both trying to turn the capstan in the same direction, the total moment to turn it will be $(x \times AC) + (y \times BC)$ foot-pounds.

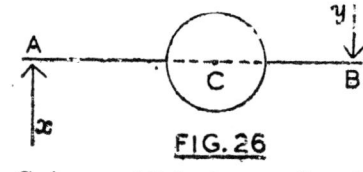

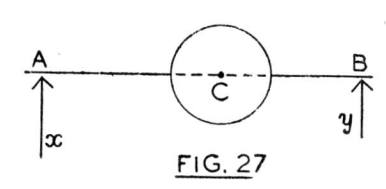

FORCES AND MOMENTS

Now, suppose that the man at B were to turn around and push with the same force, but in the opposite direction; that is, against the man at A. The total moment to turn the capstan has now become $(x \times AC) - (y \times BC)$ foot-pounds. (Fig. 27.)

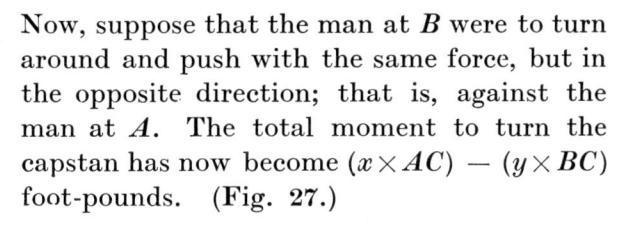

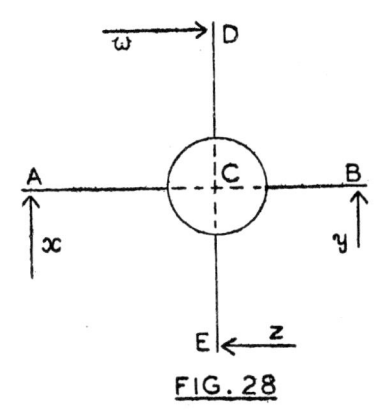

Suppose that there are four men working at the same capstan, three pushing in one direction and one in the other, against them. (Fig. 28.) The moments in one direction are $(x \times AC)$, $(w \times DC)$ and $(z \times EC)$ foot-pounds. The moment in the other direction is $(y \times BC)$ foot-pounds. The total moment to turn the capstan has become:—

$$(x \times AC) + (w \times DC) + (z \times EC) - (y \times BC)$$
foot-pounds.

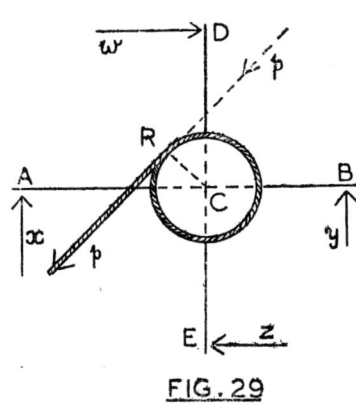

Finally, let us go one step further and consider the same capstan and men as in the last example, but with a rope around the capstan barrel, pulling against the men with a force of p pounds, as in Fig. 29. The moments trying to turn the capstan in one direction are now $(x \times AC)$, $(w \times DC)$ and $(z \times EC)$ foot-pounds. In the other direction they are $(y \times BC)$ and $(p \times RC)$ foot-pounds. So the total moment to turn the capstan is now:—

$$\{(x \times AC) + (w \times DC) + (z \times EC)\} - \{(y \times BC) + (p \times RC)\} \quad \text{foot-pounds.}$$

From the above we can see that the *final moment about a point or side of an area is the sum of the moments trying to produce rotation in one direction, minus the sum of the moments trying to produce rotation in the opposite direction.*

Centre of Gravity.—This is the point about which a body or area would balance. It may be regarded as the geometrical centre of any area, or the centre of all the weight of a body. In the case of a body, the force of gravity is considered to act vertically downwards through it, with a force equal to the weight of the body.

Centre of Gravity of an Area.—The centres of gravity of certain areas are used in ship-stability, the principal ones being as follows:—

Circle.—The centre of gravity of a circle is at its centre.

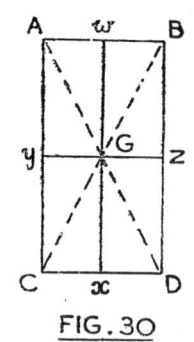

Square or Rectangle.—The centre of gravity of either of these is at the intersection of the diagonals. When we are considering the stability of box-shaped ships, we always regard the centre of gravity as being at the intersection of the centre lines. For example, the centre of gravity (*G*) of the rectangle *ABCD*, is at the intersection of the longitudinal centre line *wx* and the transverse centre line *yz*.

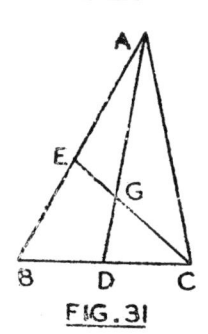

FIG. 30

Triangle.—Draw a median—that is, a line from one corner to bisect the opposite side. The centre of gravity is on this median, at a distance of one-third of its length from the bisected side.

In the triangle *ABC* (Fig. 31), let *AD* be the median, bisecting the side *BC*. Then the centre of gravity will be at *G* and *GD* will equal one third of *AD*. (Or, $AG = \frac{2}{3}AD$). Alternatively, draw a second median, *CE*, and *G* will be the point at which *AD* and *CE* intersect.

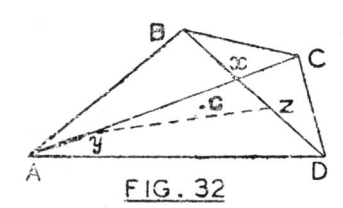

FIG. 31

Trapezium.—Draw the diagonals *AC* and *BD*. Let them intersect at *x*. Measure off *Ay* and *Dz*, so that *Ay* equals *Cx* and *Dz* equals *Bx*. Find the centre of gravity of the triangle *xyz* and this will be the centre of gravity of the trapezium.

FIG. 32

Centre of Gravity of a Waterplane.—This may be found by using moments, as follows:—

(*a*) Divide the centre line of the waterplane into a number of equal parts and draw ordinates, as for finding the area by Simpson's Rules.

(*b*) Select a suitable ordinate (usually the middle one) to act as a datum line: that is, a line from which to measure distances.

(*c*) Put the ordinates through Simpson's Rules in the ordinary way, so as to find the products for each of them. Add these together to find the sum of the products.

(*d*) Multiply each product by its distance from the datum line, to obtain what we may call the "Moment of the Product" about that line.

FORCES AND MOMENTS

(*e*) Find the sum of the moments on either side of the datum line: subtract the lesser from the greater to give a "final moment."

(*f*) The distance of the centre of gravity from the datum line is equal to the final moment divided by the sum of the products.

(*g*) The centre of gravity will be on that side of the datum line which has the greater moment.

A numerical example will best shew this. Consider the waterplane, of which half is shewn in Figure 12. Let the common interval be 30 feet and let the ordinates have the following lengths: t, 12·0': u, 27·6': v, 39·5': w, 42·0': x, 36·1': y, 22·5': z, 8·0'.

Take the middle ordinate, w, for the datum line.

Ordinate	Length	Multiplier	Product	Distance from w	Moment	Sum
t	12·0	1	12·0	90	1080	
u	27·6	4	110·4	60	6624	10074
v	39·5	2	79·0	30	2370	
w	42·0	4	168·0	—	—	
x	36·1	2	72·2	30	2166	
y	22·5	4	90·0	60	5400	8286
z	8·0	1	8·0	90	720	
	Sum of Products		539·6		Final Moment	1788

$$\text{Distance of C.G. from } w = \frac{\text{Final Moment}}{\text{Sum of products}} = \frac{1788}{539 \cdot 6}$$
$$= 3 \cdot 13 \text{ feet from } w \text{ (towards } v\text{)}$$

Centre of Gravity of a Body.—It is often necessary to find the centre of gravity of a homogeneous body—that is, a solid body, composed of the same material throughout. The three types of body, for which this is usually required are box-shapes, prismatic wedges and ship-shapes.

For convenience of calculation, we always consider the position of the centre of gravity of such bodies in the transverse and longitudinal directions separately: that is, as it would be seen from the end or from the side respectively. Fig. 33 illustrates this. Let G be the centre of gravity of the box-shape $ABCDEFH$ shown in Fig. (*a*). If we were considering this, we should first find G transversely by looking directly at the end, $ABCD$, as in Fig. (*b*) and considering its position in the plane of that area. We should then find the longitudinal position of G, by

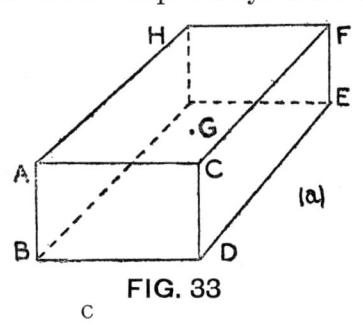

FIG. 33

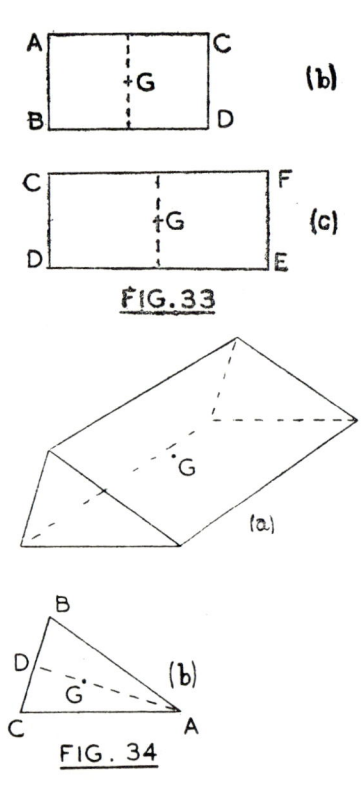

looking directly at the side *CDEF*, as illustrated in figure (*c*).

Box shapes.—We can see from the last figure, that the centre of gravity of a homogeneous box shape is at the centre-line and at the half depth of the body, both longitudinally and transversely.

Prismatic Wedges.—Consider the prismatic wedge shown in Fig. 34a. In a transverse direction, the position of the centre of gravity will be that of the triangle *ABC*. In other words, it will be on the median *AD* and at a distance of two-thirds of *AD* from the point *A*. Longitudinally, it will be at the half-length, and at the same height as in the transverse direction.

Ship-Shapes and Similar Bodies.—The calculation of the centres of gravity of such bodies, if homogeneous, is outside the scope of this book. In the case of actual ships which are not homogeneous, the methods used in practice are described later.

Effect on the Centre of Gravity of Added Weights.—Consider a see-saw, consisting of a plank balanced over a block of wood. When the block is directly under the centre of gravity of the plank (*g*), the see-saw will balance. If a weight, *w*, were now placed on the end *A*, that end would move downwards. We should probably say that this happens because the end *A* has become heavier than the other.

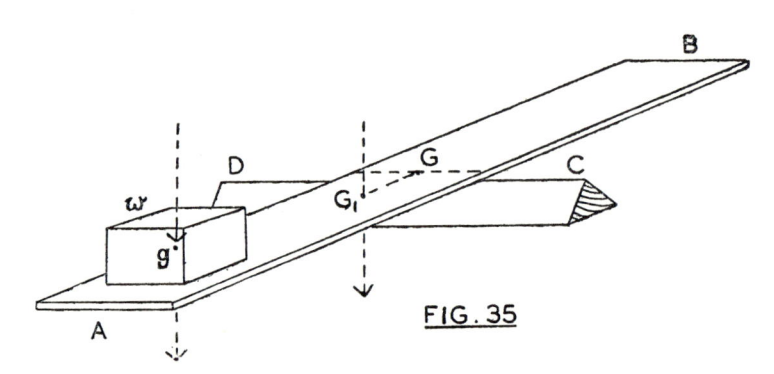

Let us see what has really happened here. We regard the force of gravity as acting vertically downwards through the centre of gravity of a body. Before the weight was added, this force acted directly over the block *CD*, and the plank balanced because there was no moment to tip it. The centre of gravity of a body is the centre of all the weight in it and since the added weight becomes, in effect, a part of the plank, *G* moves along to G_1, toward the end *A*. The force of gravity now acts vertically downward through G_1, producing a moment to cause the end *A* to move downwards. This moment will be the product of all the weight in the body and of the lever GG_1, so that if *W* is the total weight, after *w* has been added:—

$$\text{The moment} = W \times GG_1.$$

Since the see-saw balanced before the weight was added, the above effect must be entirely due to the moment of *w* about *G*. So we can also say that if *g* is the centre of gravity of the weight, *w*;—

$$\text{The moment} = w \times Gg$$

and thus $W \times GG_1 = w \times Gg$.

From this, we can derive a formula for the shift of the centre of gravity of a body when a weight is added to it—

$$GG_1 = \frac{w \times Gg}{W}$$

Two things are obvious from this:—

(a) *The centre of gravity of a body will move directly towards the centre if gravity of any weight added to it.*

(b) *The distance it will move will equal the moment of the added weight about the centre of gravity of the body, divided by the total weight after the weight has been added.*

The Effect of Removing Weights.—Suppose that in the last example, we had sawn a piece off the end, *A*, of the seesaw, instead of adding weight. The end *B* would then move downwards, because the centre of gravity of the plank would move towards it. If we use a similar process of reasoning to that which we used in the last section, we shall see that the moment of the weight removed must, again, be equal to the total moment caused by the shift of the centre of gravity of the plank. Thus, if *W* is the total weight after the piece has been sawn off,—

$$GG_1 = \frac{w \times Gg}{W}$$

Two things are again obvious:—

(a) *The centre of gravity of a body will move directly away from the centre of gravity of any weight removed from it.*

(b) *The distance it will move will equal the moment of the weight removed about the centre of gravity of the body, divided by the total weight remaining after the weight has been removed.*

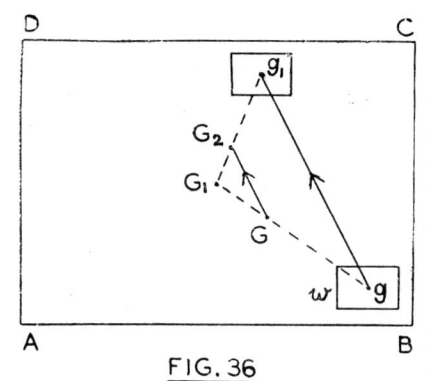

The Effect of Shifting Weights.—Consider a flat plate $ABCD$, having a weight w placed on it. Let g be the centre of gravity of this weight, and G the centre of gravity of plate and weight together. Let W be the total weight of the whole mass.

If we remove the weight from the plate, G will move directly away in the line gGG_1. If we then replace the weight so that its centre of gravity is at g_1, the centre of gravity of the whole will now move from G_1 to G_2, in the direction G_1g_1.

FIG. 36

We can shew, by working out the moments, that:—

(a) gg_1 is parallel to GG_2

(b) $W \times GG_2 = w \times gg_1$

We can say from the above that:—

(a) *The centre of gravity of a body moves parallel to the shift of the centre of gravity of any weight shifted within it.*

(b) *The distance it moves is equal to the weight shifted, multiplied by the shift of its centre of gravity, all divided by the total weight of the body.*

Inertia—A stationary body resists any attempt to move it and a moving body any attempt to change its speed or direction. This property is called "inertia" and a certain amount of force must be exerted to overcome it. If we consider what would happen if we tried to play football with a cannon ball, it should be obvious that the greater the weight of the body, the greater will be its inertia. Thus, the weight of a body gives a measure of its inertia so far as ordinary non-rotational motion is concerned. For the sake of correctness, we shall, from now on, use the word "mass" instead of "weight", but for our present purpose we may take it to mean the same thing.

Moment of Inertia and Radius of Gyration—It has been shewn earlier in this chapter that in ordinary motion, the behaviour of a body depend on the amounts of the forces applied to it, but that where a turning, or rotational, movement is attempted, the behaviour of the body depends on the *moments* of the forces applied. In a somewhat similar way, although the inertia of ordinary motion is governed by mass, the inertia of rotational motion is governed by a quantity called its "moment of inertia". There is this difference, however, that both inertia and moment of inertia are independent of the forces applied to the body. Roughly speaking, we may say that in the case of ordinary motion, the greater the mass, or inertia, the greater the resistance of the body to being moved; in the case of rotational motion, the greater the moment of inertia, the greater the resistance to that motion.

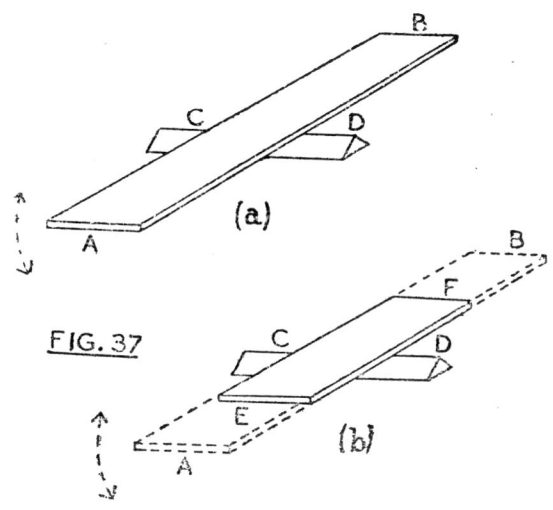

What is moment of inertia and upon what properties of bodies does it depend? Consider the see-saw shown in Fig. 37a, consisting of a wooden plank, *AB*, balanced across a block, *CD*. If it were struck a downward blow at *A*, it would start to oscillate up and down. Suppose that the wooden plank were now replaced by an iron one of exactly the same dimensions. Strike this iron "plank" a blow of exactly the same force as before and it will also oscillate, but much less than did the lighter wooden one. This shows that moment of inertia depends on mass—as a matter of fact, it is directly proportional to mass.

Suppose that we now replace the plank by a shorter one of equal weight, as shewn in Fig. 37b. If this plank is struck a downward blow with the same force as before, it will oscillate quite violently. Since the weight is the same, the increase in the rate of oscillation must be due to the decrease in length, so we can conclude that moment of inertia will also depend on length. Unfortunately, it is not proportional to actual length, but to the square of what we may term the "effective length" of the plank. This effective length is called "radius of gyration" and it can be shown that where l is the actual length:—

$$\text{Radius of gyration} = \sqrt{\frac{l^2}{12}}$$

The discoveries of the last two paragraphs indicate that

Moment of inertia = mass × (radius of gyration)².

Thus, where I is the moment of inertia, m the mass (or weight) of the plank, and l the actual length:—

$$I = \frac{ml^2}{12}$$

If the plank is of unit weight per unit length (i.e., if it had, say, a weight of one pound per foot of length), m and l will be numerically the same (i.e., a 20ft. plank would weigh 20 lbs., so that m and l would both be 20). For our purpose, we can assume this and substitute l for m in the above formula, which becomes:—

$$I = \frac{l^3}{12}$$

One factor which we have not so far considered is that moment of inertia also depends on the position of the axis about which the body is assumed to rotate. Throughout the above, we have only considered the plank of a see-saw rotating about its centre-line and the above formula only holds good for such rotation. In the case of rotation about other axes, the formula will be modified.

Moment of Inertia of a Body About Its Centre-Line.—Our discoveries about the moment of inertia of planks also extend to bodies of any size. The integral calculus is involved in most cases, but roughly speaking, the method of calculating the moment of inertia about the axis of rotation is to divide the body into strips, which may be likened to planks. The total moment of inertia of all the planks will give that of the body. For instance, the moment of inertia of the body shewn in Fig. 38 about its centre-line, AB could be found by dividing it into a number of thin "planks" as shewn. If the moment of inertia of each "plank" were then found, the sum of all of these would be the moment of inertia of the whole body.

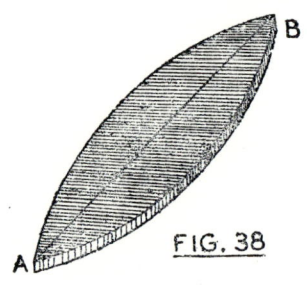

FIG. 38

Moment of Inertia of a Waterplane About Its Centre-Line.—If the body shewn in Fig. 38 were infinitely thin, it would resemble a ship's waterplane and it is obvious that the moment of inertia of such a waterplane could roughly be found as described above. For ship-shapes, this involves the use of the calculus, but for box-shapes, having a rectangular waterplane, the calculation is more simple. Consider such a waterplane, $PQRS$, having the centre-line CD. Let l be its length and b its breadth. If we consider this waterplane to be composed of a number of infinitely thin planks parallel to QR, the moment of inertia will be equal to the sum of the moments of inertia of all the planks. The moment of inertia of each plank about CD will be:—

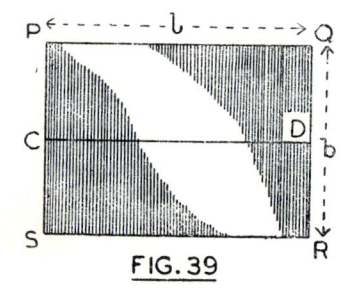

$$\frac{b^3}{12}$$

FIG. 39

Since the planks, placed side by side, extend

over the length l we can say that, where I is the moment of inertia of the area, l its length and b its breadth:—

$$I = \frac{lb^3}{12}$$

Equilibrium.—This may roughly be defined as the state of balance of a body. There are three states of equilibrium,—stable, neutral and unstable—and the body may be in either of these, according to the relative positions of the centre of gravity and the point of support.

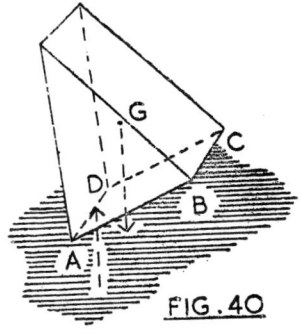

Consider a wedge which is tilted over on one edge. It will be in stable equilibrium if it tends to return to its original upright position: that is, if the centre of gravity falls vertically over some point in the base, inside the edge on which it is supported.

Fig. 40 shews a wedge tipped over on its edge AD, with G its centre of gravity and $ABCD$ its base. As long as G is vertically over some point inside the area $ABCD$, the force of gravity acting vertically downwards through G will try to pull the wedge back to its original position. Such a wedge is in stable equilibrium.

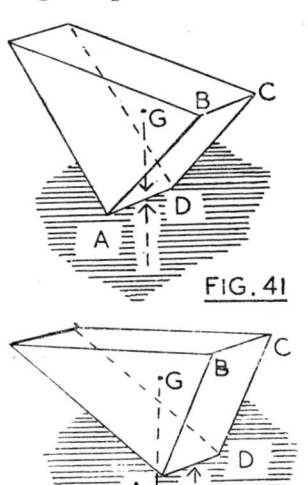

The wedge is in neutral equilibrium if it is so balanced that it neither tends to fall over, nor to return to its original position. In this case, the centre of gravity must be vertically over the point of support, as shown in Fig. 41. When G is vertically over AD, the force of gravity does not tend to turn the wedge either way. It will thus, in theory at least, remain balanced until some other force is applied to it.

The wedge is in unstable equilibrium if it tends to fall over on to its side. This will happen if the centre of gravity is vertically over some point outside the base, as is shewn in Fig. 42. If G falls vertically outside AD, the force of gravity pulling down through G will cause the wedge to fall over on to its side.

All the above are general cases, and apply to the equilibrium of any body. The special cases of ships will be considered later.

CHAPTER IV.

CENTRE OF GRAVITY OF SHIPS.

Centre of Gravity of a Ship—"**G**".—This is often defined as the point through which all the weight of the ship is considered to act vertically downwards.

A ship may be regarded as a hollow shell, inside which weights may be added, removed, or shifted about. Thus, the position of the centre of gravity will change with every condition of loading and must be calculated each time that the ship's stability is to be found. The transverse and longitudinal positions are always considered separately, as in the case of any other body (see last chapter). As far as the transverse position is concerned, G is usually assumed to be on the centre-line; since if it were not so the ship would list over. Longitudinally, it may be forward of, or abaft the centre line and is considered accordingly.

"KG".—The vertical height of the centre of gravity above the keel is usually called "KG". This is due to the fact that, in stability diagrams, K is usually taken to denote the keel and G the centre of gravity.

Light "KG".—The height of G above the keel in the light ship, before any cargo, stores or fuel are placed on board, is calculated by Naval Architects. It is given to the seaman on the stability curves or displacement scale.

Before a ship is built, the KG is estimated, usually by comparison with some existing ship of similar size and lines, although in some unusual cases it is actually calculated approximately. The KG of the completed ship, when light, is found by means of the "Inclining Experiment", which will be described later.

Shift of "G".—The centre of gravity of a ship obeys the same laws as that of any other body. Let us summarise the conclusions which we drew in the last chapter with regard to this matter.

G moves directly towards the centre of gravity of any weight added to the ship, directly away from the centre of gravity of any weight taken away from the ship and parallel to the shift of the centre of gravity of any weight moved from one place to another.

CENTRE OF GRAVITY OF SHIPS

The distance which G will move can be found from the formula:—

$$GG_1 = \frac{w \times d}{W}$$

Where GG_1 = the shift of G.

w = the weight shifted.

d = (for weights removed or added)—the distance from G to the centre of gravity of the weight.

(for weights shifted)—the distance through which the centre of gravity of the weight is moved.

W = (for added weights)—the displacement after the weight has been added.

(for weights removed)—the displacement after the weight has been removed.

(for weights shifted)—the displacement of the ship.

"KG" for any Condition of Loading.—The Naval Architects who build a ship, give the seaman her light KG and displacement. They cannot give him the KG for any other condition of loading, so he must find this for himself if he requires it.

When weights are added to the ship, G will move upwards or downwards according to whether the centre of gravity of the weight is above or below that of the ship. (Note that we are here only considering the shift of G in the vertical direction.) The KG can then be found by taking moments about a horizontal line through the keel; known in ship construction as the "base line". This is done as follows:—

(a) The light displacement is multiplied by the light KG, thus giving the moment of G about the keel.

(b) Weights added or removed are each multiplied by distance of their own centres of gravity above the baseline, giving their moments about that line.

(c) The sum of added weights is found, also the sum of their moments. The same is then done for weights removed.

(d) The sum of the added weights is added to the light displacement. That of the weights removed is subtracted from it.

(e) The sum of the moments of the added weights is added to the moment for the light displacement. The sum of those of the weights removed is subtracted.

(f) The resulting moment, divided by the resulting weight, gives the new KG.

This will be seen better from an example:—A ship has a light displacement of 5000 tons and a light *KG* of 21 feet. Find her new *KG* after the following weights have been added and removed.

Added weight,	130 tons.	Height above keel,	15 feet.
,,	450 ,,	,, ,, ,,	36 ,,
,,	240 ,,	,, ,, ,,	20 ,,
,,	1500 ,,	,, ,, ,,	12 ,,
,,	520 ,,	,, ,, ,,	25 ,,
Removed weight,	300 tons.	Height above keel	27 feet.
,,	720 ,,	,, ,, ,,	15 ,,
,,	210 ,,	,, ,, ,,	20 ,,

Light Ship: weight $5000 \times KG\ 21$ = moment 105,000.

Weights added			Weights removed.		
Weight ×	Height =	Moment.	Weight ×	Height =	Moment
130	15	1950	300	27	8100
450	36	16200	720	15	10800
240	20	4800	210	20	4200
1500	12	18000			
520	25	13000	1230		23100
2840		53950			

Ship		Weight	5000	Moment	105000
Added weights (+)		,,	2840	,,	53950
		,,	7840	,,	158950
Weights removed (−)		,,	1230	,,	23100
Final		,,	6610	,,	135850

$$\text{Final } KG = \frac{\text{Final moment}}{\text{Final weight}} = \frac{135850}{6610} = 20.6 \text{ feet}$$

We can use the above method at any time, to find the new *KG* after we have loaded or unloaded cargo. It is not necessary to start from the light *KG* in this case, as long as we know the *KG* and displacement of the ship before the weights were loaded.

Real and Virtual Centres of Gravity.—If a weight is free to move about, its effect is as if its centre of gravity were somewhere above the weight, instead of being at its real centre of gravity. This imaginary point is called the "Virtual Centre of Gravity" and for stability calculations it is regarded as being the centre of gravity of the weight.

An example of this can be found in the case of a weight which is being lifted by a derrick. Suppose the weight to be one inch off the bottom of the hold. The real centre of gravity has scarcely moved—certainly not enough to affect the centre of gravity of the ship appreciably. Since the weight is now free to swing, however, a new (virtual) centre of gravity has appeared at the head of the derrick, so that G will move as if the centre of gravity of the weight were actually at the head of the derrick and not down in the hold.

In the case of slack tanks, when the surface of the liquid is free to move, a virtual centre of gravity is caused by that free surface. This is usually at a considerable height above the real centre of gravity of the liquid and causes G to rise accordingly. A somewhat similar effect is also found when chilled meat is hung from beams in a hold and is more or less free to move.

These effects are discussed more fully in Chapter 7.

The Effect of Tanks on "G".—When a tank is filled with water or oil, weight is added to the ship and G will move directly towards the centre of gravity of the tank. When a tank is emptied, the reverse happens and G moves directly away from the centre of gravity of the tank. The distance it moves will be the same as for any other weight added or taken away and can be found by the same formula, viz:—

$$GG_1 = \frac{w \times d}{W}$$

One or two examples will illustrate this more fully.

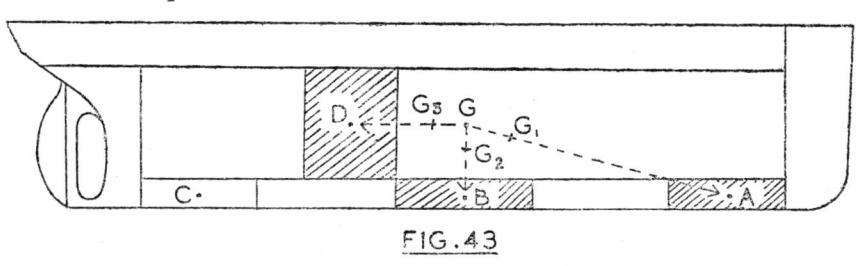

FIG. 43

If a forward double bottom tank, having its centre of gravity at A were filled, G would move forward and downward to G_1. If a double bottom tank, having its centre of gravity at B were filled, G would move vertically downward to G_2. If a tank aft, at C, were filled, G would move directly toward C, downward and aft.

In the case of a deep tank, the one shown in Fig. 43 is abaft G and has its centre of gravity (D), level with it. So in this case, G will move horizontally aft to G_3, directly towards D. The relative positions of the centre of gravity of a deep tank and that of the ship vary considerably with different ships and different conditions of loading. So the above case is only an example and not an invariable rule. Filling a deep tank may have a very different effect from that shown here and the only rule that can be laid down is that *G* will move directly toward the centre of gravity of the tank.

When tanks are emptied, *G* will move in exactly the opposite direction from the above in each case. That is, if tank *A* were emptied, it would cause *G* to move upwards and aft; tank *B* would cause it to move vertically upward; tank *C*, upward and forward; and tank *D*, directly forward.

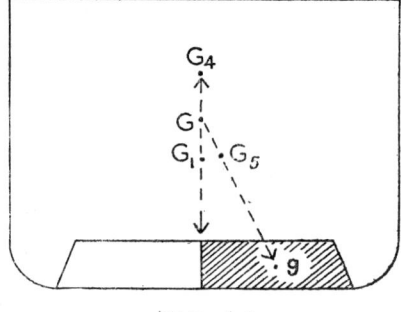

FIG. 44

Now consider the transverse effect of filling the same tanks. As long as the tanks are symmetrical about the centre-line of the ship, their centres of gravity will be on that line. Thus, so far as the transverse stability of the ship is concerned, *G* is merely assumed to move vertically upwards or downward. If the tank which has its centre of gravity at *A* were filled, *G* would move downwards to G_1. If the same tank were emptied, *G* would move upwards to G_4.

If the tank were not symmetrical about the centre-line of the ship, its centre of gravity would be to one side of that line, so that *G* would move sideways as well as up or down. For instance, if we only filled one side of a double bottom tank, with its centre of gravity at *g*, then *G* would move in the direction shown, to G_5'.

When it is necessary to calculate the effect of filling or emptying tanks they are treated as ordinary weights added or removed. The vertical shift of *G* is found by taking the weight and *KG* of the ship, weight and *KG* of the liquid in the tank and then adding or subtracting the moments (See "*KG* for any condition of loading").

It must be remembered that, in all the above cases, the tanks are considered as being completely filled or emptied. If they are not, the free surface of the liquid may cause a virtual centre of gravity, which will produce some very different effects.

CHAPTER V.

CENTRES OF BUOYANCY AND FLOTATION.

Centre of Buoyancy—"B".—This is the geometrical centre of the underwater part of the ship. That is, it is the centre of gravity of the water which has been displaced.

The force of buoyancy is considered to act vertically upward through the centre of buoyancy, with a force equal to the weight of the displaced water. Since, by the Law of Archimedes, a floating body displaces its own weight of water, this force must be equal to the weight of the ship.

The transverse and longitudinal positions of B are always considered separately. In the transverse direction, B will always be on the centre line as long as the ship is upright, but will move out to one side of this line when she heels. Longitudinally, B may be a little forward of or abaft the centre line.

"KB"—This is the vertical height of the centre of buoyancy above the keel. For box-shaped ships, floating upright, KB is always equal to one-half of the draft; this is obvious if we consider B as the centre of gravity of the underwater body. For ship-shapes, KB is usually between 0·55 and 0·60 of the draft and can be found by seamen from the ship's stability curves or scales. Its actual calculation is complicated and is beyond the scope of this book.

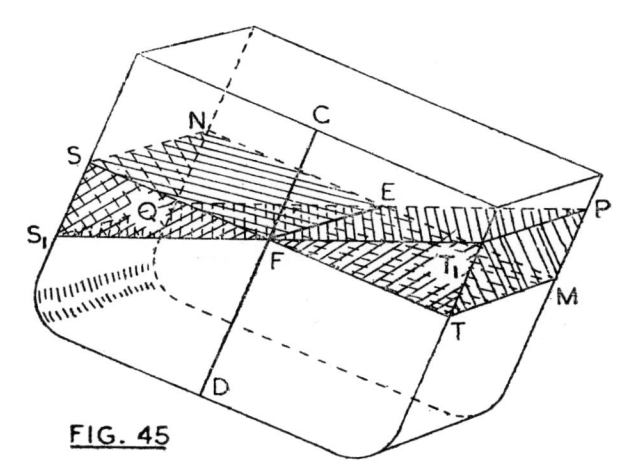

Centre of Flotation—"F". This is the point about which the ship heels and trims. Consider a ship which is heeled to a small angle, as shown in Fig. 45. Let the plane $STMN$ be the original waterplane and the plane S_1T_1PQ be the new waterplane. The wedge SS_1FNQE has emerged from the water, whilst the wedge FTT_1PME has become immersed. These are known as the "emerged wedge" and "immersed wedge", respectively.

FIG. 45

By the Law of Archimedes, a ship must displace her own weight of water at all times if she is to remain afloat. Thus, the volume which she displaces when heeled must be the same as that which she displaced when upright; so that the volumes of the immersed wedge and of the emerged wedge must be equal. When the sides of the ship are parallel, the line forming the apex of each wedge must divide each waterplane into exactly equal areas. For instance, in the figure, the line EF must be such that the area $SNEF$ is equal to the area $TMEF$ and the area S_1QEF is equal to the area T_1PEF. This will hold good whether the ship swings longitudinally or transversely, or, for that matter, in any direction. It is obvious that all such "centre lines" must cut each other at one point—the geometrical centre of each waterplane; or, in other words, its centre of gravity.

In box-shaped ships, the centres of gravity of the upright and heeled waterplanes must coincide, unless the deck-edge becomes submerged, or the bilge emerges from the water. In the case of ship-shapes this is not strictly true, but for small angles of heel or trim it can be taken as correct for all practical purposes. This gives us a new definition for the centre of flotation, namely that *the centre of flotation is the centre of gravity of a ship's waterplane.*

The transverse position of the centre of flotation is always at the centre line of the waterplane; that is, the intersection of the waterplane and the centre line of the ship. Longitudinally, it is in the waterplane and the centre line for box shapes; but may be a little abaft or forward of the centre line in ship shapes.

Shift of "B".—The centre of buoyancy has been defined as the centre of gravity of the water which has been displaced by a ship. It may, therefore, be expected to obey the same laws as any other centre of gravity.

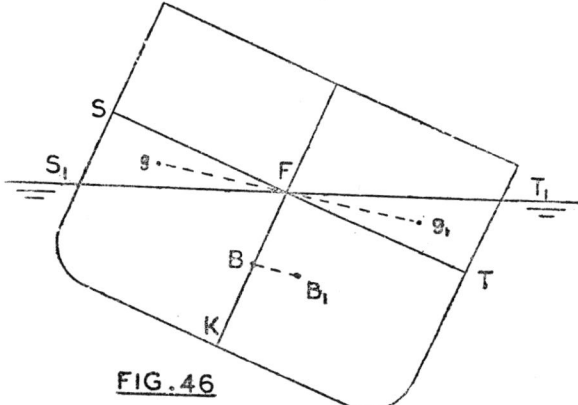

Fig. 46 represents the ship shown in Fig. 45, as it would be seen transversely. ST represents the original waterplane and S_1T_1 the new waterplane when the vessel is heeled. SS_1F is the emerged wedge and TT_1F the immersed wedge, which have their centres of gravity at g and g_1, respectively. B is the position of the centre of buoyancy before the ship heeled. The effect of heeling the ship is the same as if we took the emerged wedge away and placed it in the

FIG. 46

CENTRES OF BUOYANCY AND FLOTATION

position of the immersed wedge. Since the centre of gravity of a body moves parallel to the shift of the centre of gravity of any weight shifted, B must move out to B_1, in a direction parallel to the line gg_1.

The distance which B will shift can be found by taking moments, in the same way as for the shift of any centre of gravity. Let W be the displacement of the ship and w the weight of water in either wedge.

Now, for the centre of gravity, $W \times GG_1 = w \times d$

So, for the centre of buoyancy, $W \times BB_1 = w \times gg_1$

The weight of any body equals its volume in cubic feet multiplied by its density. So if V represents the volume of displacement of the ship; v, the volume of either wedge; and δ the density of the water; the above formula can be modified, thus:—

$$W \times BB_1 = w \times gg_1$$
$$BB_1 = \frac{w \times gg_1}{W}$$
$$BB_1 = \frac{v \times \delta \times gg_1}{V \times \delta}$$
$$BB_1 = \frac{v \times gg_1}{V}$$

All the above will also be true for longitudinal inclinations of the ship.

Horizontal and Vertical Components of the Shift of "B".—For more advanced problems in stability, it is sometimes necessary to know how far B will shift in either the horizontal or the vertical direction only, when the ship heels. Fig. 47 shows the same ship as in the last example, heeled and with B moved out to B_1. In the new vertical direction, B has moved downwards for the distance RB_1. In the new horizontal direction, it has moved out for the distance BR. These two components of BB_1 can be found as follows:—

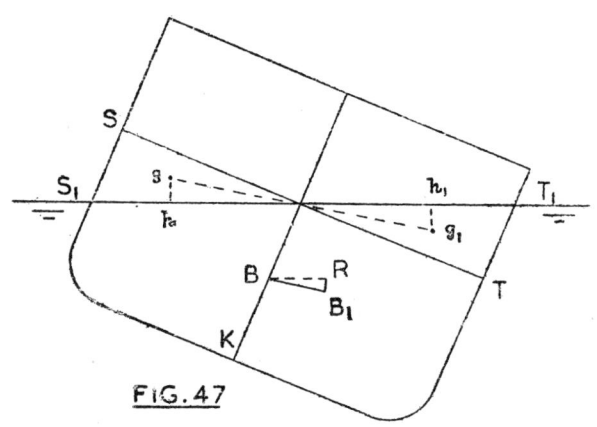

FIG. 47

Drop perpendiculars from g and g_1 on to the new waterplane S_1T_1. Let these perpendiculars be gh and g_1h_1.

For the horizontal shift, BR:—The shift of g in the horizontal direction is hh_1. If we take moments in this direction about any vertical line, the moment of the wedges must equal that of the ship. Thus, using volume in lieu of weight, as in the last example.

$$V \times BR = v \times hh_1$$
$$BR = \frac{v \times hh_1}{V}$$

For the vertical shift, B_1R:—g has risen for a vertical distance of gh above the horizontal, S_1T_1. g_1 has fallen for a vertical distance of g_1h_1 below the horizontal. Thus, the total vertical shift of g is $(gh+g_1h_1)$. If we take moments about any horizontal line, we shall see that:—

$$V \times B_1R = v(gh + g_1h_1)$$
$$B_1R = \frac{v(gh + g_1h_1)}{V}$$

CHAPTER 6.

THE RIGHTING LEVER AND METACENTRE.

Equilibrium of Ships—We have seen in Chapter 3 that a body's state of equilibrium determines whether, when it is tilted, it will right itself, remain as it is, or turn over. Seamen are, naturally, very much concerned as to whether their ships will remain upright and so the study of equilibrium forms an important part of ship stability.

In the normal ship, the centre of gravity is always higher than the centre of buoyancy; that is, KG is greater than KB. The force of gravity acts vertically downwards through the former and the force of buoyancy vertically upwards through the latter. As we have already seen, these two forces must be equal. It has been shewn in Chapter 3 that the equilibrium of a tilted body depends on the relative positions of the centre of gravity and the point of support. Unless one is vertically over the other, the body will try to turn in one direction or the other. This will hold good for ships, if we substitute "centre of buoyancy" for "point of support"; thus for a ship to remain at rest, G must be vertically over B.

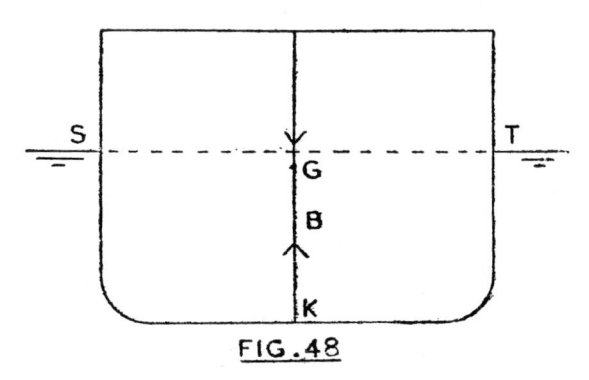

When a ship is upright and correctly loaded, B and G will both be on the centre line, as shewn in Fig. 48. The forces of gravity and buoyancy will be equal and opposite and there will be no tendency for the ship to move from the upright. As soon as any other force acts on her, however, she will heel. The centre of buoyancy will move out towards the low side and the results of this movement will decide whether the ship is in stable, neutral, or unstable equilibrium.

FIG. 48

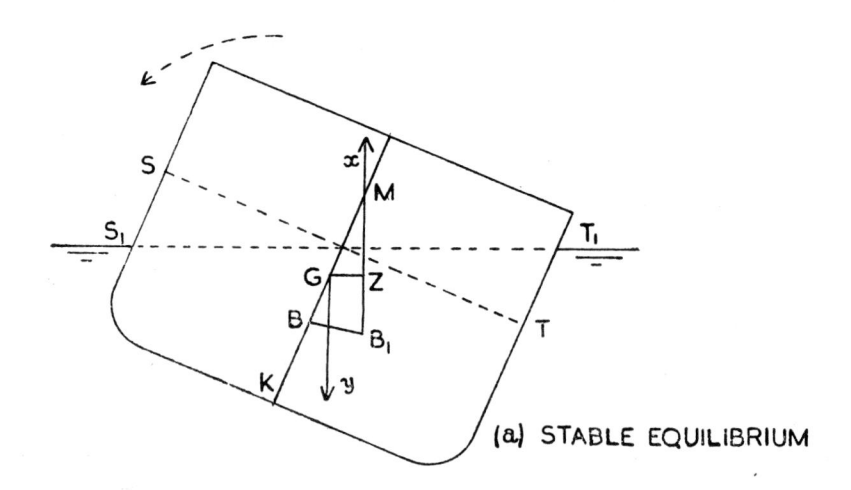

(a) STABLE EQUILIBRIUM

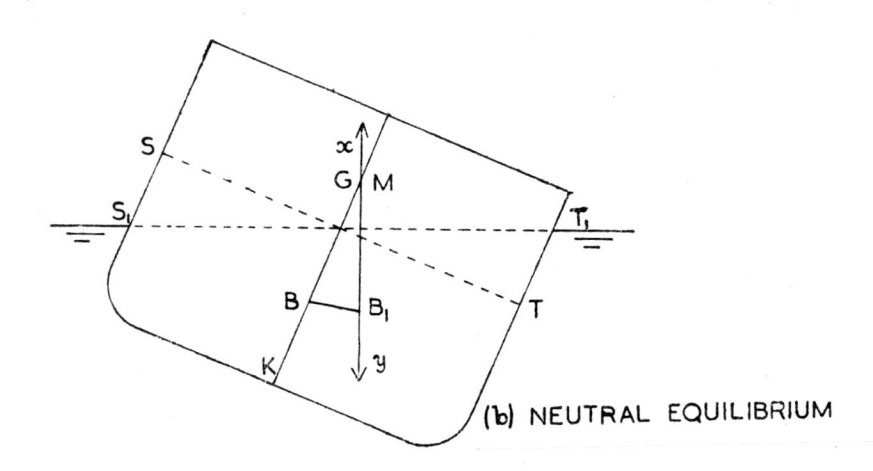

(b) NEUTRAL EQUILIBRIUM

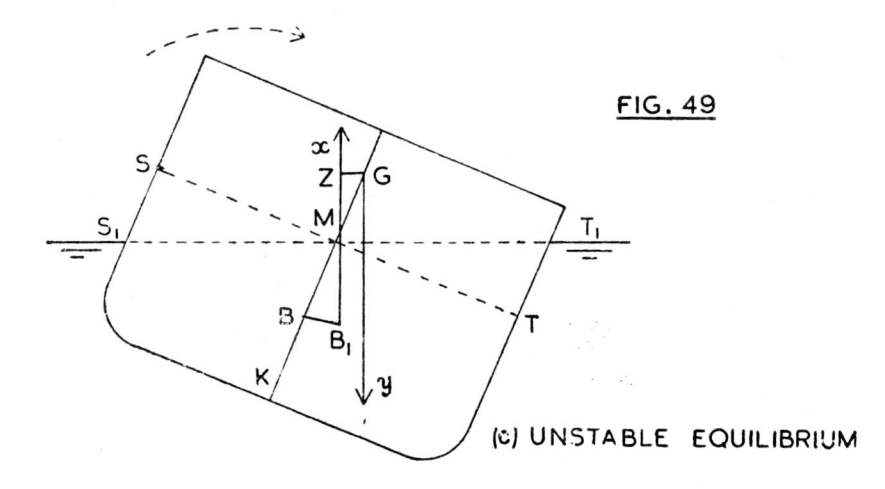

FIG. 49

(c) UNSTABLE EQUILIBRIUM

THE RIGHTING LEVER AND METACENTRE

In the next six sections we shall consider Figs. 49 (*a*), (*b*) and (*c*), which show a ship inclined by some external force such as wave action. In each case, B has moved out to B_1, but since no weights have been moved on board, G remains in its original position on the centre line. The force of gravity now acts vertically downwards through G, in the direction Gy and the force of buoyancy vertically upwards through the new centre of buoyancy, in the direction B_1x. These two forces form what is usually called a "couple", and, in the case of Figs. 49 (*a*) and (*c*), are trying to turn the ship in one direction or the other.

The Righting Lever—"GZ".—In Figs. 49 (*a*) and (*c*), a horizontal line, GZ, has been drawn perpendicular to B_1x. This perpendicular distance between G and the direction of the action of the force of buoyancy is called the "righting lever", on the ends of which the forces of gravity and buoyancy act to produce a turning movement. It can be seen that when this lever is on the immersed side of the ship, she will try to right herself (Fig. 49*a*); when it is on the other side, she will try to heel further over (Fig. 49*c*); when it does not exist, there will be no turning effect (Fig. 49*b*).

The Metacentre—"M".—In Fig. 49, the point at which the force of buoyancy, acting in the direction B_1x, cuts the centre-line of the ship, has been marked M. For small angles of heel, up to about 10 or 15 degrees, the shift of the centre of buoyancy is very small and M, which is caused by this shift, may be regarded as a fixed point. This point is called "the metacentre".

For larger angles of heel, B moves out more quickly and this causes M to move upward, so that it can no longer be regarded as a fixed point. A point called the "pro-metacentre" is sometimes considered to exist in this case. This point changes its position with every change of the angle of heel and may not be on the centre line, so it is not used for ordinary stability calculations.

Metacentric Height—"GM".—This is the distance between the centre of gravity and the metacentre. It has a definite relationship with GZ and, since it is easier to find than the latter, it is often used for calculating stability at small angles of heel. It cannot be used for angles of over about 15 degrees, since the metacentre then ceases to exist. GM is termed "positive" if G is below M and "negative" if G is above M.

NOTE.—the term "Height of the metacentre" is sometimes used in stability to denote the height of M above the keel; that is, KM. It should not be confused with metacentric height, or GM.

Stable Equilibrium.—A ship is said to be in stable equilibrium when, if she were inclined by some external force, she would try to return to the upright. If we consider Fig. 49 (a), we shall see that this condition will exist when:—

1. For small angles of heel, the ship has a positive *GM*.
2. For any angle of heel, the righting lever, *GZ*, is on the low side of the ship.

Neutral Equilibrium.—A ship which, if heeled by some external force, would have no tendency, either to return to the upright, or to heel further over, is said to be in neutral equilibrium. We can see from Fig. 49 (b) that this will occur when *G* and *M* coincide, so that there is no *GM* or *GZ*.

Unstable Equilibrium.—We say that a ship is in unstable equilibrium when, if inclined by some external force, she would try to heel still further. Fig. 49 (c) shews that this will occur when:—

1. For small angles of heel, the ship has a negative *GM*.
2. For any angle of heel, the righting lever, *GZ*, is on the high side of the ship.

It should be remembered that a ship in this condition will not necessarily capsize. As she heels further over, the centre of buoyancy will usually move further outwards and may become vertically under the centre of gravity at some larger angle of heel. She will then have developed neutral equilibrium at that angle.

Longitudinal Metacentric Height—"GM_L".—We have so far only considered transverse stability in this chapter. A ship also has a longitudinal metacentre and metacentric height, which obey the same rules as the transverse ones, although the longitudinal metacentre is not in the same position. To distinguish them, the longitudinal metacentre and metacentric height are usually denoted by M_L and GM_L. We shall consider them later, as they are used in calculating trim and for several other purposes.

The longitudinal righting lever is not considered in stability, although it obviously exists. The angles of inclination in this direction are so small that GM_L, which is more easily found, can be used for all necessary calculations.

Formulae, Etc.—The formulae for finding the positions and lengths of the various points and levers mentioned above will be given in Chapter 8.

CHAPTER 7.

TRANSVERSE STATICAL STABILITY

Moment of Statical Stability.—This is the moment which will try to return a ship to the upright when she is heeled. It is often termed "positive" if it tends to right the ship and "negative" if it tries to cause her to heel still further over.

We have seen in Chapter 3 that moment is equal to force multiplied by the length of the lever. In the case of statical stability, the lever is GZ and the force acting on this lever is equal to the weight (i.e. displacement) of the ship. So, if W be the displacement and GZ the righting lever:—

$$\text{Moment of Statical Stability} = W \times GZ.$$

For any given condition of loading, when the displacement is constant, a ship's moment of statical stability will increase or decrease, or be positive or negative, with GZ. So we can say that, whilst the measure of statical stability is $W \times GZ$, the length and direction of GZ alone is an indication of the ship's statical stability at any angle of heel.

Relation Between "GM" and "GZ".—There is a definite relationship between GZ and GM and the latter increases, decreases and becomes positive or negative with GZ.

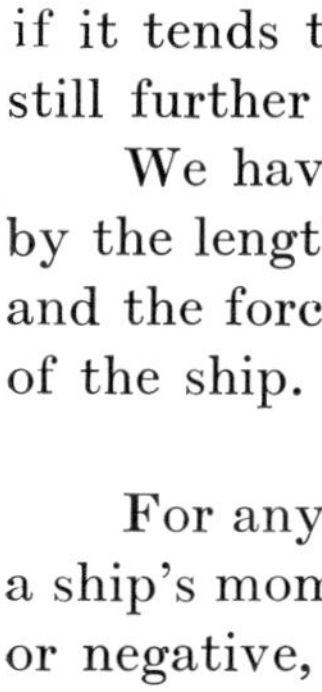

Fig. 50 represents the GZM triangle from Fig. 49 (a). The angle Z is a right angle, so that, if ø is the angle of heel:—

$$\frac{GZ}{GM} = \sin ø$$

$$GZ = GM \times \sin ø$$

FIG. 50

This means that for angles of heel of less than 10° or 15° we can use GM as the indication of statical stability, instead of GZ. This is an advantage, since the former is more easily found, but it must be remembered that M is not considered to exist for larger angles, so that we must use GZ for these latter.

Initial Stability and Range of Stability.—Initial stability is the statical stability of a ship at a very small angle of heel, and is considered to be indicated by GM. It determines whether the ship will be "stiff" or "tender" and if she is likely to develop a list during a voyage. It gives no real indication as to how the ship will behave at angles of heel for which M is not considered to exist.

Range of stability is the angular range over which a ship will have positive statical stability. It is important because it indicates the angle to which the ship could heel before she would capsize.

A ship's initial stability does not necessarily indicate what her range of stability is likely to be, or vice-versa. The two have little to connect them and a ship with a large initial stability may have either a large or small range of stability. It is also quite possible for a ship to have negative initial stability, yet to become stable at a small angle of heel and thereafter to be able to heel to quite a large angle before she capsizes.

Factors Affecting Statical Stability.—Statical stability is governed principally by:—

(*a*) The position of the ship's centre of gravity.

(*b*) The form of the ship.

The position of the centre of gravity depends on the loading of the cargo and other weights in the ship. It affects the statical stability, because it is one of the factors which determine the length of the righting lever, *GZ*.

The form of the ship decides the shape of the emerged and immersed wedges when the vessel heels. These in their turn will determine the shift of the centre of buoyancy and hence the length of *GZ*; or alternatively, the position of *M* and hence the *GM*.

An example will best show the effect of the above. Let us consider a graph, showing a ship's moment of statical stability at various angles of heel.

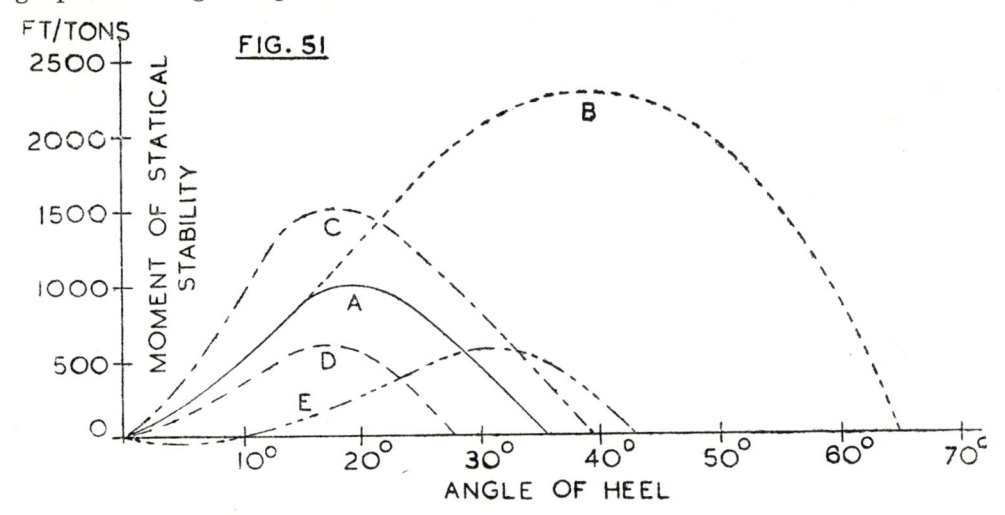

FIG. 51

Curve *A* is that of a box-shaped ship of 400 feet length, 50 feet breadth, 24 feet draft, 6 feet freeboard and having a *KG* of 18·5 feet. The maximum righting moment of this ship is just over 10,000 foot tons and occurs at about 19° of heel. The range of stability is about 36°.

TRANSVERSE STATICAL STABILITY

Curve *B* shows the effect of adding 5 feet of freeboard to the above ship, all other details being the same. Up to about 18° of heel, the point at which the deck edge becomes submerged in ship *A*, the two curves run together. Curve *B* then continues to rise, reaching its maximum statical stability of nearly 23,000 foot-tons at about 38° of heel. The range of stability is now just over 66°—an increase of about 29°.

Curve *C* shows the effect of adding 5 feet of beam to the ship in Curve *A*. The maximum statical stability has increased to nearly 15,000 foot-tons, but it still occurs at nearly 20° of heel. The range of stability has only increased by just over 3°.

The effect of raising the centre of gravity of ship *A* by 1 foot is shewn in curve *D*. The maximum statical stability is now just over 5000 foot-tons and the range about 28°—a considerable reduction in each case.

Curve *E* is an example of what would happen if the ship in curve *A* had its freeboard increased by 5 feet and its centre of gravity raised, at the same time, by 2·3 feet. She has negative initial stability, but becomes stable at an angle of heel of about $9\frac{1}{2}$°. Thereafter she has positive stability up to about 43° of heel. This example is typical of what sometimes happens when a ship carrying a deck cargo of timber develops a list. It may be likened to ship *A*, carrying a 5-foot deck cargo and having its centre of gravity raised 2·3 feet thereby.

Let us tabulate the above results, to the nearest degree of heel and 500 foot-tons of statical stability. This will give us a clear idea of what has happened in each case.

Ship	GM Feet	Stat. Stability at 20° of heel Foot-tons.	Max. Stat. Stability Foot-tons	Max. Stat. Stability Angle of heel	Range of Stability
A	+ 2·2	10,000	10,500	19°	36°
B	+ 2·2	12,500	23,000	38°	66°
C	+ 6·0	15,000	15,000	20°	40°
D	+ 1·2	5,500	5,500	17°	28°
E	− 0·1	1,500	6,000	32°	43°

From the above we can draw the following conclusions:—

(*a*) Increase of freeboard does not affect initial stability, but increases range of stability.

(*b*) Increase of beam increases initial stability, but has very little effect on range.

(*c*) Raising the centre of gravity decreases both initial stability and range.

(d) A ship which has negative initial stability will not necessarily capsize, but may become stable at some small angle of heel and may, thereafter, have a considerable range of stability before she will capsize.

It must be remembered that the curves shown are for one particular case and are intended as a demonstration only. In practice, the average merchant ship has a considerably larger range of stability than that shown, but the conclusions that we have drawn will hold good in almost all cases.

Stiff and Tender Ships.—A stiff ship may be defined as one which has a large metacentric height (GM), or righting lever (GZ). When she is inclined, the moment trying to return her to the upright will be large, owing to the length of the righting lever, and she will right herself violently. Her period of roll will be small and she will roll heavily and quickly in a seaway.

A tender ship, or "crank" ship, is one having a small GZ or GM. The moment to return her to the upright when she is heeled will be fairly small and her period of roll comparatively large. She will have an easy motion in a seaway and if her range of stability is sufficiently large, may even be safer than a stiff ship. It must be remembered, though, that if GM is decreased, the range will also usually decrease, so care must be taken that the latter is not made unduly small.

Stiffness or tenderness may be caused in almost any ship by the way in which the weights are loaded in her and we should endeavour to avoid either extreme. This will be discussed more fully in Chapter 9.

Angle of Loll (or "List").—A ship may develop a list for one of two reasons:—

(a) If the centre of gravity is out of the centre-line of the ship.

(b) If the ship has a negative GM.

These conditions are usually caused by faulty loading of the cargo and are generally avoidable if the weights in the ship are properly distributed. They are not necessarily dangerous, provided that the ship has an adequate range of stability, but are obviously bad seamanship. In either case the ship will heel over until she is in neutral equilibrium; that is, until B has moved out sufficiently to come vertically under G.

The first condition can occur in either stiff or tender ships and the list will always be towards that side of the centre line to which G has moved. In the second condition the list may be to either side and may, under the influence of external forces, change from one side to the other. It may also increase or decrease if weights are taken away from, or added to the ship.

The Effect of Free Surface of Liquids.—If a tank is completely filled with liquid, the latter becomes, in effect, a solid mass. It can be treated in exactly the same way as any other weight in the ship; that is, its weight can be regarded as being concentrated at its actual centre of gravity.

TRANSVERSE STATICAL STABILITY

In a tank which is only partly filled, the surface of the liquid is free to move and possesses inertia. The moment of inertia of this free surface about its own centre-line causes a virtual centre of gravity to appear at some height above it. The effect on the ship's stability will then be as if a weight, equal to the weight of the liquid in the tank, were placed with its centre of gravity in the position of this virtual centre of gravity.

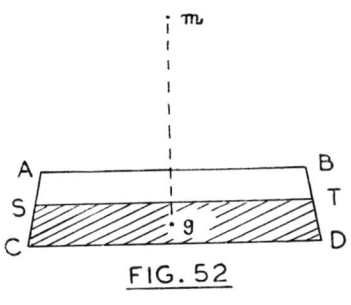

Fig. 52 shows this. The tank $ABCD$ is partly filled with water, which has its surface at ST. If the ship heels, ST is free to move and its moment of inertia causes a virtual centre of gravity at, say, m. Let w be the weight of the water. Although the actual centre of gravity of this water is at g, the effect on the ship's stability is as if a solid mass of weight w, were placed at m.

FIG. 52

It must be remembered that the position of the virtual centre of gravity is governed largely by the moment of inertia of the free surface. It is only slightly affected by the amount of water in the tank, except insofar as this will affect the shape and area of the free surface.

We shall prove, in the next chapter, that the rise of the ship's centre of gravity, due to the above, is found by the formula:

$$GG_1 = \frac{i}{V}$$

where i is the moment of inertia of the free surface and V the volume of displacement of the ship. If the free surface is not due to liquid added to, or taken away from the ship, the weight of the liquid will not affect the rise of G in any way. If the free surface is caused by liquid put into the tank, the rise of G thus caused would be decreased because:—

(*a*) If the real centre of gravity of the added liquid were below G, it would tend to lower G in the first instance, as for any added weight.

(*b*) The volume of displacement of the ship would increase and would thus slightly decrease the rise of G due to free surface. If liquid were pumped out of the tank, the effects would be the reverse of the above.

When the liquid in the tank has a different density from that of the water in which the ship floats (as in the case of a tank partly filled with oil), this will also have an effect on the shift of G. The shift will become:—

$$GG_1 = \frac{\delta_1 \times i}{\delta \times V}$$

Where δ is the density of the water in which the ship floats and δ_1 is the density of the liquid in the tank.

The rise of G due to free surface in a tank which is divided at the centre line is only about one-quarter of that in a similar, but undivided tank.

CHAPTER 8.

TRANSVERSE STATICAL STABILITY—FORMULAE AND PROOFS.

Calculation of a Ship's Stability.—When a ship is built, the naval architects calculate her displacement, deadweight and the height of the centre of buoyancy above the keel (*KB*). They also find the distance of the metacentre above the centre of buoyancy (*BM*) and, by adding this to the *KB*, obtain the height of the metacentre (*KM*). The above information is tabulated for all drafts and set out in the "Deadweight Scale"; or in the form of graphs, known as "Curves of Stability". Care is taken to see that the range of stability is sufficient to ensure that the ship will normally be safe at any reasonable angle of heel if she is loaded properly.

When the ship is completed, or nearly so, the "Inclining Experiment" is performed. This gives the metacentric height (*GM*) for the ship in the light condition and this is subtracted from the light *KM* to give the height of the centre of gravity above the keel (light *KG*). When this information is added to the scales, the naval architects have done their part of the work.

Seamen, when they wish to know the stability of their ships, can find the light *KG* and displacement from the above information. Then, knowing what weights they have added to the vessel, they can calculate the *KG* for any condition of loading, as described in Chapter 4. By further reference to the stability scales, they can find the *KM* for the ship's particular draft and hence the *GM* at any time, as will be described later.

For the examinations for Master and Mate, ship's officers are expected to know a little more than the above and should be reasonably familiar with the following formulae and proofs. Candidates for ordinary certificates are usually only asked to perform calculations for box shaped vessels; except that they may be required to find areas of waterplanes, etc., by Simpson's Rules.

KB.—We have seen, in Chapter 5, that the height of the centre of buoyancy above the keel is half the draft in box shapes and between 0·55 and 0·6 of the draft in ship-shapes.

The Inclining Experiment.—This is performed to find the ship's light *GM* and hence her light *KG*. It consists of shifting a weight, or weights transversely across the deck of a ship when the latter is free to heel. The angle of heel is measured by the shift of a plumb-bob along a batten.

TRANSVERSE STATICAL STABILITY

Certain conditions are necessary for this experiment, if it is to give good results, viz:—

(*a*) Mooring lines must be slack and the ship clear of the wharf, so that she may heel freely.

(*b*) The water must be smooth and there should be little or no wind. If there is any wind, the ship should be head-on or stern-on to it.

(*c*) There must be no free surface of water in the ship. The bilges must be dry and boilers and tanks dry or pressed up.

(*d*) All moveable weights must be properly secured.

(*e*) All persons should be ashore, except the men actually engaged in the experiment.

(*f*) The ship must be upright at the beginning of the experiment.

When this experiment is performed in practice, four weights are generally used, two on each side of the ship. These are shifted alternately, first one and then both, across the deck. Two or three plumb-lines are used and all weights and plumb lines are identical in order that they may provide a reliable check on each other.

For the purpose of proving the formula, etc., the effect of shifting one weight and of using one plumb line only is considered.

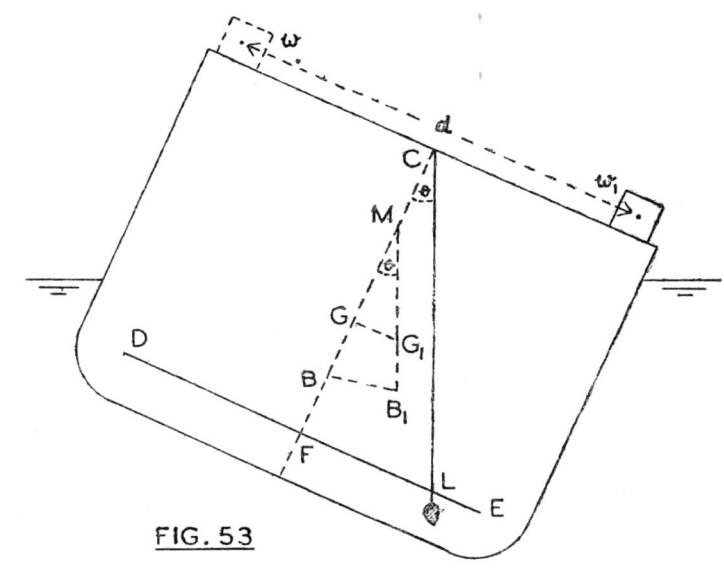

In the figure, DE represents a batten, fixed horizontally across the ship and having the point, F, at which it cuts the centre line, marked on it. CL is a plumb line, suspended at C and free to move across the batten when the ship heels.

The weight, w, is shifted across the deck to w_1, through a distance of d feet. G then moves out to G_1 and the ship heels until B has moved to B_1, vertically under both G_1 and M. The plumb line moves out across the batten for the distance FL.

FIG. 53

Let ø be the angle of heel and let W be the ship's displacement.

Consider the shift of G, as described in Chapter 4:—

$$GG_1 = \frac{w \times d}{W} \quad\quad\quad\quad\quad\quad\quad\quad (1)$$

Consider the triangle FCL:—

The angle F is a right angle and the angle C is equal to ø.

So, $\quad \dfrac{CF}{FL} = \cot ø \quad . \quad . \quad . \quad . \quad . \quad . \quad . \quad$ (2)

Consider the triangle MGG_1:—

w has been shifted across the deck at right angles to the centre line. Since G moves parallel to the shift of the weight, the angle G must be a right angle. The angle M is equal to ø.

So, $\quad \dfrac{GM}{GG_1} = \cot ø$

$\qquad GM = GG_1 \times \cot ø$

substituting for GG_1 and for Cot.ø, from formulae (1) and (2), above, this gives us:—

$$GM = \dfrac{w \times d}{W} \times \dfrac{CF}{FL}$$

Calculation of BM for Box Shapes.—The following formula and proof holds good for box shapes only.

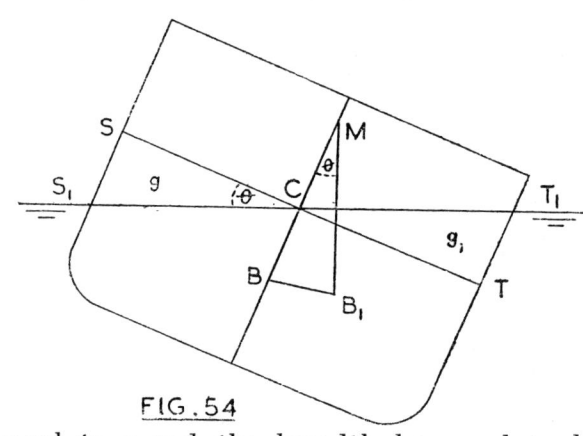

FIG. 54

Let a box-shaped ship be heeled by some external force, as shewn in Figure 54. ST is the original waterline and S_1T_1 is the new one. The original centre of buoyancy, B, has moved out to B_1. g and g_1 are the centres of gravity of the emerged and immersed wedges, SCS_1 and TCT_1, respectively.

Let the half-breadth be equal to c and the breadth be equal to b: that is, let c equal SC or TC; or $\tfrac{1}{2}b$.

$\quad$ ø $=$ angle of heel.
$\quad M =$ the metacentre.
$\quad V =$ the ship's volume of displacement.
$\quad v =$ the volume of the wedge SCS_1, or TCT_1.
$\quad l =$ the length of the waterplane.

For the purpose of this proof, it is necessary to assume that $ST = S_1T_1$ that the angle BB_1M is a right angle; and that gC and g_1C are each equal to two-thirds of a. These assumptions are approximately correct for small

TRANSVERSE STATICAL STABILITY

angles of heel, such as we are considering, and will not cause any appreciable error.

In the triangle MBB_1, if the angle B_1 is assumed to be a right angle, then:—

$$\frac{BB}{BM} = \sin ø$$

$$BB_1 = BM \times \sin ø \quad . \quad . \quad . \quad . \quad . \quad (1)$$

By mensuration (*see* Chapter 2), we can say:—

$$\text{Area of the triangle } SCS_1 = \frac{SC \times S_1C \times \sin ø}{2}$$

And, assuming that $SC = S_1C$ (*see* above):—

$$\text{Area of the triangle } SCS_1 = \frac{c \times c \times \sin ø}{2}$$

$$= \frac{c^2 \times \sin ø}{2}$$

Volume of either wedge = length × area of the end triangle.

So, $$v = \frac{l \times c^2 \times \sin ø}{2} \quad . \quad . \quad . \quad . \quad . \quad (2)$$

The centre of gravity of a triangle is on the median at a distance of two-thirds of its length from the apex (Chapter 3). But since we have said that we can safely assume that:—

$$SC = S_1C = c$$

$$gC = g_1C = \frac{2}{3}$$

$$gg_1 = gC + g_1C = \frac{4c}{3} \quad . \quad . \quad . \quad . \quad . \quad (3)$$

Reference to "Shift of B" (Chapter 3) shows that:—

$$BB_1 = \frac{v \times gg_1}{V}$$

Substituting for v and gg_1, from formulae (2) and (3), this gives us:—

$$BB_1 = \frac{\frac{l \times c^2 \times \sin ø}{2} \times \frac{4a}{3}}{V}$$

$$BB_1 = \frac{2 \times l \times c^3 \times \sin ø}{3V}$$

If we substitute for BB_1, from formula (1), this gives:—

$$BM \times \sin ø = \frac{2 \times l \times c^3 \times \sin ø}{3V}$$

So, $$BM = \frac{2 \times l \times c^3}{3V}$$

$$= \frac{2l}{3V} \times c^3$$

But $c = \frac{1}{2}b$, so:—

$$BM = \frac{2l}{3V} \times \left(\frac{b}{2}\right)^3$$

$$= \frac{2l}{3V} \times \frac{b^3}{8}$$

$$BM = \frac{lb^3}{12V} \quad . \quad . \quad . \quad . \quad . \quad . \quad . \quad (4)$$

When D equals the draft, $V = l \times b \times D$

So, $$BM = \frac{lb^3}{12 \times l \times b \times D}$$

$$BM = \frac{b^2}{12D}$$

It must be remembered that *the above formula holds good for box shapes only*.

Calculation of BM for All Shapes.—It has been shewn, in Chapter 3, that the moment of inertia of a rectangle about its centre line is

$$\frac{lb^3}{12}$$

The ship in the last case was box shaped, so that it has a rectangular waterplane. If "I" is the moment of inertia of such a waterplane, we can substitute it in formula (4) above, as follows:—

$$BM = \frac{lb^3}{12V}$$

$$= \frac{lb^3}{12} \div V$$

$$BM = \frac{I}{V}$$

The proof that we have used is for a box shape only, but the formula here deduced holds good for all shapes, although the moment of inertia of a ship-shaped waterplane is not the same as for box shapes. However, it can be proved, correctly, that *for all shapes*:—

$$BM = \frac{I}{V}$$

Approximate Formula for BM.—A close approximation for BM, which is sometimes useful, can be found by the following formula:—

Where b = the ship's breadth.
D = her mean draft.
a = a coefficient.

$$BM = \frac{ab^2}{D}$$

a is about 0·08 in very fine ships and about 0·10 in very full-formed ships. Its average value for merchant ships is about 0·09.

TRANSVERSE STATICAL STABILITY

Statical Stability at Small Angles of Heel.—The metacentre is considered to exist for angles of heel up to about 15°. For such angles, the ship's moment of statical stability can be found as follows:—

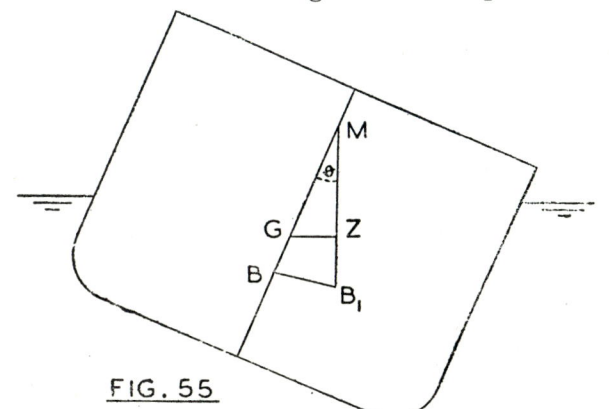

> ø = angle of heel
> GZ = the righting lever
> W = the ship's displacement.

FIG. 55

It has been shown, in Chapter 7, that since the angle GZM is a right angle,

$$GZ = GM \times \sin ø$$

Also that, moment of statical stability = $W \times GZ$

From the above it can be seen that, for small angles of heel:—

Moment of statical stability = $W \times GZ$
Moment of statical stability = $W \times GM \times \sin ø$

Statical Stability at any Angle of Heel.—The following is known as "Attwood's Formula", and holds good for any angle of heel.

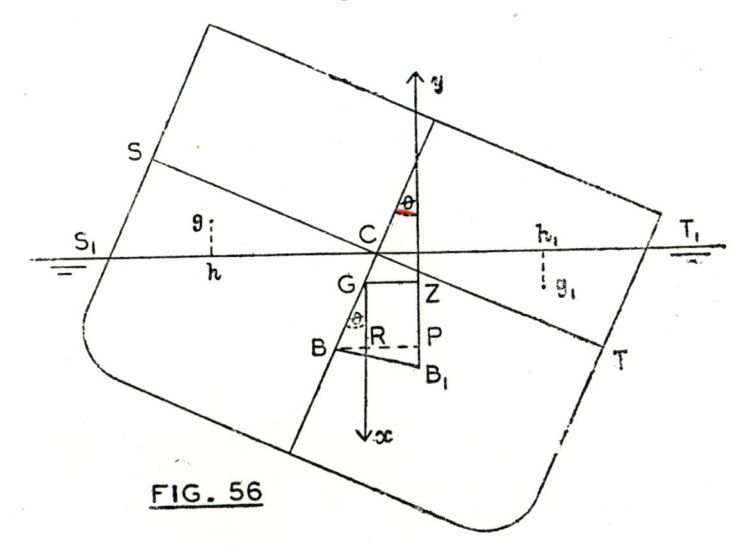

FIG. 56

Let ø = Angle of heel.
v = Volume of the immersed or emerged wedge.
V = Volume of displacement of the ship.
W = Displacement of the ship, in tons.
GZ = Righting lever.

ST = Original waterline.
S_1T_1 = New waterline.
SCS_1 = The emerged wedge.
TCT_1 = The immersed wedge.
g and g_1 = The centres of gravity of the wedges.

When the ship heels, B moves out to B_1. Let Gx and B_1y be the vertical direction of the actions of the forces of gravity and buoyancy, respectively.

From g and g_1, drop perpendiculars on to S_1T_1 and let these be gh and g_1h_1. From B draw BP parallel to S_1T_1 and let it cut Gx at R.

hh_1 is the horizontal component of the shift of g.

BP is the horizontal component of the shift of B.

It has been shown in Chapter 5 (shift of B), that in such a case:—

$$BP = \frac{v \times hh_1}{V} \qquad (1)$$

Consider the triangle GBR:—

The angle G is equal to ø and the angle R is a right angle, so,

$$\frac{BR}{BG} = \sin ø$$

$$BR = BG \times \sin ø \qquad (2)$$

To find GZ:—

GX and B_1y are parallel (construction)

BP and GZ ,, ,,

So, GZ = RP
= $BP - BR$

Substituting for BP and BR from formulæ (1) and (2), this becomes:—

$$GZ = \frac{v \times hh_1}{V} - BG \times \sin ø$$

Alternatively we can say that, since moment of statical stability is equal to $W \times GZ$, then:—

$$\text{Moment of Statical Stability} = W \left\{ \frac{v \times hh_1}{V} - BG \times \sin ø \right\}$$

"GZ" by the "Wall Sided Formula".—This formula is sometimes used to find GZ when the positions of G, B and M are known. It states that:—

$$GZ = \sin ø \, (GM + \tfrac{1}{2} BM \times \tan^2 ø)$$

Angle of Loll due to "G" being out of the Centre Line.—If a weight is shifted or loaded so that G comes out of the ship's centre line, the ship must heel until G comes vertically over B. This is precisely what happens in the "inclining experiment" and, if we refer back to that experiment, we shall see that:—

Where $\emptyset$ = The angle of heel
W = The ship's displacement.
w = The weight shifted.
d = The distance through which the weight is shifted.

$$\cot \emptyset = \frac{GM}{GG_1}$$

But, $$GG_1 = \frac{w \times d}{W}$$

So, $$\cot \emptyset = GM \div \frac{w \times d}{W}$$

$$\cot \emptyset = \frac{W \times GM}{w \times d}$$

Angle of Loll due to a Negative "GM."—It was stated in the last chapter, that a ship may develop a list through having a negative GM. In such a case, she will heel until she is in neutral equilibrium: that is, until B has moved out to a position where it is vertically under G.

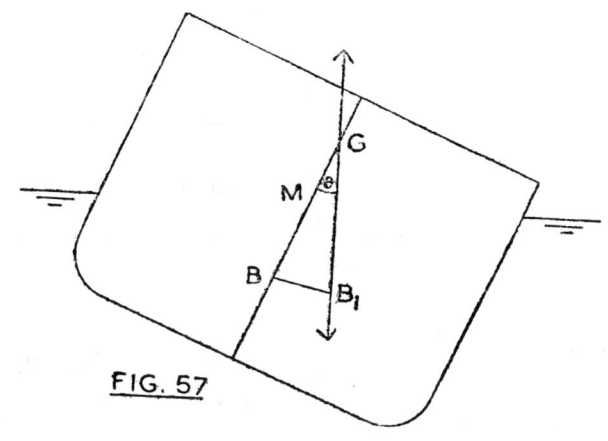

FIG. 57

The figure represents a ship in the above condition. Two things are obvious:—

1. That GM must be negative in the first instance.

2. That, after the ship has heeled and B is vertically under G, there can be no GZ.

We have seen, from the wall-sided formula, that:—

$$GZ = \sin \emptyset \, (GM + \tfrac{1}{2} BM \times \tan^2 \emptyset)$$

But it has just been shewn that $GZ = 0$, so:—

$$0 = \sin \emptyset \, (GM + \tfrac{1}{2} BM \times \tan^2 \emptyset)$$

For two quantities, when multiplied together, to be equal to 0, one at least of them must be 0. This means that either,

1. $\sin \emptyset = 0$
2. $GM + \tfrac{1}{2} BM \times \tan^2 \emptyset = 0$

If Sin ø equals O, then the angle ø must also equal O, and the ship would be upright. This is obviously impossible, since the ship has a list, so we can conclude that:—

$$GM + \tfrac{1}{2} BM \times \tan^2 ø = O$$

Since GM is negative, we get from this, that:—

$$-GM + \tfrac{1}{2} BM \times \tan^2 ø = O$$
$$\tfrac{1}{2} BM \times \tan^2 ø = GM$$
$$\tan^2 ø = \frac{2GM}{BM}$$

So,
$$\tan ø = \sqrt{\frac{2GM}{BM}}$$

The Effect of Free Surface of Liquids.—Figure 58 shows a ship which is heeled and which has free surface of water in a double bottom tank.

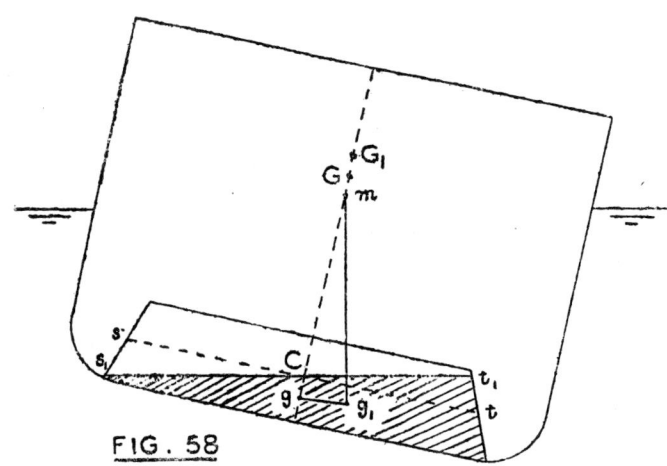

st is the original surface of the water and g its original centre of gravity. When the ship heels, its surface becomes $s_1 t_1$ and its centre of gravity shifts out to g_1. This causes a virtual centre of gravity to appear at m, and on account of this, the centre of gravity of the ship (G) rises to G_1.

FIG. 58

We have already seen that, for a ship, when I is the moment of inertia of the waterplane and V the volume of displacement:—

$$BM = \frac{I}{V}$$

If we consider figure 58, it is apparent that scs_1 and tct_1 are equivalent to the immersed and emerged wedges, respectively, of a ship: that the shift of g, out to g_1 is parallel to the shift of the centre of gravity of these wedges: that m occurs at the intersection of the centre line and the vertical line through g_1.

This is obviously similar to what happens when B moves out to produce M, in the case of a ship.

So if i is the moment of inertia of the free surface and v the volume of water in the tank:—

$$gm = \frac{i}{v} \qquad \qquad \qquad (1)$$

The effect of the virtual centre of gravity is the same as would be that of a solid weight placed at m: that is, as if the weight of the water in the tank were shifted from g to m.

So, if W is the displacement of the ship and w the weight of water in the tank:—

$$GG_1 = \frac{w \times gm}{W} \quad \text{(Shift of ``G''—Chapter 4)}$$

Let v be the volume of water in the tank and V the volume of displacement of the ship, then:—

$$w = v \times \text{density}$$
$$W = V \times \text{density}$$

If the densities are the same,

$$GG_1 = \frac{v \times gm}{V}$$

If we now substitute for gm, from formula (1), we get:—

$$GG_1 = \frac{v \times i}{V \times v}$$
$$GG_1 = \frac{i}{V}$$

The Effect of Density on Free Surface Effect.—We have assumed in the above, that the density of the liquid in the tank is the same as that of the water in which the ship floats. If these are different, the formula becomes:—

Where δ is the density of the water in which the ship floats, and δ_1 is the density of the liquid in the tank,

$$GG_1 = \frac{\delta_1 \times i}{\delta \times V}$$

The Effect of Rectangular Free Surfaces.—The free surface in a tank is often a rectangular area. In this case, the calculation of its effect is much simplified. If l is the length and b the breadth of such a surface, its moment of inertia will be found by the formula:—

$$i = \frac{lb^3}{12}$$

Since
$$GG_1 = \frac{i}{V}$$
$$GG_1 = \frac{lb^3}{12V}$$

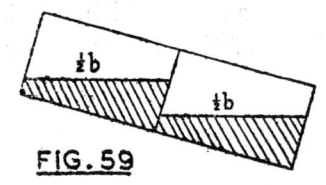

Free Surface in Divided Tanks.—Figure 59 shows a tank having a rectangular free surface and divided at the centre line. Let l be the length and b the breadth of the tank. The breadth of the free surface on either side of the tank will thus be $\tfrac{1}{2}b$.

FIG. 59

$$\text{Rise of } G \text{ due to free surface on one side} = \frac{l \times (\tfrac{1}{2}b)^3}{12V}$$

$$= \frac{l}{12V} \times \frac{b^3}{8}$$

GG_1 is due to the free surface on two sides, however, so:—

$$GG_1 = 2 \times \frac{l}{12V} \times \frac{b^3}{8}$$

$$= \frac{2}{8} \times \frac{lb^3}{12V}$$

So

$$GG_1 = \frac{1}{4} \times \frac{lb^3}{12V}$$

If we compare this with the formula found in the last section, we shall see that it is one quarter of the latter. So, in the case of a rectangular free surface, dividing the tank at the centre line will decrease the rise of G to one quarter of what it would be in an undivided tank. Since that rise is only due to free surface, it does not matter whether the tank is divided by a watertight bulkhead or only by a washplate, as long as the latter extends to below the surface. In the case of surfaces other than rectangular ones, the decrease may not be the same, but it will be considerable in any case.

It can be proved, in the same way, that dividing the tank into three would decrease the rise of G due to free surface to approximately one-ninth of that for an undivided tank. Dividing the tank into four parts will decrease the free surface effect to about one-sixteenth of the above.

Free Surface Effect when Tanks are Filled.—Three things must be considered when we wish to calculate the new position of G after water has been run into a tank in such a way as to leave a free surface:—

1. G will move toward the real centre of gravity of the water in the same way as for any other weight added.

2. The volume of displacement of the ship will increase on account of the weight of water added.

3. There will be a rise of G due to free surface.

Consider the effects of the above in the case of a double bottom tank below G

TRANSVERSE STATICAL STABILITY

Let w = The weight of water put into the tank.
W = The new displacement of the ship after the tank has the water added.
g = The real centre of gravity of the water in the tank.
G = The original centre of gravity of the ship.
V = The volume of displacement of the ship after the water has been put into the tank.

Downward shift of G, due to added weight $= \dfrac{w \times Gg}{W}$ . . (1)

Rise of G, due to free surface effect $= \dfrac{i}{V}$ . . . (2)

The final shift of G will be found by taking the difference of (1) and (2) above.

Free Surface Effect when Tanks are Emptied.—Let us consider the effect if the above tank were at first full and was then pumped partly out so as to leave a free surface.

Let g = The centre of gravity of the water removed.
V = The volume of displacement of the ship after the water has been removed from the tank.

Formula (1), above, remains as $\dfrac{w \times Gg}{W}$

Formula (2), becomes $\dfrac{i}{V}$

G moves upwards in each case, so that the final shift of G is the sum of (1) and (2).

CHAPTER 9.

TRANSVERSE STATICAL STABILITY IN PRACTICE.

Placing of Weights.—The naval architects who design a ship, make sure that she will be reasonably safe if she is properly loaded, as regards both her statical stability and her range of stability. They can, however, only fix the position of the centre of gravity for the ship when she is in her light condition. Its position during and after the loading of cargo will depend on the distribution of the weights, which is the duty of the ship's officers. It has already been seen that both the statical stability and the range of stability depend partly on the position of the centre of gravity, so those who load the ship must always remember that the final responsibility is on them.

It is not always possible to load ships exactly as we would wish, since we do not control the kind of cargo we receive, or the order in which it comes alongside. Thus, we sometimes have to "make the best of a bad job"; but even in the worst cases we can do quite a lot to control the stability of our ships by the judicious distribution of weights. If the seaman loads his ship so that she has a reasonably large metacentric height, he need not worry unduly about the range of stability, since the naval architects can be relied on to do their part of the work faithfully. In practice, the average merchant ship, when properly loaded and with a sufficient metacentric height, usually has a range of at least sixty to seventy degrees. Many still have a large righting lever even at ninety degrees of heel.

The metacentric height of the average merchant ship should be between one and three feet. If it is less than this, the ship may be too tender; if it is more, she will probably be too stiff. A metacentric height of about one foot is usually considered to be the ideal condition, provided that it will not decrease to much less than this on account of fuel and stores used during the voyage. The officer in charge of the loading of a ship should, therefore, aim to finish a voyage with approximately this metacentric height.

A "rule of thumb" method commonly used at sea, is to place about one-third of the weight in the 'tween decks and two-thirds in the holds. This is quite a good rule and a reasonably safe one in most cases, but it must be remembered that all ships have their peculiarities and what is good for the average ship is not necessarily good for every one. The only truly reliable method is that of calculating the metacentric height.

TRANSVERSE STATICAL STABILITY

The Effect of "Winging-Out" Weights.—"Winging-out" means placing weights well out from the centre-line towards the sides of a ship. Most seamen know that a ship so loaded is steadier in a seaway than one in which the heaviest weights are concentrated at the centre-line, all other things being equal.

A ship's period of roll depends largely on her moment of inertia. We have seen, in Chapter 3, that the greater the moment of inertia of a seesaw, the less quickly will it swing. Similarly with a ship; if her moment of inertia is increased, her period of roll will also become greater. If the weights in the ship are winged well out, they will cause her to have a greater radius of gyration than she would have if they were nearer to the centre-line. This will increase her moment of inertia and period of roll, so that she will be steadier in a seaway.

It must be remembered, to avoid confusion, that we are here considering the moment of inertia of the ship herself; not that of the waterplane, as we did when we were finding BM.

Ships in Ballast.—When a ship has to make a voyage with no cargo on board, it is usually considered advisable to carry a certain amount of ballast. This makes the ship more seaworthy generally and immerses the propeller more deeply, thus increasing its efficiency and decreasing vibration. Modern ships invariably use water ballast carried in tanks for this purpose.

When the normal ship is light, she is comparatively stiff. If double bottom tanks were used for water ballast in such a ship, they would lower the centre of gravity still further and thus make her unduly stiff. In order to avoid this, most modern ships are fitted with deep tanks, which will carry a considerable amount of water ballast without lowering the centre of gravity. These deep tanks are usually placed at, or a little abaft, the centre of flotation of the ship, so that she either sinks bodily, or trims a little by the stern when they are filled.

Stiff Ships.—A ship which is unduly stiff will be very uncomfortable at sea, is liable to strain herself and may cause cargo to shift or to be damaged. Such a condition should be avoided, but if a ship is found to be too stiff when she gets to sea, a good remedy is to work out bunkers from the lowest possible points.

The question is sometimes raised as to whether it is advisable to pump out double bottom tanks in a stiff ship. In most such cases it would be perfectly safe and good practice, since the centre of gravity would thus be raised and the metacentric height correspondingly decreased. Whilst the tank is being pumped out, free surface effect will cause the centre of gravity to rise somewhat above its final position, but this should do no harm in the circumstances.

Tender Ships.—A ship which is slightly tender will behave well in a seaway and will be quite safe, as long as she has sufficient freeboard to give her an adequate range of stability. This does not mean that it is good practice for a ship to be in a very tender state: on the contrary, such a condition should be avoided as much as undue stiffness. It is important to remember that the consumption of fuel and stores during a voyage usually causes the ship's centre of gravity to rise, so that she will probably arrive in port with a smaller *GM* than that with which she set out. If the ship is tender to begin with, this may cause her to become more so and she may even develop a negative *GM* before she finishes her voyage.

If a ship should become tender at sea, the best cure is to work down bunkers and/or to fill double-bottom tanks, in order to lower the centre of gravity. Whilst tanks are being filled, free surface effect will cause G to rise slightly and the ship to become more tender, but this will disappear when the tank becomes nearly full. In modern ships the double bottoms are usually well divided-up by the centre-line and side girders, which will reduce free surface even though they are not necessarily watertight. It is advisable, if possible, first to fill tanks which have a watertight division at the centre line, in such cases.

Unstable Ships.—In British law, Masters and Officers are expected to make sure that their ships will be stable at all times. The fact that a ship was stable at the outset of a voyage is not accepted as extenuation, should she suffer loss or damage through becoming unstable during that voyage, unless the circumstances are extraordinary and unforeseeable. Apart from this, good seamanship demands that a ship should be so loaded as to ensure that the *GM* will not become negative at any time. Ships do sometimes become unstable, however, and if this happens, every effort must be made to rectify matters. The necessary steps are simple and obvious to those who understand stability, but unfortunately the wrong thing is often done because it seems logical. Many blunders have been made in attempts to take a list out of ships, sometimes with serious results.

Let us consider the causes of instability in practice:—

(*a*) Weights may be placed too high in the ship when cargo is being loaded and thus cause a negative *GM* at the outset of the voyage.

(*b*) Fuel and stores consumed at sea are often taken from a position low down in the ship. This may cause G to rise sufficiently, in a tender ship, to give her a negative *GM*.

(*c*) When a deck cargo is carried, it may soak up water during the voyage and thus increase its weight. This may also cause G to rise sufficiently to give the ship a negative *GM*.

(*d*) Water or oil may be taken from double bottom tanks at sea. In this case, there will be a rise of G due to the removal of weight from the bottom and a further rise due to free surface effect in the slack tanks. This is particularly liable to happen in ships carrying oil fuel in the double bottoms. The free surface effect is then unavoidable, but the other effect can be minimised by filling each tank with water ballast as it becomes empty.

It is obvious from the above that the cause of instability is, eventually, a negative metacentric height and the only cure for this is to lower the ship's centre of gravity. It is necessary to take great care in doing this, since it is at its best, difficult, and at its worst, a dangerous operation. Weights such as bunkers, stores and cargo must, if possible, be trimmed down and/or double bottom tanks filled, whilst in extreme cases it may become necessary to jettison cargo. The best general rule is to *add weight as low as possible or to remove it from the highest possible point*.

The most common and practical method of curing instability in a ship is to fill a double bottom tank or tanks, but this may be dangerous if it is not done properly. Tanks which are divided at the centre line should always be filled first, in order to minimise the effect of free surface. One tank should be filled at a time, commencing with the low side and when this is about two-thirds full, it will be safe to start running-up the high side. Free surface effect and the added weight on the low side will probably cause the ship to increase her list at first, but as the tank fills, she will gradually come upright. The high side of a tank should never be filled first, even though it may eventually achieve the desired result. There are two reasons against this: that G will not be lowered so quickly, as by filling the low side first: that at some time the added weight on the high side will cause the ship to change her list, suddenly and violently, from one side to the other.

It is extremely dangerous and worse than useless to pump out double bottom tanks in an attempt to correct a list. It might seem at first sight that if we pump out a tank on the low side of the ship, the removal of weight from that side would allow her to right herself. We must remember, however, that an unstable ship lists because her centre of gravity is too high and if we remove weight from the bottom of the ship, we shall only cause G to rise still higher. This rise of G will probably be aggravated by free surface effect. When sufficient weight has been removed from the low side of the tank, the ship will give a sudden "heave" and develop an even greater list to the other side; or she may even capsize.

A ship rarely becomes unstable when all the double bottom tanks are full, but if this does occur, it is obvious that they should on no account be pumped out. If the ship is still dangerously unstable in such a case, after all possible cargo, fuel and stores have been shifted downwards, the only resort is to jettison cargo. When this is done, the cargo should first be taken from the high side of the ship and levelled off later. The reasons for this are the same as those for filling double bottom tanks on the low side first.

Deck Cargoes.—Ships carrying deck cargoes are very liable to become unstable, since the additional weight is placed high in the ship. If the cargo is of a type which is likely to soak up water during the voyage, the consequent increase of weight on deck may cause G to rise sufficiently to make the vessel unstable. When such a cargo is being loaded, therefore, a sufficient margin of safety must be allowed for this eventuality.

Timber Deck Cargoes.—The remarks made in the last paragraph also apply to the particular case of a timber deck cargo. When such a cargo is properly secured, however, it becomes in effect an addition to the ship's hull and thus increases the freeboard. It has been shewn in Chapter 7 that an increase in freeboard will increase the range of stability so that a ship carrying a timber deck cargo may be perfectly safe, even though she is tender. In Fig. 51, curve E shows that such a ship may even have a small list on account of the extra weight on deck, and yet have quite a large range of stability. This would be bad seamanship, but not necessarily dangerous as far as stability is concerned.

The advantage of increased range of stability can obviously only be gained if the deck cargo is efficiently secured so as to form a solid block with the ship's hull. It is worth noting that the regulations with regard to deck cargoes of timber carried on ordinary ships lay down that such cargo must be compactly lashed, stowed and secured and that it must not render the vessel unstable during the voyage.

Ships marked with lumber load lines are allowed to load more deeply when carrying a timber deck cargo, than at other times. Since the additional weight will normally be on the deck in such cases, it is important that the stability of these ships should be even more carefully considered. Three points from the regulations with regard to this are worth noting particularly:—

(a) The double bottoms must have adequate longitudinal sub-divisions. This is obviously a precaution against undue free surface effect when the tanks are filled, to prevent the ship from becoming unduly tender.

(b) The timber must be stowed solid to a certain minimum height. This ensures sufficient freeboard to give an adequate range of stability, if the ship becomes very tender. It also means that if she were to lose the deck cargo, she would rise approximately to her ordinary load lines.

(c) The lashings have to conform to very stringent rules, which ensure that the deck cargo forms a solid mass with the ship.

Free Liquid in Tanks.

Free Liquid in Tanks.—The importance of longitudinal subdivisions in tanks which are to be filled in tender ships, has been referred to several times. A study of Chapter 7 will shew that the less the area of free surface in a tank, the less will be the rise of the ship's centre of gravity due to such surface; also that a decrease in its breadth will have a much greater effect than a decrease in length. Hence, the best way of minimising the effect is to use a tank which has as many longitudinal subdivisions as possible. Washplates are quite as effective as watertight subdivisions for this purpose, provided that they extend to below the surface of the liquid. The modern cellular double bottom tank has, at least, a watertight centre girder and two side girders, which will act as washplates, so that the free surface is divided into at least four parts. Slack double bottom tanks should always be avoided if possible, but they will not usually be dangerous, unless the ship is very tender.

The amount of liquid in a tank will not appreciably affect the position of the virtual centre of gravity due to free surface, unless it changes the shape of that surface. The weight of the liquid does, however, affect the final position of the ship's centre of gravity for two reasons. In the first place, it will have an influence on the original position of G. Secondly, it will change the volume of displacement of the ship and will thus cause a slight change in the rise of G due to free surface. In theory, one inch of water in a double bottom tank would cause the centre of gravity of the ship to rise much higher than, say, one foot of water. The free surface effect would be the same in each case, but in the second case, the original centre of gravity would be lower, on account of the extra weight in the bottom of the ship. This would hold good in practice, as long as the ship were perfectly upright, but as soon as she heeled slightly, the water would run down into one corner. If the tank were nearly empty, or nearly full, this would cause a considerable decrease in the free surface.

There is always a large free surface effect when deep tanks are being filled. This is not normally dangerous, since, in the average ship, such tanks are only filled when she is light and, therefore, stiff. Some modern ships carry liquid cargoes and/or bunkers in deep tanks and peak tanks, however, and may only have a small metacentric height when such tanks are filled. In this case, free surface effect becomes important and must be considered carefully.

Free liquid in tanks, as distinct from pure free surface effect, is not usually considered, because it has peculiar and apparently unpredictable effects on the rolling of ships. There is no doubt, however, that the period of surge of the liquid is sometimes the same as the ship's period of roll and when this happens, it increases the rolling.

Apart from any question of stability, it must be remembered that slack tanks are always bad from a structural point of view. Free liquid exerts a considerable lifting effect on the tank tops and may cause considerable damage to them.

It can be seen from the above that free liquid in tanks is always objectionable, even when the free surface effect is not dangerous and should always be avoided if possible. When it does occur, it is important to keep one's sense of proportion and neither to underestimate, nor to overrate its possibilities.

Free Surface Effect in Oil Tankers.—This effect presents a special problem in the case of oil tankers, since, when tanks are "full", a certain amount of space (or "ullage") must be left between the surface of the oil and the tank-top to allow for expansion of the cargo due to changes of temperature. The usual methods of minimising free surface effect, in this case, are shown diagrammatically in figures 60a and 60b.

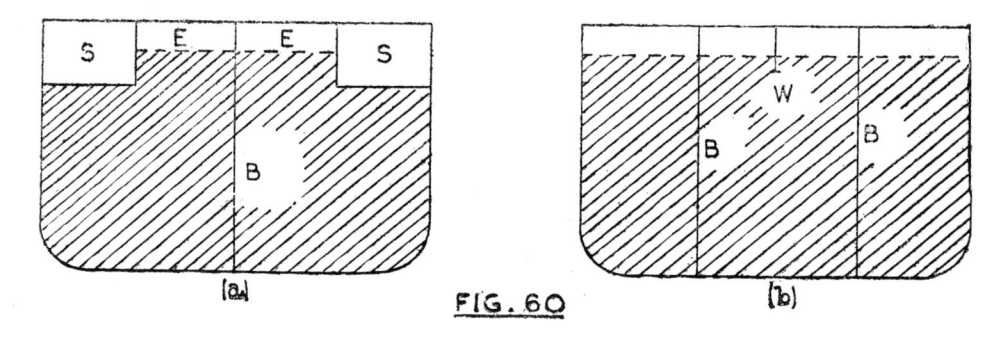

FIG. 60

Fig. 60a shows an arrangement which was very common at one time and which is still frequently seen. A longitudinal bulkhead, B, is fitted at the centre-line and "summer tanks", S, are built in the upper corners of the ship. The space between the summer tanks is called the "expansion trunk", E. When the main tanks are full, the free surface is confined to the expansion trunk and is there subdivided by the bulkhead. The summer tanks are only used when light oils are being carried, when the filling of the main tanks alone will not bring the ship down to her loadlines.

Fig. 60b shows an arrangement which is often adopted in modern tankers. There are no summer tanks, but two longitudinal bulkheads B are fitted, one at each quarter line and also a washplate W at the centre-line. When the tank is partly full, the free surface is divided into three nearly equal parts; when it is nearly full, so that the washplate extends to below the surface of the oil, that surface is divided into four parts.

CHAPTER 10.

DYNAMICAL STABILITY.

Definition.—Dynamical stability is the amount of work done in inclining a ship to a given angle of heel.

Work.—Suppose that we wish to push a weight across the deck of a ship. The weight will resist our efforts to move it on account of inertia, friction with the deck, etc., and we shall have to exert force, in order to start it moving. If we then stop pushing, the friction between the deck and the weight will soon cause the latter to stop moving, so we must continue to push until it is in the desired position. The greater the weight, the harder we must push and the greater the distance, the longer we must push. In other words, we must do work and the amount of work done depends on the distance we have to move the weight and the amount of force we have to exert in order to move it. Thus, work done is equal to the force exerted, multiplied by the distance over which it is exerted.

Dynamical Stability.—Consider a ship which is being heeled by some external force. As soon as she heels to a small angle, her moment of statical stability will try to force her back to the upright. In order to heel her further, sufficient force must be exerted to overcome this statical stability and must continue to be exerted for as long as the ship continues to heel. We can liken this case to that of the weight mentioned in the last paragraph and say that the work done to heel the ship to any given angle is equal to all the force exerted, over all the distance through which the ship has heeled. This is obviously only another way of expressing the definition of dynamical stability which is given above.

Dynamical Stability from a Curve of Statical Stability.—Fig. 61 shows a curve of statical stability, in which the moment of statical stability ($W \times GZ$) is plotted against the angle of heel. The statical stability at any angle is found by the perpendicular distance from the base line to the curve at that angle. For instance, the moment of statical stability at 30° of heel is found by drawing the perpendicular line, AB, and then the horizontal one, BD. The required moment is then CD—in this case about 13,000 foot-tons.

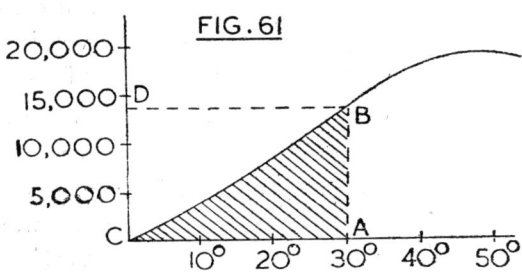

We have just said that dynamical stability is equal to all the force exerted over all the distance through which the ship has heeled. This can be taken to mean the sum of all the moments of statical stability, for every minute angle of heel, up to the given angle. If we consider Fig. 61 again, we shall see that the sum of all the moments of statical stability up to 30° of heel, will be equal to the shaded area *ABC*. Similarly for other angles. This means that the *dynamical stability at any angle is equal to the area under the curve of statical stability up to that angle.* For this purpose, the vertical distances to the curve are always measured in terms of statical stability and the length along the base line in terms of circular measure (or "radians"). A radian is equal to 57·3°, so that the length along the base line becomes:—

$$\frac{\text{Angle of heel, in degrees}}{57 \cdot 3}$$

The above method is very convenient and is often used for finding dynamical stability.

Calculation of Dynamical Stability.—Dynamical stability can, if desired, be found by direct calculation.

When a ship heels, the centres of gravity and buoyancy separate vertically. *G* moves slightly upwards with the ship, whilst *B* moves outward and downwards, because its shift is parallel to the shift of the centres of gravity of the immersed and emerged wedges. The upward shift of *G* is resisted by the weight of the ship, which acts vertically downwards through it. The downward shift of *B* is resisted by the upward thrust of the force of buoyancy, which is also equal to the weight of the ship. Thus, when a ship heels, *B* and *G* are forced apart against a resistance equal to the ship's weight, or displacement. The work done, or dynamical stability, is thus equal to the displacement, multiplied by the vertical separation of the centres of gravity and buoyancy.

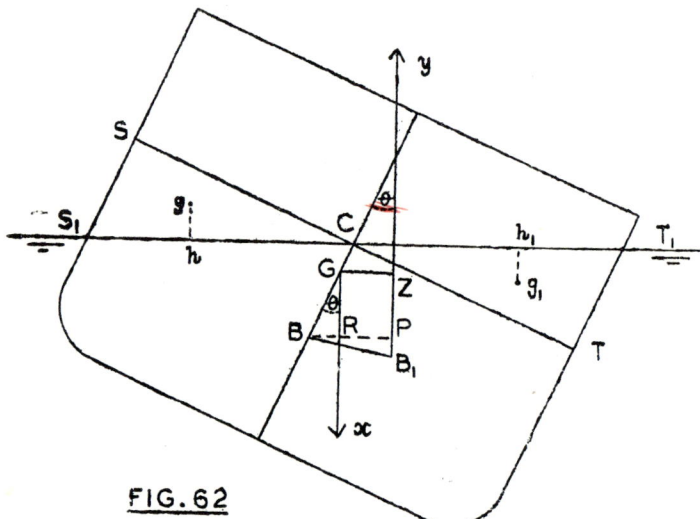

Consider Fig. 62. When the ship was upright, the vertical distance between the centres of buoy-

FIG. 62

DYNAMICAL STABILITY

ancy and gravity was BG. With the ship heeled to the angle ø, B has moved out to B_1, and the vertical distance has become B_1Z. So the vertical separation of B and G, due to the heel of the ship is—

$$(B_1Z - BG).$$

If W is the ship's displacement, this means that:—

Dynamical Stability at the angle ø $= W(B_1Z - BG)$.

Moseley's Formula.—This is a development of the above formula. Consider Fig. 62 again:—

Let g and g_1 be the centres of gravity of the emerged and immersed wedges. Drop the perpendiculars gh and g_1h_1 on to the new waterline, S_1T_1. Draw the horizontal line BP and drop the vertical line GRx on to it.

Let $W =$ the ship's displacement.

$V =$ her volume of displacement.

$v =$ the volume of the immersed wedge or of the emerged wedge (SCS_1 or TCT_1).

ø $=$ the angle of heel.

Now, $gh + g_1h_1 =$ the total vertical fall of the centre of gravity of the wedges.

$PB_1 =$ the vertical fall of the centre of buoyancy of the ship.

So, from our study of the vertical component of the shift of B, in Chapter 5, we can see that:—

$$PB_1 = \frac{v(gh + g_1h_1)}{V} \quad . \quad . \quad . \quad . \quad . \quad . \quad (1)$$

In the triangle BGR, the angle G equals ø and the angle R is equal to 90°, so:—

$$GR = BG \times \cos ø$$

But, by construction, $GR = PZ$, so:—

$$PZ = BG \times \cos ø \quad . \quad . \quad . \quad . \quad . \quad . \quad (2)$$

It is obvious that:—

$$B_1Z = PB_1 + PZ$$

If we substitute for PB_1 and PZ from formulae (1) and (2) above, we get:—

$$B_1Z = \frac{v(gh + g_1h_1)}{V} + BG \times \cos ø \quad . \quad . \quad . \quad (3)$$

In the last section, it was seen that:—

Dynamical stability $= W(B_1Z - BG)$

Substituting for B_1Z from formula (3), above, this gives:—

$$\text{Dynamical stability} = W \left\{ \frac{v(gh + g_1h_1)}{V} + BG \times \cos ø - BG \right\}$$

$$= W \left\{ \frac{v(gh + g_1h_1)}{V} - BG(1 - \cos ø) \right\}$$

But $(1 - \cos ø)$ is equal to Versine ø, so:—

$$\text{Dynamical stability} = W \left\{ \frac{v(gh + g_1h_1)}{V} - BG \times \text{versine } ø \right\}$$

Notes.—Dynamical stability is important in ship-stability for two reasons. Since it is the measure of the work that must be done to heel a ship:—

(*a*) It is a big factor in deciding how a ship will roll; in this case the waves are doing the work.

(*b*) It determines the ability of a sailing ship to stand-up under sail; the pressure of the wind on the sails supplying the work in this case. This is not of much interest to the average merchant seaman today, but is important to a large number of yachtsmen and others who have to deal with sailing craft.

It must always be remembered that anything which reduces statical stability will also reduce dynamical stability. This is yet another count against our old enemy, the free surface of liquids.

CHAPTER 11.

LONGITUDINAL STABILITY.

Recapitulation.—It is now time to consider the effects of what may be called the longitudinal stability of a ship. Before we begin, it will be as well to refresh our memories on certain matters which were discussed in Chapters 4, 5 and 6.

The centre of gravity (G) and centre of buoyancy (B) will not necessarily be on the longitudinal centre line of the ship, but may be forward or aft of it.

The centre of flotation (F) is the centre of gravity of the ship's water plane and is the point about which the ship heels and trims. In box-shape, it is always on the longitudinal centre-line: in ship-shapes it may be a little abaft or forward of the centres of buoyancy and gravity. Its longitudinal position changes with change of draft and sometimes with change of trim also. It is sometimes called the "tipping centre".

The longitudinal metacentre (M_L) is a different point from the transverse metacentre, although it is found in a similar way and obeys similar laws.

The longitudinal metacentric height (GM_L) is always very large, often several hundred feet. If the position of G is not known, BM_L can often be used instead of GM_L, the error thus caused being negligible in practice.

Trim.—This is the longitudinal equivalent of heel, but whereas the latter is measured in angle, trim is measured by the difference of the drafts fore and aft. In many ways, the calculation of a ship's trim is simpler than that for heel, but there is one complication that we do not meet with in transverse calculations. A ship heels and trims about her centre of flotation and when she is upright, the transverse positions of the centres of gravity, buoyancy and flotation are all vertically over one another, on the centre-line. Longitudinally, none of them will necessarily be at the centre line; and further, although B and G must be in the same vertical line, the centre of flotation is very rarely directly over them. We shall shortly consider the effect of this on trim and sinkage due to added weights.

Inch Trim Moment.—"I.T.M."—We all know that if we add, remove, or shift a weight forward or aft, the ship will change her trim. The greater the weight, or the greater the distance it is shifted or placed away from the tipping centre, the greater the change of trim. Moment is weight, or force, multiplied by the length of the lever on which it acts. In this case the weight is that added, removed, or shifted; the length of the lever is the distance that the weight has been moved, or the distance between the centre of gravity of the weight added or removed and the centre of flotation. If we add or remove a weight of w tons at a distance of x feet from the centre of flotation, or shift it for a distance of x feet, then the moment changing the trim is wx foot-tons. *The inch trim moment is the moment which will change a ship's trim by exactly one inch.* Its amount will vary in the same ship with change of draft.

Tons per Inch Immersion—"T.P.I."—A ship must always displace her own weight of water. If a weight is added to her, it will cause her to sink until she displaces an extra layer of water of equal weight. *The tons per inch immersion is the weight which must be added to cause the ship to sink one inch bodily*—that is, to increase her mean draft by one inch. The amount of this will vary with the draft, as we shall see later on.

Change of Draft due to Change of Trim.—When a ship changes her trim, she can be considered to increase her draft at one end and to decrease it at the other. The sum of the changes at both ends is the change of trim, assuming that there is no increase of draft due to added weights.

The change of draft due to change of trim will depend on the position of the centre of flotation. When this is at the longitudinal centre line, the ship will increase her draft at one end by exactly half the change of trim and will decrease it by a like amount at the other end. The mean draft will not change.

When the centre of flotation is not at the centre line, the draft will change more at one end than at the other, because the ship will be tipping about a point which is not midway between the ends. In this case, the change of draft can be found by a simple proportion, as will be shown in the next chapter.

Change of Mean Draft due to Change of Trim.—When the centre of flotation is not at the centre line of the ship, it will be found that the mean draft may change slightly with change of trim. At first sight, this would appear to be an impossibility, since we usually consider the ship's displacement to be the same for the same mean draft. This latter is not strictly correct, unless the centre of flotation is at the centre line; otherwise the form of the ship is more "full" at one end than at the other. If the "full" end becomes more deeply immersed, the ship will rise slightly; if the finer end becomes more immersed, the ship must increase her mean draft, in order to displace the same volume of water.

LONGITUDINAL STABILITY

The Effect of Shifting a Weight.—We have already seen that for a ship to be in transverse equilibrium, her centre of gravity must be vertically over her centre of buoyancy. This applies equally in the longitudinal direction. If a weight is shifted forward or aft, the centre of gravity will move parallel to it and will no longer be vertically over the centre of buoyancy, unless the ship changes her trim.

This can be seen from Fig. 63 (A). The weight, w, has here been moved forward to w_1 and G has moved out to G_1. The force of gravity now acts vertically downwards through G_1, in the direction xG_1, whilst the force of buoyancy acts vertically upward through B, in the direction yB. The effect of this is to force the ship's head downwards, so that she starts to change her trim about the centre of flotation, F.

If we now refer to Fig. 63 (B), we can see that as the ship trims, the wedge SFS_1 will emerge from the water and the wedge TFT_1 will become immersed. B will move out parallel to the shift of the centres of gravity of the wedges (g and g_1), until it reaches B_1, vertically under G_1. The ship is then in equilibrium and floats at the new waterline S_1T_1. Note how the longitudinal metacentre, M_L, has appeared.

The moment changing the trim is the weight, in tons, multiplied by the distance, in feet, through which it has been shifted. The change of trim will be:—

$$\frac{\text{Moment changing trim}}{\text{Inch trim moment.}}$$

The Effect of Adding A Weight at the Centre of Flotation.—Suppose that, as in Fig. 64 (*A*), a ship floats at a waterline, ST, and that a weight, w, is then added directly over the centre of flotation, F. Let B and G be vertically under F. When the weight is added, G will move vertically

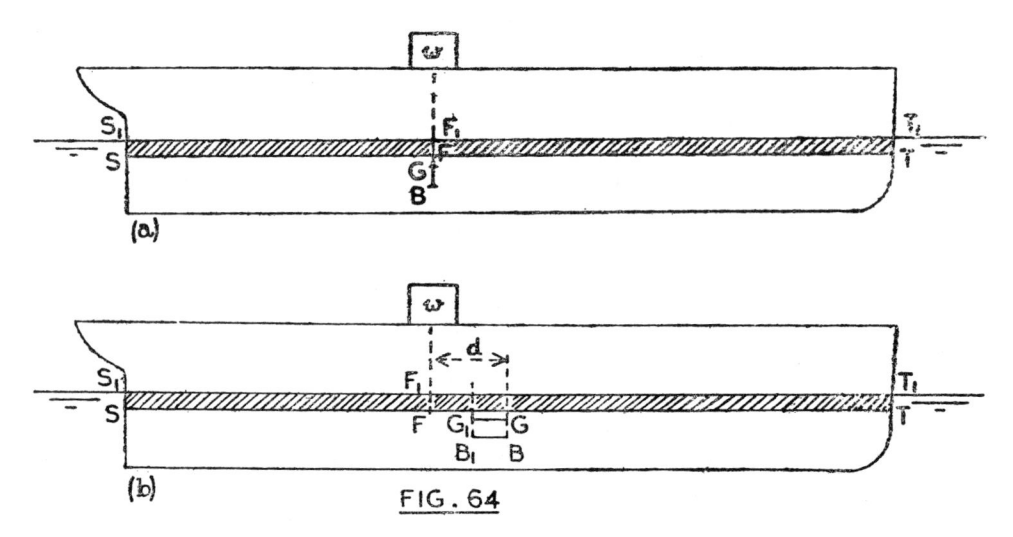

FIG. 64

upwards, towards the centre of gravity of the weight. The ship will sink to the new waterline S_1T_1, so that the weight of the added layer, SS_1T_1T, is equal to that of the added weight. The new centre of flotation is at F_1, but if the weight is not too large, it will be approximately over the old centre of flotation. B will move vertically upwards towards the centre of gravity of the added layer, which is somewhere between F and F_1. In this case, both B and G have merely moved upwards and are still in the same vertical line. Consequently, there will be no reason for the ship to change her trim and she will merely sink bodily, increasing her draft by the same amount at each end.

Now consider what will happen when B and G are not vertically under the centre of flotation, as shown in Fig. 64 (*B*). G will move directly towards the centre of gravity of the weight and B towards the centre of gravity of the added layer, SS_1T_1T; so they both move aft and upwards. Their upward movement will not affect the trim, so we need only consider the fore and aft movement. Thus, we can consider G as moving to G_1 and B to B_1. The horizontal distance between the centre of gravity of the ship and that of the added weight, (d), is the same as that between the centre of buoyancy of the ship and the centre of gravity of the added layer. The shift of B and G can be found in the same way as in transverse stability, that is:—

When W is the weight of the ship; w, the weight added; V, the volume of displacement of the ship; and v, the volume of the layer:—

$$GG_1 = \frac{w \times d}{W}$$

$$BB_1 = \frac{v \times d}{V}$$

But the weight of the layer must be equal to the added weight, so:—

$$BB_1 = \frac{w \times d}{W}$$

Therefore $\qquad GG_1 = BB_1$

Thus B and G will move aft for the same distance and will remain in the same vertical line, so that the ship will again merely sink bodily and will not change her trim.

In either of the cases mentioned above, the sinkage of the ship will be:—

$$\frac{\text{Weight added}}{\text{T.P.I.}}$$

The Effect of Adding a Weight Away from the Centre of Flotation.—When a weight is added at some point forward of, or abaft the centre of flotation, the ship will both change her trim and increase her mean draft. The easiest way to find what happens in this case is to consider these two effects separately. Thus:—

(*a*) First consider the weight as being added directly over the centre of flotation, causing the ship to sink bodily as described in the last section.

(*b*) Secondly, imagine the weight to be shifted forward or aft from the above position, causing the ship to trim, as described under "effect of shifting a weight".

The calculation of the above will be described fully in the next chapter It is quite simple, unless the weight added is very large.

Loading Weights to Obtain a Desired Trim.—It is often desirable to obtain a certain trim when the ship is loaded. Generally, we do not require the trim to exact limits, but merely to about, say, "a foot by the stern". In this case, it is usually sufficient to load weights as desired during the earlier stages of loading. Later on, we can get the trim roughly as we want it by using a combination of experience and common sense. Finally, near the end of the loading, we can trim our ship exactly as we want her by "juggling" with the inch trim moment and the amount of weight to come on board.

Sometimes, as when a ship has to cross a bar, we require a certain maximum draft, or wish to keep the after draft constant. This can be done quite easily, as we shall see in the next chapter.

The Effect of Removing Weights.—If a weight is removed from a ship, the effects on trim and mean draft will be the reverse of those described for added weights.

The Effect of Bilging a Compartment.—When a hold or compartment is bilged (i.e., holed, so that it becomes flooded), a number of things can happen.

(a) The ship will increase her mean draft in order to compensate for the buoyancy which she has lost, since she must displace her own weight of water in order to float. If an empty hold is bilged, it will cease to displace any water and so the ship must sink until the remaining, intact part of her has made up this loss and displaces a weight of water equal to the the weight of the ship. If the hold has cargo in it, such cargo will continue to displace a certain amount of water, so that the bilged compartment only loses a part of its displacement. The amount of displacement then lost, expressed as a percentage of that which would have been lost had the hold been empty, is called the "*Permeability*" of the hold.

An example will illustrate this. Suppose that a hold has an underwater volume of 50,000 cubic feet. If it were bilged when empty, the ship would lose that much volume of displacement and would sink until the remaining holds, etc., displaced an extra 50,000 cubic feet. If the hold were filled with cargo, the actual solid material in that cargo would continue to displace water after the hold was bilged. Suppose that the total solid material in the cargo amounted to 30,000 cubic feet, then only 20,000 cubic feet of water could find its way into the space left. Thus the displacement which would actually be lost on bilging, or permeability, will only be—

$$\frac{20000}{50000} \times 100 \text{ per cent.}$$

or 40 per cent of the volume of the hold.

(b) If the centre of gravity of the compartment is in the same vertical line as the centre of buoyancy of the ship, the latter will merely sink bodily to a new waterline. If these two points are not in the same vertical line, B will shift forward or aft, as the case may be. As the bilging is the cause of loss of buoyancy only and not actual addition of weight to the ship, G will not move, so the ship must change her trim in order to bring B back into the same vertical line as G.

Note the difference between this case and that of weights added, removed, or shifted. In the latter case, G moves as well as B, so that the relative positions of the weight and the centre of flotation govern whether the ship will change her trim. In this case, where G does not shift, the change of trim, if any, is governed by the relative positions of the bilged compartment and the centre of buoyancy.

(c) If the compartment is divided longitudinally, the ship may list on account of the lost buoyancy being out of the transverse centre line.

CHAPTER 12.

LONGITUDINAL STABILITY—FORMULAE AND PROOFS.

Longitudinal Metacentric Height—"GM_L".—The calculations to find this are very similar to those used for transverse metacentric height. BM_L is first calculated, whilst KB and KG will have already been found for the transverse calculations, so that GM_L can be found by addition and subtraction.

For instance, suppose that a ship's BM_L is found by calculation to be 428 feet, that KB is 11 feet and KG is 19 feet. Then:—

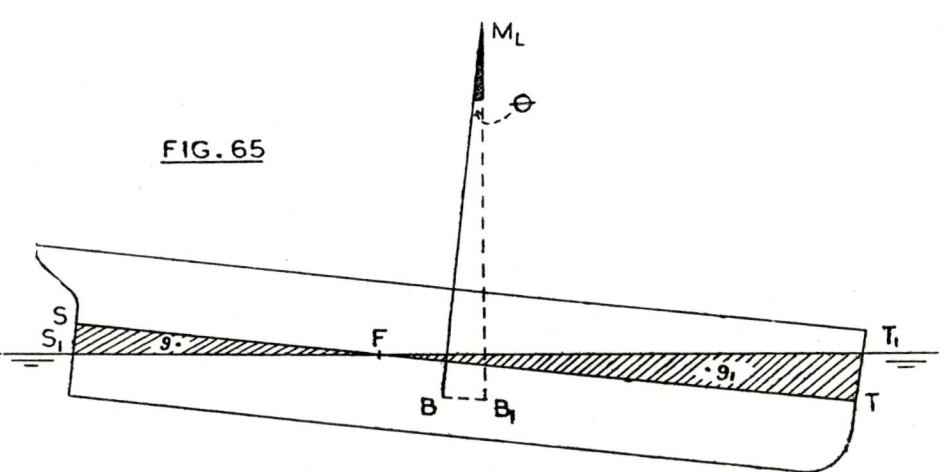

$$
\begin{aligned}
BM_L &= 428 \text{ feet} \\
KB &= \underline{11 \text{ ,,}} \\
KM_L &= 439 \text{ ,,} \\
KG &= \underline{19 \text{ ,,}} \\
GM_L &= 420 \text{ feet}
\end{aligned}
$$

FIG. 65

The Calculation of "BM_L" for all Shapes.—Figure 65 shows a ship which has tipped longitudinally through a small angle, φ. B has moved out to B_1 and the longitudinal metacentre, M_L, has appeared.

Compare this figure with Figure 54, Chapter 8, which shows the transverse metacentre appearing as the ship heels. In each case there is an emerged and an immersed wedge; a shift of B to B_1, parallel to the shift of the centres of gravity of the wedges; and a heel or trim to the angle φ. The transverse centre of flotation, about which the ship heels, is on the centre line, at C. The longitudinal centre of flotation, about which she trims, may or may not be on the longitudinal centre line—in Fig. 65 it is shewn at F, abaft that centre line. The only other difference is one of perspective, so that where we considered breadth before, we now have length, and vice-versa.

It can be seen from the above that we could show by means of a proof similar to that for transverse *BM*, that:—

Where I_L is the moment of inertia of the waterplane, longitudinally, about the centre of flotation, and V the ship's volume of displacement; then for all shapes, including ship shapes,

$$BM_L = \frac{I_L}{V}$$

The calculation of "BM_L" for Box Shapes.—In the case of box shapes, the centre of flotation is on the longitudinal centre line of the ship. If we consider the moment of inertia of a rectangle about its centre line, it follows that if l is the ship's length, b her breadth and D the draft at which she floats:—

$$I_L = \frac{bl^3}{12}$$

but $$BM_L = \frac{I_L}{V}$$

so $$BM_L = \frac{bl^3}{12V}$$

but $V = l \times b \times D$, so the above becomes:—

$$BM_L = \frac{bl^3}{12l \times b \times D}$$

$$BM_L = \frac{l^2}{12D} \quad \text{(for box shapes only)}$$

Tons Per Inch Immersion—"T.P.I".—We have already seen that this is the number of tons required to cause the ship to sink one inch bodily. Let us deduce a formula for finding it.

It is safe to assume that, for all practical purposes, two waterplanes which are one inch apart will have the same areas and also that the ship's sides will be vertical between them. The volume of the layer between such waterplanes can thus be considered as having the area of one waterplane and as being one inch thick. One inch is one twelfth of a foot so, if A is the area of one waterplane, the volume of the layer will be:—

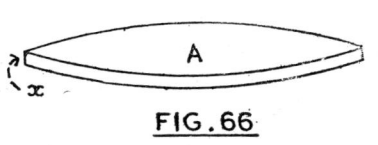

$$\frac{A}{12} \text{ cubic feet}$$

FIG. 66

Fig. 66 illustrates this. The body shewn has flat sides, each having an area, A, and has a depth of x. If we consider the area of the ship's water-plane to be A, and one inch, or one twelfth of a foot to represent x, we can see how the above is arrived at.

LONGITUDINAL STABILITY

In order to submerge the above layer, it is necessary to add to the ship a weight equal to the weight of water which the layer will displace. Since the layer is one inch thick, this weight is that which is necessary to sink the ship one inch bodily, or the "Tons per inch immersion". Since ships are designed to float in salt water, of which 35 cubic feet weigh one ton:—

$$\text{Tons per inch immersion} = \text{Volume of layer} \div 35$$
$$= \frac{A}{12} \div 35$$
$$\text{Tons per inch immersion} = \frac{A}{420}$$

Inch Trim Moment.—Figure 67 represents a ship in which a weight, w, has been shifted forward to w_1, through a distance of d feet. B and G have moved to B_1 and G_1, respectively, and the longitudinal metacentre, M_L, has appeared. ST is the original waterplane and S_1T_1 the new waterplane, the ship trimming about the centre of flotation, F.

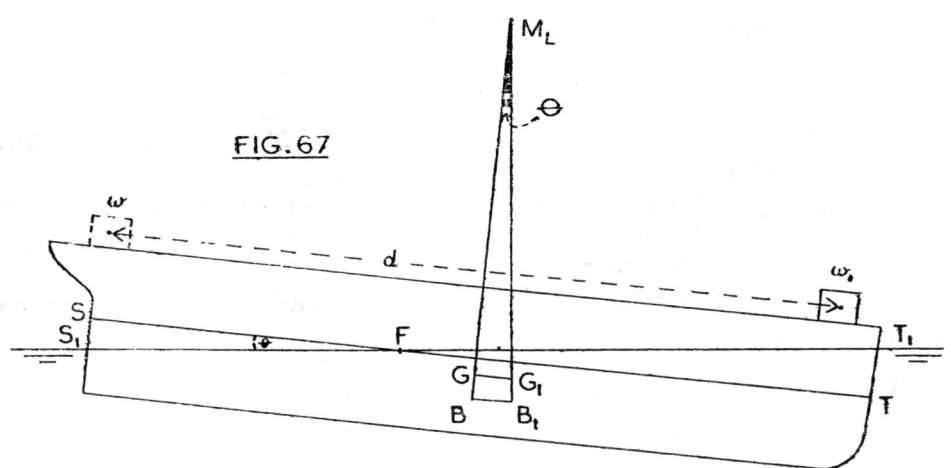

FIG. 67

Let φ be the angle between the original and new waterplanes, W the ship's displacement and l her length.

Let us do a little simple trigonometry:—In the triangle GG_1M_L, the angle G is equal to 90° and the angle M_L to φ. So:—

$$GG_1 = GM_L \times \text{Tan } \varphi \quad . \quad . \quad . \quad . \quad . \quad . \quad (1)$$

And yet more trigonometry:—In the triangle FTT_1, the angle T is equal to 90° and the angle F to φ. In the triangle FSS_1, the angle S is equal to 90° and the angle F to φ. So:—

$$TT_1 = FT \times \text{Tan } \varphi$$
$$SS_1 = FS \times \text{Tan } \varphi$$

Adding these, we get:—
$$TT_1 + SS_1 = FT \times \tan \varphi + FS \times \tan \varphi$$
$$= (FT + FS)\tan \varphi$$
But $(TT_1 + SS_1)$ equals the change of trim, whilst $(FT + FS)$ is equal to the ship's length, so:—
$$\text{Change of trim} = l \times \tan \varphi$$
If the trim is to change one inch—i.e. one-twelfth of a foot:—
$$l \times \tan \varphi = \frac{1}{12}$$
$$\tan \varphi = \frac{1}{12l} \qquad \qquad \qquad (2)$$

The change of trim is due entirely to the shifting of the weight, so we can say that:—
$$\text{Moment changing trim} = w \times d$$
But, $\qquad w \times d = W \times GG_1$
So, Moment changing trim $= W \times GG_1$
Substituting for GG_1 from formula (1), we get:—
$$\text{Moment changing trim} = W \times GM_L \times \tan \varphi$$
Substituting for $\tan \varphi$ from formula (2), this gives:—
$$\text{Moment to change trim } 1'' = W \times GM_L \times \frac{1}{12l}$$
$$\textit{i.e. Inch trim moment} = \frac{W \times GM_L}{12l}$$

If GM_L is not known, we can substitute BM_L for it in the above formula without causing any appreciable error.

Approximate Formulae for "I.T.M."—There are two very useful approximations, which are reasonably accurate for ship shapes and which may be used according to the information available.

Where T is the "T.P.I.," b the ship's breadth, and A the area of the waterplane:—

(1) $\qquad$ I.T.M. $= \dfrac{30.84\, T^2}{b}$

(2) $\qquad$ I.T.M. $= 0.000175 \dfrac{A^2}{b}$

Change of Draft Due to Change of Trim.—Change of trim is the sum of the changes of draft forward and aft. If the centre of flotation is at the ship's centre line, this change will be the same at each end; if not, the change will be greater at one end than at the other.

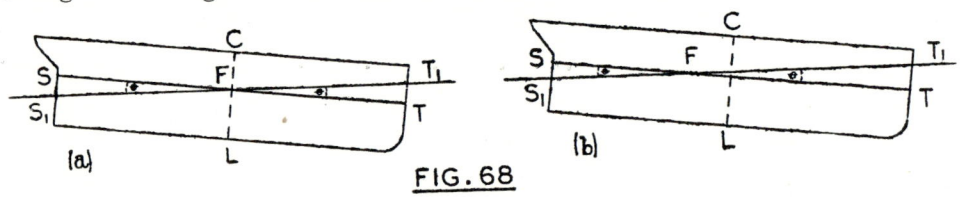

FIG. 68

Figures 68 (*A*) and (*B*) show what happens in the above cases. *F* represents the centre of flotation and *CL* the centre line of the ship, whilst

ST and S_1T_1 are the old and new waterlines, respectively. In each case the change of trim is SS_1+TT_1.

In Fig. 68 (A), F is on the centre line. It can be seen that, for all practical purposes, SF equals TF, S_1F equals T_1F, whilst the angle φ is the same on either side of F. The triangles SS_1F and TT_1F are, therefore, equal in all respects, so:—

$$SS_1 = TT_1$$
But $SS_1+TT_1=$ the change of trim
So, $SS_1=TT_1=$ half the change of trim.

This means that when the centre of flotation is on the longitudinal centre line, the change of draft at either end is equal to half the change of trim.

Fig. 68 (B) shows what happens when F is not on the centre line. In the triangles SS_1F, and TT_1F the angles φ are equal and the angles at S and T may be considered to be right angles, so that the triangles are similar but not equal. One of the properties of similar triangles is that the sides are proportional to each other, so:—

$$SS_1 : TT_1 :: SF : TF$$

Now, $SS_1+TT_1=$ the change of trim (call this t).
and $SF+TF=$ the length of the ship on the waterline (call this l)

So, $$SS_1 = \frac{SF}{l} \times t$$

and $$TT_1 = \frac{TF}{l} \times t$$

Change of Trim Due to Weights Shifted—When a weight is shifted, a moment is set up to cause a change of trim. This moment is the product of the weight shifted and of the distance through which it is shifted forward or aft. Since inch trim moment (I.T.M.) is the moment to change the trim by one inch, we can say that:—

Where w is the weight, in tons, and d the distance through which it is shifted forward or aft,

$$\text{Moment changing trim} = w \times d$$
$$\text{Change of trim, in inches} = \frac{w \times d}{\text{I.T.M.}}$$

The change of draft due to this can be found from the change of trim, as shown in the last section. If the weight is shifted aft, the after draft will increase and the forward draft decrease; if the weight is shifted forward, the reverse will happen. If the position of the centre of flotation is not known, we usually assume it to be at the centre line, since the error thus caused, if any, is generally small.

Change of Draft Due to Loading Weights at the Centre of Flotation.— If a weight is added at the centre of flotation, the ship may be assumed to sink bodily, without changing her trim.

When w is the added weight:—

$$\text{Bodily sinkage} = \frac{w}{\text{T.P.I.}}$$

The vessel will increase her draft at each end by the amount of the bodily sinkage.

Moderate Weights Loaded Off the Centre of Flotation.— When a weight is loaded at any point which is not in the same vertical line as the centre of flotation, the ship will change both her draft and trim. If the weight is of moderate amount the mean draft will only be altered by a few inches, so that the inch trim moment and the tons per inch immersion will be nearly the same for both the old and the new drafts. In such a case, we can calculate the new draft and trim as follows:—

(*a*) First, assume the weight to be added at the centre of flotation and calculate the sinkage by the formula:—

$$\text{Bodily sinkage} = \frac{w}{\text{T.P.I.}}$$

(*b*) Next, assume the weight to be shifted from the centre of flotation, forward or aft, to its new position. Calculate the change of trim caused by this by the formula:—

$$\text{Change of trim} = \frac{w \times d}{\text{I.T.M.}}$$

(*c*) Calculate the change of draft at either end, due to the above change of trim, as described in "Change of draft due to change of trim".

(*d*) Add the results of (*a*) to the draft at each end; then apply the results of (*c*). This will give the ship's new drafts after the weight has been added.

Large Weights Added Off the Centre of Flotation.— When large weights are added to a ship, the methods described in the last section must be modified. This is necessary because, as the ship changes her draft, there may be considerable changes in the position of the centre of flotation and in the amounts of the tons per inch immersion and inch trim moment. The following are the modifications which must be applied to the four stages mentioned in the last section:—

(*a*) Find the approximate bodily sinkage, as shown in (*a*) above, using the original tons per inch immersion. Apply this sinkage to the old draft to find an approximate new mean draft and find the tons per inch immersion for this new draft. Find the mean of the two tons per inch immersion

LONGITUDINAL STABILITY

by adding them together and dividing by two. Use this mean T.P.I. to find the true sinkage, using the formula:—

$$\frac{w}{\text{T.P.I.}}$$

(Strictly speaking, even this is not quite accurate, but it is good enough for all practical purposes). Find, also, the new mean draft.

(b) Find the position of the centre of flotation for this new mean draft, using the ship's stability curves. Also the inch trim moment at this draft. Use these to find the change of trim by the formula:—

$$\text{Change of trim} = \frac{w \times d}{\text{I.T.M.}}$$

(c) Calculate the change of draft due to the change of trim, using the new position of the centre of flotation.

(d) Find the new drafts fore and aft by applying sinkage and changes, as in the last section.

A Rough Approximation.—A "rule of thumb" method is sometimes used to determine the number of tons of cargo which must be loaded right forward or right aft in order to change the trim by one inch. The rule is:—

$$\text{Number of tons required} = \frac{\text{T.P.I.}}{4}$$

This rule, like most of its kind, is simple but very approximate. It may be useful in an emergency, but should not be used if full data is available, since it is always better to work these things out properly.

Loading a Weight to Produce a Desired Trim.—If it is desired to produce a certain trim, or to bring the ship to an even keel, we must proceed as follows:—

First, find the difference of the drafts forward and aft, thus finding the existing trim. The difference between this and the desired trim is the change of trim required.

Let t be the existing trim and t_1 the desired trim. Let w be the added weight and d its distance from the centre of flotation.

$$\text{Change of trim required} = t \sim t_1$$

but,
$$\text{Change of trim} = \frac{w \times d}{\text{I.T.M.}}$$

so,
$$\frac{w \times d}{\text{I.T.M.}} = t \sim t_1$$
$$w \times d = \text{I.T.M.} (t \sim t_1)$$

Thus, according to which we wish to find:—

$$d = \frac{\text{I.T.M.} (t \sim t_1)}{w}$$

$$w = \frac{\text{I.T.M.} (t \sim t_1)}{d}$$

Position to Load Weight so as not to Change the Draft Aft.—When a weight is loaded, there is usually a bodily sinkage of the ship and also a change of trim. The bodily sinkage tries to increase the draft aft: whilst if the weight is loaded forward of the centre of flotation, the change of trim tries to decrease the after draft. It is possible, by balancing these effects against each other, to keep the after draft constant when a weight is loaded.

Let w be the added weight and d its distance forward of the centre of flotation. Let L be the length of the ship and l the distance of the centre of flotation from aft.

$$\text{Bodily sinkage} = \frac{w}{\text{T.P.I.}}$$

This is equivalent to an increase of draft aft.

$$\text{Total change of trim} = \frac{w \times d}{\text{I.T.M.}}$$

$$\text{Change of draft aft, due to trim} = \frac{w \times d}{\text{I.T.M.}} \times \frac{l}{L}$$

This is equivalent to a decrease of draft aft.

For the after draft to remain constant, the increase due to the sinkage must be equal to the decrease due to the change of trim. That is:—

Bodily sinkage = Change of draft aft, due to trim.

$$\frac{w \times d}{\text{I.T.M.}} \times \frac{l}{L} = \frac{w}{\text{T.P.I.}}$$

$$\frac{w \times d}{\text{I.T.M.}} = \frac{w \times L}{\text{T.P.I.} \times l}$$

$$d = \frac{w \times L \times \text{I.T.M.}}{w \times \text{T.P.I.} \times l}$$

$$d = \frac{\text{I.T.M.} \times L}{\text{T.P.I.} \times l}$$

Note that the after draft will remain constant if the weight is loaded in the position so found, irrespective of how much weight is added, within reasonable limits.

Loading a Weight to Produce a Desired Draft Aft.—This may be achieved by a little modification of the above. When a weight is loaded, the bodily sinkage causes an increase of draft aft, whilst the change of trim may cause an increase or decrease, according to whether the weight is loaded forward of or abaft the centre of flotation. So:—

To obtain a decrease of draft, aft:
  Change of draft aft = change due to trim − bodily sinkage.
To obtain an increase of draft, aft:
  Change of draft aft = Bodily sinkage ± change due to trim.

LONGITUDINAL STABILITY

In the latter case, if the bodily sinkage is less than the change required, the sign will be $+$ and the weight loaded abaft the centre of flotation. If it is greater, the sign will be $-$ and the weight loaded forward of the centre of flotation.

A little thought should make this clear.

Increase of Draft Due to Bilging a Compartment.—Fig. 69 represents a vessel in which a compartment at the centre line has been bilged. The vessel is shewn as box shaped, for the sake of simplicity, but the effect will be the same for ship-shapes.

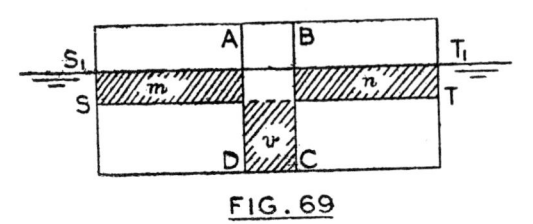

FIG. 69

Suppose that the ship floated originally at the waterline ST and that an empty compartment $ABCD$ is bilged. The buoyancy of this compartment is now lost to the ship. Call this lost buoyancy, v. The ship must continue to displace her own weight of water and so must displace the same volume as before. In order to do this, she will sink to the new waterline S_1T_1, so that the total volume of the layers, m and n, which have become immersed must be equal to that of the lost buoyancy. This means that:—

$$m+n=v$$

If the total areas of the original and the new waterplanes are the same, the volumes of m and n are together equal to the area of intact waterplane multiplied by the increase of draft (SS_1, or TT_1). So, if A is the total area of waterplane, a the area within the compartment and X the increase of draft, in feet:—

$$m + n = v$$
But, $$m + n = (A - a) X$$
so, $$v = (A - a) X$$
$$X = \frac{v}{A-a}$$

If there is cargo in the bilged compartment, it will still continue to displace a certain amount of water and we shall not lose the whole of the buoyancy in the compartment. We shall also gain a little buoyancy by submerging more cargo between the old and new waterplanes. In such a case, we must consider the permeability, which was discussed in the last chapter.

Thus, if p is the permeability, the formula becomes:—

$$X = \frac{v\,p}{A-ap}$$

CHAPTER 13.

ROLLING.

The Formation of Waves.—Officers of the modern Merchant Navy are not prone to fall into grave social errors and it is not recommended that they attempt to prove the following theory in the presence of passengers. At the same time, we all know that if we pour our tea into the saucer and then blow on it, waves are formed. Friction between the wind and the sea surface has a similar effect in producing sea-waves. The wind blows, to a greater or less degree, in gusts and also appears to blow somewhat obliquely down on to the sea surface. The effect of this is to cause slight depressions in that surface in some places, with corresponding elevations elsewhere so that "ripples" are formed. The wind will now act directly on these ripples, and if it blows long enough and strongly enough it will turn them into waves. It appears that, within certain limits, the size of the waves will depend largely on the force of the wind and on the distance from the point at which the waves originated.

The Trochoidal Theory.—This theory is generally used to explain the construction of waves and also certain phenomena connected with them. It is rather too complicated for us to consider fully here, so we will merely extract two points from it.

(*a*) The shapes of waves are approximately the same as a "trochoid", which is the curve traced out by a point inside a circle, rolling along a straight line. This is shewn in Fig. 70. Suppose that a wheel, with centre C, be rolled along the level surface AB, from left to right. A point, x, on the wheel

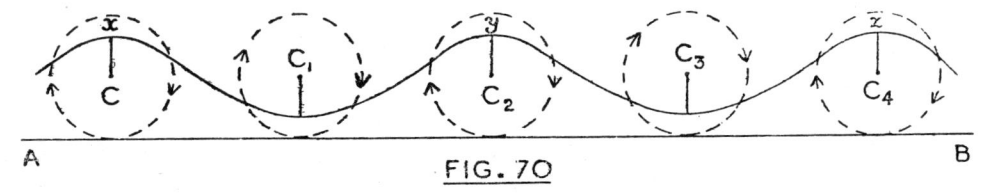

FIG. 70

would trace out the trochoid xyz, which has approximately the same shape as the surface of the waves—notice that the crests are sharper than the troughs.

(*b*) The water in a wave is not considered to have any appreciable horizontal motion; that is, it does not travel along with the wave in a horizontal direction. Each particle of water moves in a circular orbit, forward at the crest, backward in the trough, upwards in front of the wave and downward behind it. This produces a progressive "heaping-up" of the water, which causes the wave-outline to travel along, although the water itself is not doing so. For our purposes, we can consider waves as comparatively shallow, vertical movements of water.

The True Period of Waves.—This is the interval between the passage of any two consecutive wave crests at a stationary point. If a ship were stopped and had no movement, the period of the waves would be the interval between the time she was on one wave-crest and the time she was on the next. In theory, it is often assumed that a series of waves all have the same period; in practice, this very rarely occurs and successive groups of waves often have slightly different periods. The period usually increases with the size of waves, but rarely exceeds ten or twelve seconds.

The Apparent Period of Waves.—When a ship is moving through the water, the period of the waves may appear to those on board to be greater or less than the true period. A ship which is steaming head-on into a sea will be moving to meet each successive wave, which will thus reach her more quickly and will appear to have a shorter period than it actually has. A ship which has the sea aft, on the other hand, is moving away from the waves, so that these will take longer to catch up with her and will appear to have a longer period. When the sea is exactly abeam of the ship, her motion will have no effect and the apparent period will be the same as the true period. The apparent period will thus depend on the ship's speed through the water and on her course relative to the direction of the waves.

The apparent period is important, because it is the one which is actually felt by the ship and which thus affects her rolling.

The Period of a Ship.—This is the time taken by a ship to roll from one side to the other and back again. When the period is exactly the same for every roll, the rolling is termed "isochronous." It is often assumed that isochronous rolling occurs in every ship for any angle of roll, but this is not correct. We may accept the following general rules:—

(*a*) Different ships have different periods of roll.

(*b*) The same ship will have a different period for different conditions of loading.

(*c*) The same ship will have a longer period when she is tender than when she is stiff.

(*d*) "Winging out" weights will increase the period, all other things being equal.

(*e*) Rolling is isochronous for small angles of roll, up to about ten degrees, but the period increases slightly for larger angles.

Synchronism.—This is said to occur when the ship's period of roll is the same as the apparent period of the waves. When it occurs, the waves give the ship a "push" each time she rolls, in the direction in which she is rolling, causing her to roll more and more heavily. In theory, it would continue until she capsized, but this does not happen in practice because of certain resistances, which we shall consider later.

Unresisted Rolling.—Let us assume for a moment that there are no forces in existence to damp a ship's roll and that she merely rolls under the influence of the waves and of her own period. Let us also assume that the period of the waves is the same throughout and that the ship's period is isochronous for all angles of roll.

If the ship's period is much less than that of the waves, she will always take up a position at right angles to the wave-slope and will not roll to either greater or smaller angles than this. In other words, she will behave in exactly the same way as a raft would do.

If synchronism occurs, the ship will roll through increasingly greater angles until she capsizes.

When the ship's period is much greater than that of the waves, she will roll easily and never to large angles. The waves would set her rolling, but would soon become out of time with the roll and would thus cause her to steady-down again.

In practice, we find that the ship's period increases with the angle of roll and also that we rarely meet a long series of waves of exactly the same period. So, even if the ship herself offered no resistance to rolling, synchronism would seldom exist for long. A normal ship might roll heavily, but she would be unlikely to capsize.

Resistances to Rolling.—We all know that it is possible to set a boat rolling by leaning from side to side in time with her period. If we first start her rolling and then sit upright and without moving, the roll will gradually decrease and will finally die out altogether.

A ship can be set rolling in still water, in a similar way, by shifting weights or bodies of men from side to side. Similarly also, if we stop moving them, the ship's roll will die out. For this to happen, the boat or ship must be setting up resistance to its own roll; otherwise it would merely continue to roll to the same angle and with the same period. These resistances are usually considered to be as follows:—

(*a*) A rolling ship creates waves and these require a considerable amount of work to produce them. This work is provided by the ship and would otherwise have formed part of the forces producing the rolling. Instead, it now passes away with the waves and is lost. This wave-formation is one of the chief resistances to be considered.

(*b*) Friction between the water and the hull of the ship sets up a slight resistance. The effect is very slight in a ship having a much rounded bottom. In a ship which has a full bilge, or particularly bilge keels, it is much greater but is never very considerable.

(*c*) There is a certain amount of resistance between the hull and the air, but its effect is negligible.

(*d*) Properly fitted bilge keels have a great damping effect on rolling. Their exact effects are complicated and will be considered more fully in the next section.

It can be seen that since the above resistances are capable of eliminating the ship's roll in still water, they will also resist the forces causing the ship to roll in a seaway. They will not eliminate rolling, but they can damp it considerably.

The Effects of Bilge Keels.—These may be said to have three main effects in resisting rolling, namely:—

(*a*) They offer a certain amount of direct resistance to the water, but this effect is comparatively weak.

(*b*) They cause the ship's period of roll to increase slightly.

(*c*) They set up eddy currents and pressure under water.

The latter effect is by no means simple and may be considered to produce a number of subsidiary effects:—

1. The wave formation due to rolling, described in subdivision (a) of the last section, is considerably increased.

2. The water pressure on the hull is increased on that side of each bilge keel towards which the ship is rolling. This pressure acts at right angles to the hull and its direction is such that it forms a resistance to the roll of the ship.

3. Water is unable to run around the hull in an uninterrupted streamline. This will also reduce rolling, since any upsetting of streamline effects will cause eddy currents and resistance to motion.

Bilge keels have a greater effect when the ship is moving than when she is stationary, and the greater the speed the greater the effect. This is usually considered to be due to the fact that as the ship moves ahead she is passing out of the water which has been disturbed by her rolling. A certain amount of the bilge keel is thus working in undisturbed water and the effect of this part is increased accordingly. The faster the ship moves, the more of the keel is in such water and the greater the anti-rolling effect.

Cures for Heavy Rolling.—When, for any reason, a ship is found to be rolling heavily, the proper cure is to alter course and/or speed. This will alter the apparent period of the waves and destroy synchronism, which is nearly always the cause of such rolling.

It is usually futile, and sometimes dangerous, to attempt a cure by working water ballast in these circumstances.

CHAPTER 14.

MISCELLANEOUS MATTERS.

Drydocking.—When a ship is drydocked, her support has to be transferred from the water to the keel blocks and shores. She may be considered safe whilst she is waterborne, or once the shores have been set up, but there is a danger that she may become unstable during the intervening period, which is often termed the "critical period".

Whilst the dock is being pumped out, the ship at first sinks bodily as the water level falls, but as soon as she touches the keel blocks she stops sinking and the water falls around her. She thus loses displacement so that weight, equal to the amount of the lost displacement, is transferred to the blocks. As far as the ship's stability is concerned, this weight is equivalent to a force acting vertically upwards at the keel and it will decrease the metacentric height. The latter must, sooner or later, become negative and if this were to happen before the shores were properly set up, the ship might capsize in the dock. It is thus of the utmost importance to keep full control of the ship during the critical period and to get the shores set up as soon as possible. To assist in this, it is usual to have the ship trimmed a little by the stern when she enters the dock, so that the heel of the stern post is the first part to touch the blocks.

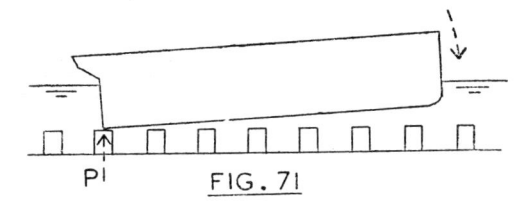

Fig. 71 illustrates what happens in the above case. As soon as the ship's stern touches the blocks the upward force, *P*, comes into existence. This force is small at first, but gradually increases as the water level falls and the ship's bow comes down. The advantage of this is that the decrease in metacentric height, caused by the force *P*, is more gradual than it would be if the ship suddenly sat flat on the blocks fore and aft, so that we have more control over the ship's stability. Also, although the shores cannot be set up before the ship comes down flat on the blocks, we can start to put-in the after shores loosely as soon as the stern touches. By the time that the ship is right down on the blocks a large number of shores are already in place, so that the remainder can be put in and all set up with the minimum of delay. This decreases the risk of the ship falling over in the dock.

It is important to have the ship upright when she enters a drydock. If she were not, this could be due to one of two causes; a negative metacentric height, or the weights on board not being symmetrical about the centre line.

MISCELLANEOUS MATTERS

In the first case, the ship would be certain to fall over as soon as her keel touched the blocks. In the second, she might fall over at some time during the critical period on account of the excess of weight on one side.

Before the ship is floated again, it is very important to check any weights which may have been shifted whilst she is in the dock; otherwise we may have a similar effect to the above whilst the dock is being filled. In this respect, do not forget to make sure that boilers have not been filled or emptied, or to check-up on any weights shifted in the engine room.

The procedure of drydocking is, briefly, as follows. As soon as the ship enters the dock she usually comes under the control of the foreman carpenter or shipwright, who manoeuvres her into the position he requires. The dock gates are then closed and pumping-out commences. When the ship's stern is nearly on the blocks, pumping is stopped whilst the ship is aligned so that her centre line is exactly over them. Pumping is then resumed slowly until the stern touches the blocks, when the after shores are put-in loosely. As the ship settles down, more shores are put-in, working from aft forward, and as soon as the keel comes flat on the blocks any remaining shores are put in place and all are set-up as quickly as possible. The heads of shores should always be placed on frames and not between them, in order to eliminate the risk of denting the ship's plating. Once the shores have been set-up, pumping is continued quickly until the dock is dry.

The following formula will give the ship's metacentric height at any time during the process of drydocking:—

Where P = the force acting upwards through the keel.
KM = height of the metacentre on entering the dock.
W = ship's displacement on entering dock.

$$\text{New } GM = \text{Old } GM - \frac{P \times KM}{W}$$

The force P is the difference between the displacement of the ship on entering the dock and her displacement at the time for which we wish to calculate her GM. After the ship has come flat on the blocks, this calculation is quite simple, since the two displacements will be those for the respective mean drafts: that is—

P = displacement at original draft − displacement at new draft.

It is more difficult to find P during the critical period, after the ship's stern has touched the blocks, but before she comes flat on them. The most dangerous part of this period, and hence the one with which we are most concerned, occurs at the instant before the ship takes the blocks fore and aft. For this instant, P can be found approximately by the following formula:—

Where t = the trim, in inches, on entering the dock.
l = the distance between the after block and the centre of flotation.

$$P = \frac{\text{I.T.M.} \times t}{l}$$

Grounding.—When a ship runs ashore, her metacentric height will decrease or become negative as in drydocking, but the exact effect of this on her stability is almost unpredictable. It will vary according to the nature of the ground, how the ship is placed on the bottom, what damage she has sustained and the nature and state of the tides. In practice, we can only attempt to get the ship afloat again as soon as possible, if it appears safe to do so.

The Effect of Density on Stability.—When there is a change in the density of the water in which a ship floats, she will change her draught. This will generally have the following effects on her stability:—

(*a*) When the ship is near her light draft, the centre of buoyancy will be lowered and the metacentre will probably rise. Thus there will be an increase of *BM* and probably of *GM* also.

(*b*) When the ship is near her load draft, the centre of buoyancy will fall and the metacentre will probably do likewise. There will usually be little change in *BM*, but *GM* may decrease.

(*c*) The trim may change, usually so as to cause an increase of the draft aft and a decrease forward.

It should be remembered that all the above effects are comparatively small, so that they can safely be ignored in practice.

The Effect of Density on the Draft of Ships.—In Chapter 1, we considered this effect in box shapes and also with regard to fresh water allowance. Now let us consider it in relation to ship shapes.

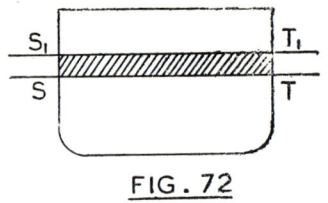

In Fig. 72, let the ship be first floating at the waterline ST, in water of density δ. Then let her pass into water of a lesser density, δ_1 and sink to the new waterline S_1T_1. Let X be the increase of draft, in inches—that is, the distance between the two waterlines. Let W be the ship's displacement: since the ship must always displace her own weight of water, this will remain the same for both drafts.

FIG. 72

$$\text{Volume} = \frac{\text{Weight}}{\text{Density}}$$

So, volume below the waterline $ST = \dfrac{W}{\delta}$

And volume below the waterline $S_1T_1 = \dfrac{W}{\delta_1}$

The difference between these two volumes must be equal to the volume of the layer SS_1T_1T, so:—

$$\begin{aligned}
\text{Volume of the layer } SS_1T_1T &= \frac{W}{\delta_1} - \frac{W}{\delta} \\
&= \frac{W\delta - W\delta_1}{\delta\delta_1} \\
&= \frac{W}{\delta\delta_1}(\delta - \delta_1) \quad . \quad . \quad (1)
\end{aligned}$$

The weight of a layer such as SS_1T_1T must be equal to its depth in inches multiplied by the tons per inch immersion.

Weight of the layer $SS_1T_1T = X \times $ T.P.I.

Volume of the layer $SS_1T_1T = \dfrac{X \times \text{T.P.I.}}{\delta}$ . . . (2)

If we now combine formulæ (1) and (2) above, we can see that:—

$$\dfrac{X \times \text{T.P.I.}}{\delta} = \dfrac{W}{\delta \delta_1}(\delta - \delta_1)$$

$$X \times \text{T.P.I.} = \dfrac{W}{\delta_1}(\delta - \delta_1)$$

$$X = \dfrac{W(\delta - \delta_1)}{\delta_1 \times \text{T.P.I.}}$$

Derivation of the Fresh Water Allowance.—It has been stated in Chapter I. that the formula $\dfrac{\Delta}{40T}$ is used for finding a ship's fresh water allowance. The derivation of this can easily be seen if we consider the formula above.

Since we are dealing with a change from salt water to fresh water, δ becomes 1025 and δ_1 becomes 1000. Δ is the displacement at the summer draft, so it can be substituted for W in the above formula. If T represents the tons per inch immersion and X the fresh water allowance, then:—

$$X = \dfrac{W(\delta - \delta_1)}{\delta \times \text{T.P.I.}}$$

$$X = \dfrac{\Delta(1025 - 1000)}{1000T}$$

$$X = \dfrac{\Delta}{40T}$$

Reserve Buoyancy.—In the case of a ship, this is the volume of the hull between the waterline and the freeboard deck. It amounts, approximately to the difference between the actual displacement and that which the ship would have if she were submerged to her freeboard deck.

We can calculate the reserve buoyancy for any floating body by finding the difference between the total watertight volume of the body and the volume of water which it displaces.

Continuous Watertight Longitudinal Bulkheads.—These give great longitudinal strength to a ship and also reduce free surface effect when liquids are carried in bulk. They have one serious disadvantage, however, in that if the ship is holed on one side and the bulkhead remains intact, the compartment will become flooded on one side only. This will give the ship a list, which may be dangerous if the compartment is large.

In ordinary cargo ships, having large holds, there would be considerable risk of the ship capsizing in the above circumstances. There is normally no free surface effect to be reduced in the holds and the bulkheads have the additional disadvantage that they interfere with the handling of cargo. Consequently continuous longitudinal bulkheads are not fitted in ordinary cargo ships, since the disadvantages outweigh the gain in longitudinal strength.

In the case of oil-tankers, carrying bulk liquid cargoes, some form of longitudinal subdivision is necessary to minimise free surface effect. Interference with the stowage of cargo does not have to be considered and great longitudinal strength is required. In such ships, the advantages of continuous longitudinal bulkheads are obvious and one or two are always fitted. The danger of the vessel's capsizing in the event of her being bilged is overcome by reducing the length of the tanks to a maximum of thirty feet between transverse bulkheads.

Non-Continous Longitudinal Bulkheads.—These are often fitted in ordinary ships, as they have a number of structural advantages. Since they are not continuous throughout any hold, they do not affect the ship's stability.

Bulkhead Subdivision and Sheer.—The subdivision of a ship into compartments by means of transverse bulkheads is a great factor in determining her safety if she is holed. It is not generally realised by seamen that sheer also plays an important part in this if the ship is holed forward or abaft the centre of the flotation.

In 1912, a committee was set up to investigate the spacing of bulkheads and the suggestions which were made in their report are now compulsory for passenger ships. It was not possible to apply them to cargo ships also and the bulkheads in the latter are usually more widely spaced than would be allowed in passenger vessels. The committee introduced the "Margin Line" and the "Curve of Floodable Lengths".

The Margin Line is an imaginary line, three inches below the bulkhead deck. It is assumed that a ship which was sunk to this line would still be navigable in fine weather.

The Curve of Floodable Lengths is a graph from which can be found the floodable lengths for any part of the ship, i.e., that length of the ship which, if flooded, would cause her to sink to her margin line. When this is calculated, allowance is made for an assumed average permeability in each of the various compartments. The length allowed for any compartment is found by multiplying the floodable length by a factor which depends on the length of the ship and on a number of other things.

Sheer is the upward rise of the ship's deck from amidships towards the bow and stern. If a compartment becomes bilged at one end of the ship so

MISCELLANEOUS MATTERS

that she changes her trim, the sheer helps to prevent the margin line from becoming submerged at that end. It thus increases the floodable lengths forward and aft.

Pressure on Bulkheads.—When a compartment is flooded, the water pressure on the end bulkheads is greatest at the bottom and decreases to nothing at the water level. The greatest support is needed at a point somewhere between the bottom and the surface level, such that the total pressure above it is equal to the total pressure below it. This point is known as the "Centre of Pressure" and its position is as follows:—

(a) For rectangular bulkheads, at the two-thirds depth of the bulkhead below the water level.

(b) For triangular bulkheads (apex downwards), at the half-depth of the bulkhead below the water level.

(c) In the case of ship shapes, the majority of the bulkheads are nearly rectangular and need shoring most strongly at about the two-thirds depth. Some of the bulkheads are, however, of an intermediate shape and in this case the centre of pressure falls between the half-depth and the two-thirds depth.

Three formulae may be useful here:—Where h is the depth below the surface of any point on a bulkhead; H, the depth below the surface of the centre of gravity of the underwater part of the bulkhead; A, the underwater area of the bulkhead; W, the weight of the water in pounds per cubic foot:—

Pressure at any given point $= Wh$ (lbs. per square foot.)
Average pressure on the bulkhead $= WH$ (lbs.)
Total pressure on the bulkhead $= WHA$ (lbs.)

Note that H, which is sometimes called the "Centroid", must not be confused with the centre of pressure. For instance, in a rectangular bulkhead, the centre of pressure is at the two-thirds depth, whilst the centroid is at the half depth below the water level.

The Effect of Water in Sounding Pipes, etc.—When water rises in sounding pipes or air pipes to above the top of a tank, pressure is set up on the tank-top. Many seamen assume that this pressure will be negligible, because such pipes are usually of comparatively small diameter and the weight of water in them is correspondingly small. This is not the case, however. Water exerts pressure equally in all directions and so the pressure per square inch at the bottom of the pipe is transmitted over the whole of the tank top. This pressure will not depend on the actual weight of water in the pipe, but on the head of water and will be approximately the same whatever the diameter of the pipe.

CHAPTER 15.

STABILITY CURVES AND SCALES.

When a ship is built, the Naval Architects calculate certain data affecting her stability and set it out in the form of curves and scales. Copies of these are handed over to the Owners and should eventually reach the Masters and Officers. The information given and the methods of setting it out vary considerably, but usually consist of a set of curves, a deadweight scale and sometimes a "metacentric diagram." The Ministry of Transport now specify that certain information must be supplied to ships.

Occasionally, a set of sample "conditions" is drawn up. These consist of a number of diagrams showing the ship in different states of loading and give information about her stability in each state shown. The objection to the use of these is that the ship is rarely exactly in any of the conditions shown, so that the information thus obtained is usually only approximate.

Information to be Supplied to Ships.—A Ministry of Transport Notice (M.375) requires that certain stability information be supplied to all ships. The following is a summary of the requirements:—

(a) A plan of the ship to shew the capacity and Kg of each space: weight and Kg of passengers and crew; weight, disposition and Kg of any anticipated homogeneous deck cargo.

(b) The light displacement and KG; also the weight, disposition and Kg of permanent ballast, if any.

(c) Curves or scales to shew displacement, deadweight, KM, T.P.I., and I.T.M.

(d) A statement of the free surface effect in each tank.

(e) Cross curves, stating the assumed KG.

(f) Statements and diagrams to shew displacement, disposition and weights of cargo, etc., drafts, trim information, KG, KM, GM, free surface corrections, and curves of statical stability when the ship is:—

    (i) Light.
    (ii) In ballast condition.
    (iii) Loaded with homogeneous cargo.
    (iv) In service loaded conditions.

(g) Written instructions concerning any special procedure necessary to maintain adequate stability throughout the voyage.

Curves of Displacement, etc.—In the back of this book will be found a set of curves of a type often supplied to ships. These are often called "Hydrostatic Curves." As we have already mentioned, such curves vary considerably in detail, but are fundamentally the same, so that anyone who can understand those given here should have no difficulty in taking-off information from any others he may encounter.

A scale of mean drafts of the ship runs vertically up the left-hand side of the sheet, lines being drawn horizontally across the plan at every foot. The main body of the plan consists of a number of curves, each showing the amount or position of any one item for any mean draft on the scale. Along the bottom edge are scales from which the amounts of the various items can be read off. The curves for the various coefficients are usually shown plain, but are here given as pecked lines, in order to avoid confusion due to too many similar lines.

To obtain information, find the ship's mean draft on the left-hand scale and draw a line horizontally across the plan from this, until it cuts the curve required; or use dividers to measure up to this point from the nearest horizontal line. From the point thus found, drop a perpendicular line to the appropriate scale on the bottom of the plan, or again use dividers, and read off the required information. For example, to find the tons per inch immersion at a mean draft of 18 feet 6 inches. we run horizontally across the plan from that draft on the scale and find the point A on the T.P.I. curve. We then find the point on the T.P.I. scale which is vertically under A, which tells us that the required T.P.I. is about 39·8.

It will be noticed that the curves have their descriptions written on them in full, whilst, to save space, abbreviations have been used for naming the scales. Sometimes abbreviations are used along the curves also, but this should not cause any difficulty, since they are standardised and should be known by anyone studying stability. Those used in the curves given here are as follows:—

Height of the centre of buoyancy above the keel	KB
Height of the transverse metacentre above the keel ..	KM
Height of the longitudinal metacentre above the keel ..	KM_L
Inch trim moment	I.T.M.
Tons per inch immersion	T.P.I.
Centre of buoyancy abaft amidships	C.B. abaft amidships.
Centre of flotation abaft amidships	C.F. abaft amidships.
Displacement	"Displacement."
Block coefficient of fineness	
Prismatic coefficient of fineness	
Waterplane coefficient of fineness .. .. (all)	"Coefficients."
Midships section coefficient of fineness	

Always be careful that you take off information from the proper scale.

Use of the Hydrostatic Curves.—The uses of the information which we can obtain from the curves are fairly obvious to anyone who has read through this book. Let us consider an example of the information that it is possible to obtain.

Suppose that we wish to find all possible stability information from the curves given in the back of this book, assuming that the ship is floating at a mean draft of 21 feet 5 inches. We draw a horizontal line across the plan at this draft and can then take off the following information from the scales at the foot:—

Displacement	8750 tons
KB	11·9 feet
KM	23·0 ,,
KM_L	531 ,,
I.T.M.	945 ft.-tons
T.P.I.	40·65
Centre of flotation abaft amidships	9·4 feet
Centre of buoyancy abaft amidships	6·4 ,,
Midships section coefficient of fineness	0·95
Waterplane	0·79
Prismatic	0·69
Block	0·66

We can also, if we wish, find the ship's GM as follows:—From the deadweight scale we find that the light KG is 23·18 feet and, from the curves that the light displacement is 3460 tons. If we know what weights have been loaded in the ship and the heights of their centres of gravity, we can calculate the existing KG, as shown in Chapter 4. The difference between this KG and the KM found above will be the ship's GM.

The Deadweight Scale.—This scale is familiar to most ship's officers and is another method of giving certain stability information which they are most likely to need. A typical scale will be found in the back of this book, with the displacement scale, and is made out for the same ship as the latter. It contains a scale of mean draft, against which is placed one of deadweight, marked to read to each 100 tons. The tons per inch immersion is given for each foot of draft, shown at the 6-inch marks. The inch-trim moment is shown for each 25 tons, against the corresponding mean draft. The heights of the metacentre and of the centre of buoyancy above the keel (KM and KB) are given for every 6 inches of mean draft. In the lower margin we are told the light KG —that is, the height of the centre of gravity above the keel when the ship is light.

Use of the Deadweight Scale.—It is quite a simple matter to obtain information from the scale, although a little interpolation must be done some-

STABILITY CURVES AND SCALES

times if great accuracy is required. For most practical purposes, however, this is not necessary and it is sufficient to take the nearest figure and reading on the scale. This is the reason why the T.P.I. is shewn at the 6-inch marks, because the figure thus given may be taken as the average over the whole foot. For example we could say that, for all practical purposes, the T.P.I. for drafts of between 20 feet and 21 feet is about 40·4.

Suppose that we wish to find all possible information from the curves, for a mean draft of 16 feet 6 inches. This will be:—

Deadweight	Just over 2900 tons—say, 2910.
T.P.I.	39·01.
I.T.M.	Just under 875—say, 870 foot-tons.
KM	23·70 feet.
KB	9·21 feet.

We can see that the light KG is 23·18 feet and if we know the light displacement, can find the existing KG and GM, as described in "Use of the Curves."

Curves of Statical Stability.—These are graphs which shew the ship's statical stability at all angles of heel. Each curve is given for one displacement only, using an assumed KG. The curves sometimes shew righting moments ($W \times GZ$), or sometimes righting levers (GZ), according to the purpose for which they are intended.

There is a theorem which says that we can find the shape of the curve at its origin (*i.e.*, 0°) by drawing a perpendicular at 1 radian (57·3°) and on this, marking off the GM from the GZ scale. A straight line from the point so found to the point of origin will form a tangent to the curve at that point.

Figure 73 shews a single curve, on which the righting levers have been plotted. It has been constructed by calculating the GZ's at various angles of heel and plotting these as a graph. The dotted lines illustrate the method of finding the shape of the curve at its origin, referred to in the theorem above: the assumed GM has been marked off on the perpendicular at 57·3° and the line from here to the point of origin forms the tangent to the curve.

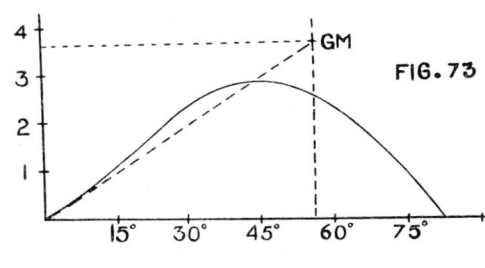

FIG. 73

A single curve of statical stability enables us to find the range of stability, or angle of vanishing stability; the angle and amount of maximum stability; the approximate GM for which the curve has been drawn. The latter is found by drawing a tangent to the curve at the point of origin and then measuring off the *GM* at the point where this tangent meets the perpendicular at 1 radian.

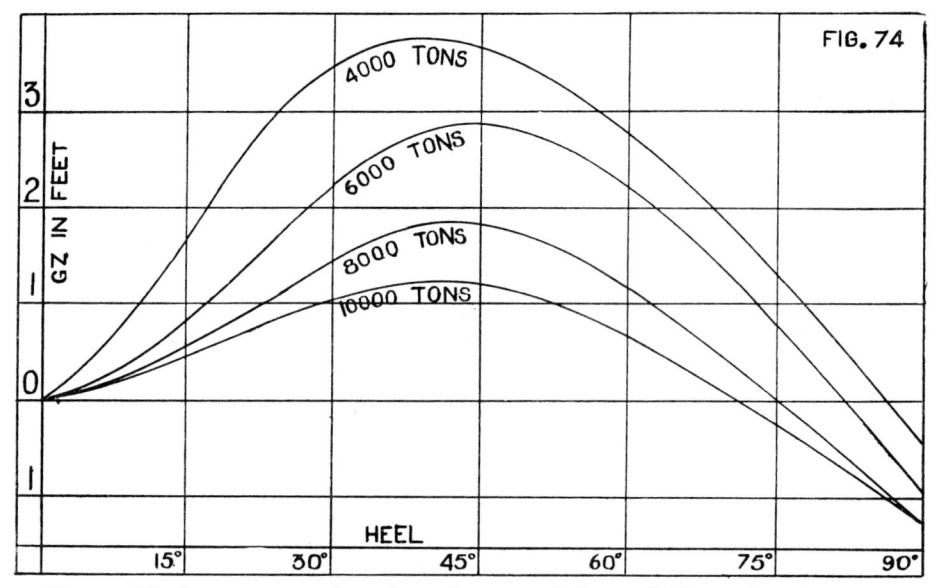

FIG. 74

If we wish for a comprehensive picture of the stability of a ship we may, construct a series of curves of statical stability, using the same *KG* for all, but a different displacement for each. A typical set of such curves, drawn for one ship, is shewn in Figure 74, above.

Cross Curves.—These are another common method of drawing graphs of righting levers. They are different from the ordinary curves of statical stability, however, because each curve shews the righting levers for one angle of heel only, but at different displacements. The principle on which they are constructed is shewn diagrammatically in Figure 75; in which the curves of statical stability are represented as standing-up, one behind the other, at equal distances apart. Points 15° apart have been marked on each curve

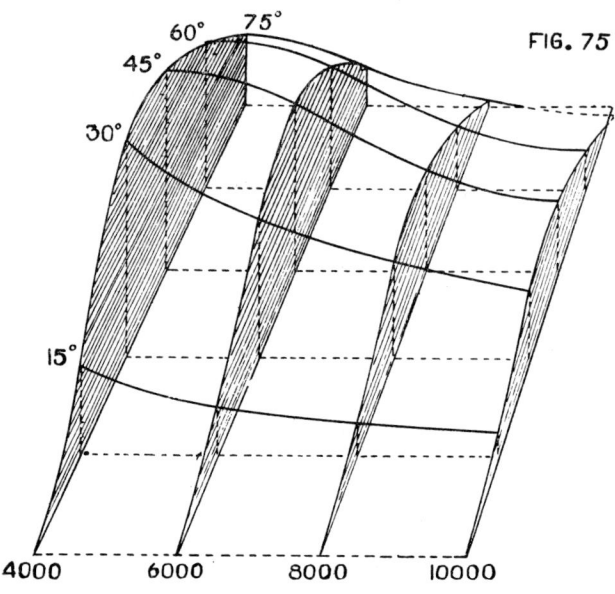

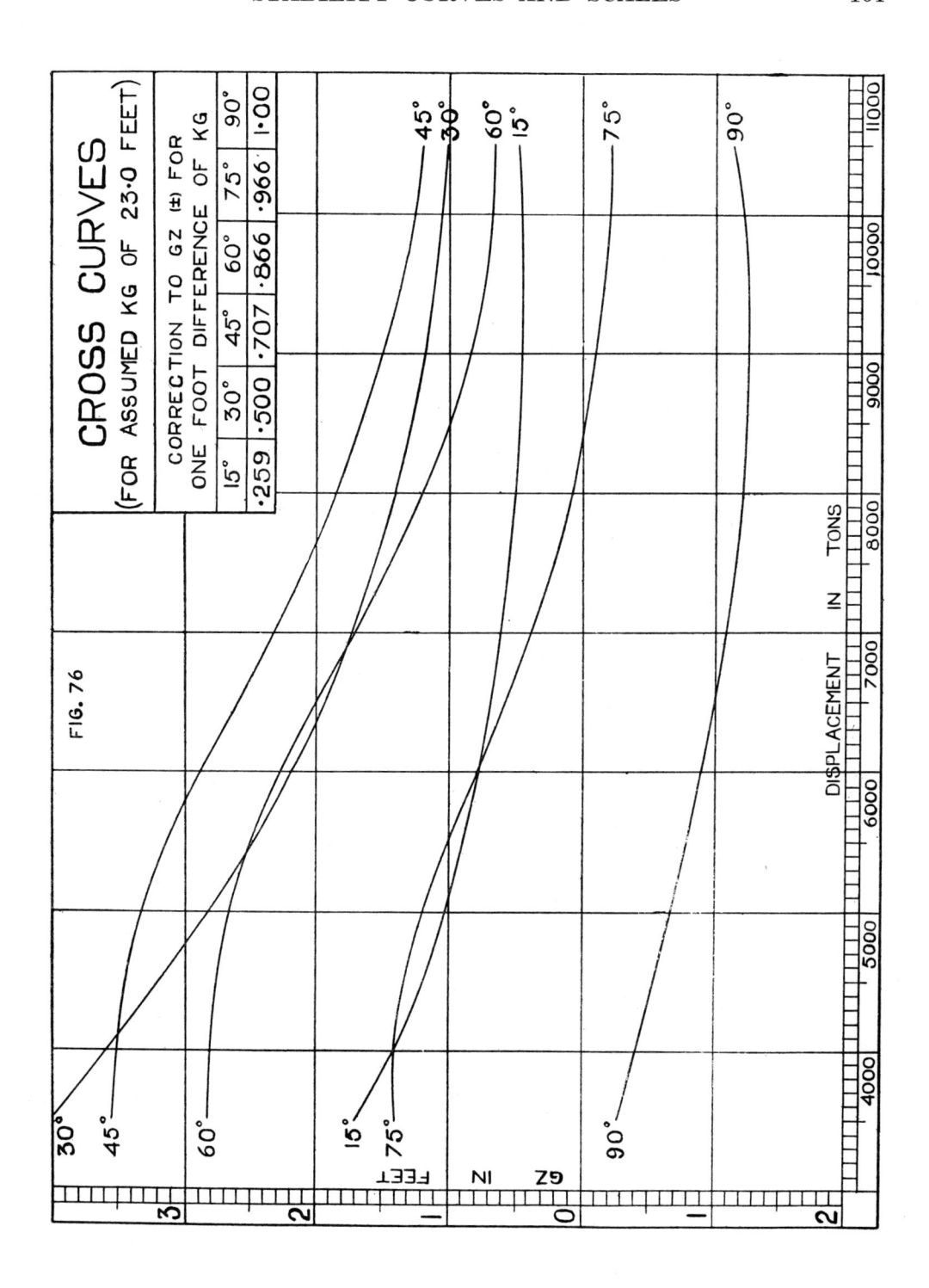

STABILITY CURVES AND SCALES

FIG. 76

CROSS CURVES
(FOR ASSUMED KG OF 23·0 FEET)

CORRECTION TO GZ (±) FOR ONE FOOT DIFFERENCE OF KG					
15°	30°	45°	60°	75°	90°
·259	·500	·707	·866	·966	1·00

and each "set" of points has been joined by a fair curve, which is the cross curve for that angle of heel. It can be seen from this that their name is derived from the fact that these curves, in effect, cut across the curves of statical stability.

Figure 76, on page 101, shews a typical set of cross curves, which has been derived from the curves of statical stability given in Figure 74. The *GZ* can be found from these, for any angle for which a curve is given, by measuring vertically upwards to the curve, at the displacement chosen, and then reading off the *GZ* from the scale on the left hand side. For example, the *GZ* for 30° of heel at 7000 tons displacement would be 1·75 feet.

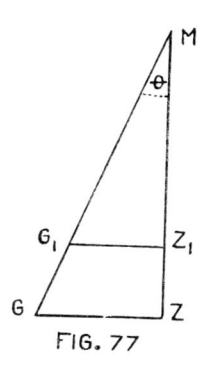

Effect of Height of G.—If the actual height of the ship's centre of gravity is different from the assumed height used in constructing the curves, the *GZ*'s obtained from the curves will be incorrect. If we consider the *GZM* triangle, it is obvious that if *G* be raised, *GZ* will be decreased: if *G* is lowered, *GZ* will be increased. Suppose that, in Figure 77, *G* is the assumed position of the ship's centre of gravity, whilst G_1 is its actual position. Then, if the angle of heel is θ:—

FIG. 77

$$GZ = GM \times \sin \theta$$
$$G_1Z_1 = G_1M \times \sin \theta$$
$$\overline{GZ - G_1Z_1} = \overline{(GM - G_1M)} \sin \theta$$

So decrease (or Increase) of $GZ = GG_1 \times \sin \theta$

This means that if the actual *KG* is different from the assumed *KG*, each *GZ* found from the curves must be amended by $GG_1 \times \sin \theta$. In practice, a table of corrections is often given with a set of cross curves; as in the right hand top corner of Figure 76. This gives the correction for each foot of difference in *KG*: for other differences, the correction will be proportional; for example, if *G* is 0·5 of a foot higher or lower, the correction to *GZ* will be 0·5 of that shewn in the table.

The Metacentric Diagram.—This diagram is another method of showing the heights of the metacentre and centre of buoyancy for various mean drafts. A scale of mean drafts is drawn up and a line is drawn across the paper at an angle of 45° to it—this is called "the 45° line." A curve of centres of buoyancy is drawn in below this line, so that the distance from the curve to any point on the line is equal to the distance of the centre of buoyancy below the water line at that point. The curve of metacentres is drawn in a similar way above the 45° line.

STABILITY CURVES AND SCALES 103

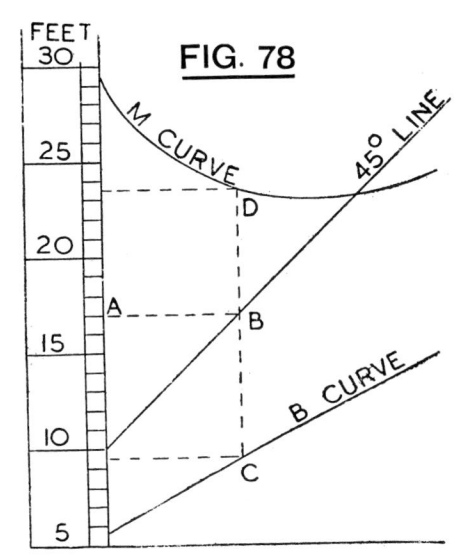

FIG. 78

This is best seen from Fig. 78. To find the positions of *B* and *M* for any particular draft, draw a horizontal line through that draft. Then, through the point where this cuts the 45° line, draw a vertical line to meet the *B* and *M* curves. The scale readings opposite the points thus found give the positions of the centre of buoyancy and the metacentre, whilst the distance between the points is equal to the *BM*.

For example, in Fig. 78, to find the *KB*, *KM* and *BM*, at a draft of 17 feet. Draw the horizontal line, *AB*, through the 17 feet mark and then the vertical line, *CBD*. *C* then represents the height of the centre of buoyancy, *D* that of the metacentre above the keel and *CD*, the ship's *BM*. We can see from the scale that *KB* equals 9·5 feet, *KM* equals 23·5 feet and *BM* is 14·0 feet.

H

WORKED EXAMPLES

Increase of Pressure with Depth.—A rectangular plate in the bottom of a ship is 26 feet long and 6 feet wide. If it is 18 feet below the sea surface, find the pressure per square foot and also the total pressure on the plate.

$$\begin{aligned}
\text{Pressure per square foot} &= 64D \text{ lbs.} \\
&= 64 \times 18 \\
&= 1152 \text{ lbs., or } 0\cdot 514 \text{ tons} \\
\text{Total pressure} &= 64AD \text{ lbs.} \\
&= 64 \times 26 \times 6 \times 18 \\
&= 179712 \text{ lbs., or } 80\cdot 23 \text{ tons}
\end{aligned}$$

Floating Bodies and Density.—1. A log of wood weighs 550 lbs. and floats in the water of density 1000. Find its underwater volume.

$$\begin{aligned}
\text{Underwater volume} &= \frac{\text{Weight of the body, in ounces}}{\text{Density of water}} \\
&= \frac{550 \times 16}{1000} \\
&= 8\cdot 8 \text{ cubic feet}
\end{aligned}$$

2. A floating body displaces 255 cubic feet of water of density 1005. What volume will it displace if placed in water of density 1025?

$$\begin{aligned}
\frac{\text{New volume displaced}}{\text{Old volume displaced}} &= \frac{\text{Old density}}{\text{New density}} \\
\text{New volume displaced} &= \frac{\text{Old density} \times \text{old volume displaced}}{\text{New density}} \\
&= \frac{1005 \times 255}{1025} \\
&= 250 \text{ cubic feet}
\end{aligned}$$

Effect of Density on Draft.—1. A box-shaped lighter has a draft of 3 feet 8 inches in water of density 1024. What would her draft be in water of density 1008?

$$\begin{aligned}
3' \, 8'' &= 44'' \\
\frac{\text{New draft}}{\text{Old draft}} &= \frac{\text{Old density}}{\text{New density}} \\
\text{New draft} &= \frac{\text{Old density} \times \text{old draft}}{\text{New density}} \\
&= \frac{44 \times 1024}{1008} \\
&= 44\cdot 7 \text{ inches, or 3 feet } 8\cdot 7 \text{ inches}
\end{aligned}$$

WORKED EXAMPLES

2. A ship floats at a draft of 17 feet $8\frac{1}{2}$ inches in water of density 1005. If her fresh water allowance is $7\frac{1}{4}$ inches, what will be her draft on passing into water of density 1025?

$$x = \frac{F(1025 - \delta)}{25} = \frac{7 \cdot 25 (1025 - 1005)}{25} = 5 \cdot 80 \text{ inches}$$

$$\begin{aligned}
\text{Old draft} &= 17' \ 8\frac{1}{2}'' \\
\text{Rise} &= 5\frac{3}{4} \\
\hline
\text{New draft} &= 17' \ 2\frac{3}{4}''
\end{aligned}$$

Areas of Waterplanes.—1. Use the Trapezoidal Rule to find the area of a waterplane which has the following ordinates, spaced 10 feet apart:—8·0; 14·6; 17·2; 16·2; 11·8; 4·4 feet.

$$\text{Area} = h \left\{ \frac{a+f}{2} + b + c + d + e \right\}$$

$$= 10 \left\{ \frac{8 \cdot 0 + 4 \cdot 4}{2} + 14 \cdot 6 + 17 \cdot 2 + 16 \cdot 2 + 11 \cdot 8 \right\}$$

$$= 660 \text{ square feet}$$

2. Use Simpson's Rules to find the area of a waterplane which has the following half-ordinates, spaced 12 feet apart:—1·7; 5·9; 7·0; 5·2; 1·3 feet.

Since there are 5 ordinates we can use Simpson's First Rule.

$$\text{Half area} = \frac{h}{3} \left\{ a + 4b + 2c + 4d + e \right\}$$

$$= \frac{12}{3} \left\{ 1 \cdot 7 + (4 \times 5 \cdot 9) + (2 \times 7 \cdot 0) + (4 \times 5 \cdot 2) + 1 \cdot 3 \right\}$$

Ordinate	Multiplier	Product
1·7	1	1·7
5·9	4	23·6
7·0	2	14·0
5·2	4	20·8
1·3	1	1·3
		61·4

$$\text{Half area} = \frac{12}{3} \times 61 \cdot 4$$

$$\text{Area} = 2 \times \frac{12}{3} \times 61 \cdot 4$$

$$= 491 \cdot 2 \text{ square feet}$$

3. Find the area of a waterplane, using Simpson's Second Rule. The common interval is 15 feet and the ordinates are:—0; 9·0; 13·3; 14·7; 12·8; 7·5; 0·6 feet.

$$\text{Area} = \frac{3}{8} h \left(a + 3b + 3c + 2d + 3e + 3f + g \right)$$

Ordinate	Multiplier	Product
0·0	1	0·0
9·0	3	27·0
13·3	3	39·9
14·7	2	29·4
12·8	3	38·4
7·5	3	22·5
0·6	1	0·6
		157·8

$$\text{Area} = \frac{3}{8} \times 15 \times 157\cdot 8$$

$$= 887\cdot 6 \text{ square feet}$$

4. Three ordinates, a, b and c, are 12 feet apart and have lengths of 29·2, 33·5, and 37·6 feet, respectively. Find the area contained between a and b.

$$\text{Area} = \frac{h}{12}(5a + 8b - c)$$

$$= \frac{12}{12}(5 \times 29\cdot 2 + 8 \times 33\cdot 5 - 37\cdot 6)$$

$$= 376\cdot 4 \text{ square feet}$$

Forces and Moments.—1. A force of 60 lbs. is applied to one end of a lever, which is 7 feet long. What is the moment about the other end?

Moment = force × distance = 60 × 7 = 420 foot-lbs.

2. Three men are working at a capstan and push on bars 10 feet long with forces of 70, 95 and 86 lbs., respectively. Find the moment to turn the capstan.

Moment produced by first man = 70 × 10 = 700 foot-lbs.
,,   ,,   ,, second ,, = 95 × 10 = 950   ,,
,,   ,,   ,, third ,, = 86 × 10 = 860   ,,

Total moment to turn capstan = 2510 foot-lbs.

3. A seesaw is exactly balanced about its centre line. Weights of 50 lbs. and 90 lbs. are placed on one side at distances of 18 feet and 22 feet, respectively, from the centre-line. What weight must be placed on the other side, at a distance of 20 feet from the centre, to cause the seesaw to balance once more?

Moment of weights on one side about centre-line = (50 × 18) + (90 × 22) foot-lbs.

Let X be the weight on the other side.

Then, moment of weight on the other side, about the centre-line = $20X$

For the seesaw to balance, these moments must be equal.

So $20X = (50 \times 18) + (90 \times 22)$

$$X = \frac{(50 \times 18) + (90 \times 22)}{20}$$

$$= 144 \text{ lbs.}$$

WORKED EXAMPLES

Shift of the Centre of Gravity.—1. Find the shift of the centre of gravity of a ship of 7000 tons displacement, if a weight of 50 tons is shifted for a distance of 80 feet.

$$GG_1 = \frac{w \times d}{W} = \frac{50 \times 80}{7000} = 0.57 \text{ feet}$$

2. A ship has a displacement of 3200 tons. What would be the shift of her centre of gravity if a weight of 200 tons is added at a distance of 60 feet from the original position of her centre of gravity?

$$GG_1 = \frac{w \times d}{W} \quad \text{(Where } W \text{ equals the displacement after adding the 200 tons)}$$

$$GG_1 = \frac{200 \times 60}{3400} = 3.53 \text{ feet}$$

3. A weight of 48 tons is removed from a lighter, the centre of gravity of this weight being 2·0 feet above the keel. What will be the new KG of the lighter if its original displacement and KG were 690 tons and 6·2 feet, respectively?

$$d = 6.2 - 2.0 = 4.2 \text{ feet}$$
$$W = \text{Displacement after weight has been removed}$$
$$= 690 - 48 = 642 \text{ tons}$$
$$GG_1 = \frac{w \times d}{W} = \frac{48 \times 4.2}{642} = 0.31 \text{ feet}$$

G moves vertically upwards, away from the weight removed, so :—

$$\text{New } KG = \text{Old } KG + GG_1 = 6.2 + 0.3$$
$$= 6.5 \text{ feet}$$

Shift of the Centre of Buoyancy.—1. A ship displaces 288,000 cubic feet and is heeled so that the volume of the immersed wedge is 15,500 cubic feet. The distance between the centres of gravity of the immersed and emerged wedges is found to be 27 feet. Find the shift of B.

$$BB_1 = \frac{v \times gg_1}{V} = \frac{15500 \times 27}{288000} = 1.45 \text{ feet}$$

2. A box shaped lighter is 100 feet long, 30 feet wide, and floats at a draft of 5 feet fore and aft. What will be the shift of her centre of buoyancy if she takes a list of 12°? (Assume that the shift of the centres of gravity of the wedges is two-thirds of the beam).

If we refer back to figure 45, we can see that the volume of the immersed wedge is equal to the area of the triangle FTT_1, multiplied by the length of the vessel.

Since FTT_1 is right-angled at T its area is equal to $\frac{1}{2}FT \times TT_1$ and, if φ equals the angle of heel, $TT_1 = FT \times \tan \varphi$

So, area of $FTT_1 = \dfrac{FT^2 \times \tan \varphi}{2}$

And, volume of wedge $=$ length $\times \dfrac{FT^2 \times \tan \varphi}{2}$

$FT = \frac{1}{2}$ beam $= 15$ feet

Volume of wedge $= \dfrac{100 \times 15^2 \times \tan 12°}{2}$

Volume of vessel $=$ length $\times$ breadth $\times$ draft $= 100 \times 30 \times 5$

$gg_1 = \dfrac{2}{3} \times 30 = 20$ feet

$BB_1 = \dfrac{v \times gg_1}{V} = \dfrac{100 \times 15^2 \times \tan 12° \times 20}{2 \times 100 \times 30 \times 5}$

$BB_1 = 3\cdot 195$ feet

The Inclining Experiment.—A weight of 15 tons is moved horizontally across the deck of a ship for a distance of 35 feet. The ship heels so that a pendulum, suspended 26 feet above a horizontal batten, moves out along the batten for a distance of 10 inches. The ship's displacement is 3150 tons and her KM is 20·2 feet. Find the GM and KG.

$GM = \dfrac{w \times d}{W} \times \dfrac{CF}{FL} = \dfrac{15 \times 35}{3150} \times 26 \div \dfrac{10}{12} = 5\cdot 2$ feet

$KG = KM - GM = 20\cdot 2 - 5\cdot 2 = 15\cdot 0$ feet

BM.—1. A box shaped vessel is 160 feet long, 30 feet broad and floats at a draft of 10 feet. Find her BM and height of the metacentre.

$BM = \dfrac{b^2}{12d} = \dfrac{30^2}{12 \times 10} = 7\cdot 5$ feet

$KB = \frac{1}{2}$ draft $= 5\cdot 0$ feet

$BM = 7\cdot 5$,,

$KM = \underline{\underline{12\cdot 5}}$ feet

2. The Inclining experiment is performed on a ship and her GM is found to be 6·3 feet. Her displacement in salt water is 3200 tons and the moment of inertia of her waterplane was 2,880,000. If her KB was 5·9 feet, what was the KG?

WORKED EXAMPLES

$$\text{Volume of displacement} = 3200 \times 35$$

$$BM = \frac{I}{V} = \frac{2880000}{3200 \times 35} = 25 \cdot 7 \text{ feet}$$

$$BM = 25 \cdot 7 \text{ feet}$$
$$KB = 5 \cdot 9 \text{ ,,}$$
$$KM = 31 \cdot 6 \text{ ,,}$$
$$GM = 6 \cdot 3 \text{ ,,}$$
$$KG = 25 \cdot 3 \text{ feet}$$

3. An ordinary merchant ship has a beam of 42 feet and floats at a mean draft of 12·0 feet. Find her *BM* by approximate formula.

$$BM = \frac{ab^2}{d} = \frac{0 \cdot 09 \times 42^2}{12} = 13 \cdot 23 \text{ feet}$$

Moment of Statical Stability.—1. A ship of 6240 tons displacement has a *GM* of 2·2 feet. Find her moment of statical stability at an angle of heel of 9°.

$$\text{Moment of statical stability} = W \times GM \times \sin \varphi$$
$$= 6240 \times 2 \cdot 2 \times \sin 9°$$
$$= 2148 \text{ foot-tons}$$

2. A vessel of 1370 tons displacement is heeled to an angle of 18°. Her *KB* is 4·2 feet and her *KG* 6·7 feet. The volume of the immersed wedge is found to be 4200 cubic feet and the horizontal shift of the centres of gravity of the wedges is 18·0 feet. Find the moment of statical stability.

$$BG = KG - KB = 6 \cdot 7 - 4 \cdot 2 = 2 \cdot 5 \text{ feet}$$

$$\text{Moment of statical stability} = W \left\{ \frac{v \times hh_1}{V} - BG \times \sin \varphi \right\}$$

$$= 1370 \left\{ \frac{4200 \times 18 \cdot 0}{1370 \times 35} - 2 \cdot 5 \times \sin 18° \right\}$$

$$= 1370 (1 \cdot 577 - 0 \cdot 773)$$

$$= 1102 \text{ foot-tons}$$

Angle of Loll.—1. A ship has a *GM* of 8·7 feet and a displacement of 3200 tons. A weight of 160 tons is loaded into the wing of the 'tween deck, so that it is 14 feet above the centre of gravity of the ship and 21 feet off the centre line. Find the angle to which the ship will heel, assuming that *M* does not move.

To find the new GM:—

$$GG_1 = \frac{w \times d}{W} = \frac{160 \times 14}{3200 + 160} = 0.67 \text{ feet}$$

New GM = old $GM - GG_1$ = $8.7 - 0.7$ = 8.0 feet

To find the heel:—

$$\cot \varphi = \frac{W \times GM}{w \times d} = \frac{3360 \times 8.0}{160 \times 21} = 8.00$$

Angle of heel = $7°$

2. A ship of 6000 tons displacement has a list of 9° to starboard and her KG is 21·4 feet. 300 tons of cotton are to be loaded into a 'tween deck, so that its centre of gravity will be 35·4 feet above the keel and 18·0 feet on either side of the centre line. The KM is 22·8 feet. Find what weight of cotton to place in each wing in order to bring the ship upright.

Excess weight to load on one side:—

$$\cot \varphi = \frac{W \times GM}{w \times d}$$

$$w = \frac{W \times GM}{d \times \cot \varphi} = \frac{6000 \times 1.4}{18 \times 6.31} = 74 \text{ tons}$$

Total weight to load	=	300 tons.
Excess on Port side	=	74 ,,
Distribute on 2 sides	=	226 ,,
,, ,, 1 side	=	113 ,,

Load on the Starboard side - - 113 tons
Excess on port side - - - - 74 tons

Load on port side - - - - 187

Note: The original heel, displacement and GM will give the correct answer, used as above. It can be shown that the result is not affected by the height at which the weight is loaded.

3. A ship has a displacement of 4500 tons and a GM of 0·6 feet. A weight of 270 tons is then loaded on deck, so that its centre of gravity is 15 feet above that of the ship and the BM is then found to be 14·4 feet. Find the new GM and the angle of loll, if any.

WORKED EXAMPLES

New displacement $= 4500 + 270 = 4770$ tons.

$$GG_1 = \frac{w \times d}{W} = \frac{270 \times 15}{4770} = 0.8 \text{ feet}$$

New $GM = 0.6 - 0.8 = -0.2$ feet

To find the angle of loll:—

$$\tan \varphi = \sqrt{\frac{2GM}{BM}} = \sqrt{\frac{2 \times 0.2}{14.4}} = 0.0167$$

Angle of loll $= 9\frac{1}{2}°$

Free Surface Effect.—1. A deep tank is half full of water, which has a rectangular free surface, 60 feet long and 55 feet wide. The ship displaces 6050 tons and her KG, if the effect of the free surface were ignored, would be 18·7 feet. Find her actual KG, allowing for the free surface.

Volume of displacement $= 6050 \times 35$

Rise of G, due to free surface:—

$$GG_1 = \frac{i}{V} = \frac{lb^3}{12V} = \frac{60 \times 55^3}{12 \times 6050 \times 35} = 3.9 \text{ feet}$$

True KG = estimated $KG + GG_1 = 18.7 + 3.9$
$= 22.6$ feet

2. A rectangular double bottom tank is 42 feet long, 40 feet wide and 4 feet deep. Sea water is run into it to a depth of 2 feet and the ship's KM is then found to be 25·1 feet. If the ship had a displacement of 5154 tons and a KG of 22·0 feet before the water was let into the tank, find the new GM when the ship is upright.

Weight of added water $= \dfrac{\text{volume}}{35} = \dfrac{42 \times 40 \times 2}{35} = 96$ tons

New displacement of ship $= 5154 + 96 = 5250$ tons.

Height of CG of ship above that of water $= 22.0 - 1.0 = 21.0$ feet

Fall of G due to added weight:—

$$GG_1 = \frac{w \times d}{W} = \frac{96 \times 21}{5250} = 0.4 \text{ feet}$$

Rise of G due to free surface:—

$$GG_1 = \frac{i}{V} = \frac{lb^3}{12V} = \frac{42 \times 40^3}{12 \times 5250 \times 35} = 1.2 \text{ feet}$$

Original KG	22·0 feet
Fall of G due to added weight	0·4 ,,
	21·6 ,,
Rise of G due to free surface	1·2 ,,
New KG	22·8 ,,
KM	25·1 ,,
GM	2·3 feet

3. A box shaped lighter is 120 feet long, 30 feet beam and has a *GM* of 3·1 feet. A tank, 15 feet long and extending right across the lighter, has 20 tons of water pumped out of it, the centre of gravity of the water removed being 2 feet below that of the lighter. The draft was then 4 feet. Find the new *GM*, assuming that the height of the metacentre does not change.

$$\text{New volume of displacement} = 120 \times 30 \times 4 \text{ cubic feet}$$

$$\text{New displacement} = \frac{120 \times 30 \times 4}{35} \text{ tons}$$

Rise of *G* due to weight removed:—

$$GG_1 = \frac{w \times d}{W} = \frac{20 \times 2 \times 35}{120 \times 30 \times 4} = 0.1 \text{ feet}$$

Rise of *G* due to free surface:—

$$GG_1 = \frac{i}{V} = \frac{lb^3}{12V} = \frac{15 \times 30^3}{12 \times 120 \times 30 \times 4} = 2.3 \text{ feet}$$

$$\begin{aligned}
\text{Total rise of } G &= 0.1 + 2.3 = 2.4 \text{ feet} \\
\text{Original } GM &= 3.1 \text{ ,,} \\
\text{New } GM &= 0.7 \text{ feet}
\end{aligned}$$

Longitudinal BM_L.—Find the BM_L and GM_L of a box shaped vessel, 240 feet long, 40 feet beam, which floats at a draft of 12 feet, the *KG* being 7·0 feet.

$$BM_L = \frac{l^2}{12d} = \frac{240^2}{12 \times 12} = 400 \text{ feet}$$

$$\begin{aligned}
KB &= \text{half draft} = 6 \text{ ,,} \\
KM_L &= 406 \text{ ,,} \\
KG &= 7 \text{ ,,} \\
GM_L &= 399 \text{ feet}
\end{aligned}$$

Tons per inch Immersion.—1. A box shaped lighter is 100 feet long and 28 feet wide. Find her T.P.I.

$$\text{T.P.I.} = \frac{A}{420} = \frac{100 \times 28}{420} = 6.7$$

2. A ship is 540 feet long, 63 feet beam and the coefficient of fineness of her waterplane is 0·788. What is the T.P.I. at her existing draft?

$$\text{T.P.I.} = \frac{A}{420} = \frac{540 \times 63 \times 0.788}{420} = 63.8$$

WORKED EXAMPLES

Inch trim Moment.—1. A ship is 432 feet long and has a displacement of 3618 tons and a GM_L of 576 feet. Find her I.T.M.

$$\text{I.T.M.} = \frac{W \times GM_L}{12l} = \frac{3618 \times 576}{12 \times 432} = 402 \cdot 0 \text{ foot-tons}$$

2. Use the approximate formula to find the I.T.M. of a ship having a beam of 54 feet and a T.P.I. of 48.

$$\text{I.T.M.} = \frac{30 \cdot 84 T^2}{b} = \frac{30 \cdot 84 \times 48^2}{54} = 1315 \cdot 8 \text{ foot-tons}$$

3. A ship is 476 feet long, 58 feet beam and the coefficient of fineness of her waterplane is 0·762. Find her I.T.M.

$$\text{Area of waterplane} = l \times b \times 0 \cdot 762 = 476 \times 58 \times 0 \cdot 762$$

$$\text{I.T.M.} = 0 \cdot 000175 \frac{A^2}{b} = \frac{0 \cdot 000175 \times (476 \times 58 \times 0 \cdot 762)^2}{58}$$

$$= 1335 \text{ foot-tons}$$

Change of Draft Due to Change of Trim.—1. A box shaped vessel has its centre of flotation on the longitudinal centre line and floats at drafts of 15 feet 6 inches forward and 15 feet 10 inches aft. A weight is shifted forward and causes a change of trim of 3 inches. Find the new drafts.

Since the centre of flotation is on the centre line, the draft at each end will change by half the change of trim. The draft forward increases and that aft decreases, so:—

Old drafts - - -	Forward 15' 6"	Aft	15' 10"
Half change of trim -	+ 1½	−	1½
New drafts - - -	15' 7½"		15' 8½"

2. A ship is 400 feet long and her centre of flotation is 10 feet abaft the centre line. She floats at drafts of 21 feet 7 inches forward and 22 feet 3 inches aft. Find the new drafts if a weight is shifted aft so as to change the trim by 15 inches.

The centre of flotation is 210 feet from forward and 190 feet from aft.

$$\text{Change of draft} = \frac{TF}{l} \times t$$

$$\text{Change forward} = \frac{210}{400} \times 15 = 7 \cdot 9 \text{ inches (call this 8 inches)}$$

$$\text{Change aft} = \frac{190}{400} \times 15 = 7 \cdot 1 \text{ inches (call this 7 inches)}$$

Original drafts -	F. 21' 7"	A. 22' 3"	M. 21' 10"
Change of drafts -	− 8	+ 7	
New drafts -	F. 20' 11"	A. 22' 10"	M. 21' 10½"

Note that in the above case, although no weight has been added, the mean draft has increased by ½ inch. The cause of this is discussed in chapter 11.

Change of Trim due to Shifting Weights.—1. A ship has an I.T.M. of 960 foot-tons and drafts of 17 feet 5 inches forward and 18 feet 1 inch aft. If a weight of 60 tons is shifted forward for a distance of 160 feet, what will be the change of trim and the new drafts fore and aft, the centre of flotation being on the centre line of the ship?

$$\text{Change of trim} = \frac{\text{moment changing trim}}{\text{inch trim moment}} = \frac{60 \times 160}{960}$$
$$= 10 \text{ inches}$$

Change of draft at either end = half change of trim = 5 inches

Original drafts	F. 17′ 5″	A. 18′ 1″
Change of drafts	+ 5	− 5
New drafts	F. 17′ 10″	A. 17′ 8″

2. Find the change of trim and the new drafts in a ship of 400 feet length, when a weight of 100 tons is shifted aft for a distance of 150 feet. The centre of flotation is 10 feet abaft the ship's centre line, the inch trim moment is 900 foot-tons and the original drafts were 16 feet 2 inches forward and 16 feet 0 inches aft.

$$\text{Change of trim} = \frac{\text{moment changing trim}}{\text{inch trim moment}} = \frac{100 \times 150}{900}$$
$$= 16\tfrac{1}{2} \text{ inches}$$

The centre of flotation is 210 feet from forward and 190 feet from aft.

$$\text{Change of draft forward} = \frac{210}{400} \times 16\tfrac{1}{2} = 8\tfrac{3}{4} \text{ inches}$$

$$\text{Change of draft aft} = \frac{190}{400} \times 16\tfrac{1}{2} = 7\tfrac{3}{4} \text{ inches}$$

Original drafts	F. 16′ 2″	A. 16′ 0″	M. 16′ 1″
Change	− 8¾	+ 7¾	
New drafts	F. 15′ 5¼″	A. 16′ 7¾″	M. 16′ 0½″

Change of Draft on Loading or Discharging Weights.—1. A ship has a T.P.I. of 54·0 and her drafts are 14 feet 7 inches forward and 15 feet 4 inches aft. What will be her new drafts if a weight of 117 tons is added directly over the centre of flotation?

$$\text{Bodily sinkage} = \frac{\text{weight added}}{\text{T.P.I.}} = \frac{117}{54} = 2\tfrac{1}{4} \text{ inches}$$

Original drafts	F. 14′ 7″	A. 15′ 4″
Bodily sinkage	+ 2¼	+ 2¼
New drafts	F. 14′ 9¼″	A. 15′ 6¼″

WORKED EXAMPLES

2. Find the new drafts in a ship which has a T.P.I. of 28, if 70 tons of cargo are discharged from a point vertically below the centre of flotation. The original drafts were 9 feet 10 inches forward and 10 feet 1 inch aft.

$$\text{Bodily rise} = \frac{\text{weight discharged}}{\text{T.P.I.}} = \frac{70}{28} = 2\frac{1}{2} \text{ inches}$$

Original drafts   -   F. 9' 10"   A. 10' 1"
Bodily rise   -   —   2½   —   2½

New drafts   -   F. 9' 7½"   A. 9' 10½"

Moderate Weights Loaded off the Centre of Flotation.—1. A box shaped vessel is 140 feet long, has a T.P.I. of 10 and an I.T.M. of 100 foot-tons. Her drafts are 6 feet 2 inches forward and 6 feet 3 inches aft. What will be her new drafts after a weight of 60 tons has been discharged from a point 60 feet from the bow?

$$\text{Bodily rise} = \frac{\text{weight removed}}{\text{T.P.I.}} = \frac{60}{10} = 6 \text{ inches}$$

Since the ship is box shaped, the centre of flotation will be on the centre line.

Distance of centre of flotation from stem   -   -   -   -   70 feet
Distance of weight removed from stem   -   -   -   -   60 „

Distance of weight removed from centre of flotation   -   10 „

$$\text{Change of trim} = \frac{\text{moment changing trim}}{\text{I.T.M.}} = \frac{60 \times 10}{100}$$
$$= 6 \text{ inches}$$

Since the centre of flotation is on the centre line, the drafts fore and aft will each change by half the trim.

Change of draft at either end = ½ × 6 = 3 inches.

Original drafts   -   F. 6' 2"   A. 6' 3"   M. 6' 2½"
Bodily rise   -   —   6   —   6

                      F. 5 8   A. 5 9
Change due to trim   —   3   +   3

New drafts   -   F. 5' 5"   A. 6' 0"   M. 5' 8½"

2. A weight of 100 tons is loaded into a ship at a distance of 220 feet abaft the stem. The ship's length is 350 feet, her T.P.I. is 40, her I.T.M. is 800 foot-tons and the centre of flotation is 10 feet abaft the centre line. If the original drafts were 17 feet 10 inches forward and 18 feet 0 inch aft, find the new drafts.

Bodily sinkage = $\dfrac{\text{added weight}}{\text{T.P.I.}}$ = $\dfrac{100}{40}$ = $2\frac{1}{2}$ inches

Distance of centre line from stem - - - - 175 feet
Distance of centre of flotation from centre line - - 10 ,,
Distance of centre of flotation from stem - - - 185 ,,
Distance of added weight from stem - - - - 220 ,,
Distance of added weight from centre of flotation - 35 ,,

Change of trim due to added weight = $\dfrac{\text{moment changing trim}}{\text{I.T.M.}}$

$= \dfrac{100 \times 35}{800} = 4\frac{1}{2}$ inches

Change of draft forward = $\dfrac{185}{350} \times 4\frac{1}{2} = 2\frac{1}{2}$ inches

Change of draft aft = $\dfrac{165}{350} \times 4\frac{1}{2} = 2$ inches

Original drafts	F. 17' 10"	A. 18' 0"	M. 17' 11"	
Bodily sinkage	+ $2\frac{1}{2}$	+ $2\frac{1}{2}$		
	F. 18' $0\frac{1}{2}$	A. 18' $2\frac{1}{2}$		
Change due to trim	− $2\frac{1}{2}$	+ 2		
New draft	F. 17' 10"	A. 18' $4\frac{1}{2}$"	M. 18' $1\frac{1}{4}$"	

3. A ship is 420 feet long, has a T.P.I. of 50 and an I.T.M. of 1000 foot-tons, whilst the centre of flotation is 10 feet abaft the centre line. The draft is 23 feet 1 inch forward and 24 feet 5 inches aft. The following cargo is then loaded and discharged:—

    (a) Loaded   120 tons, 60 feet abaft the stem.
    (b) Loaded   70 ,, 300 ,, ,, ,, ,,
    (c) Discharged 90 ,, 150 ,, ,, ,, ,,

Find the new drafts.

Weight loaded - - - - 120 tons.
Weight loaded - - - - 70 ,,
Total Loaded - - - - 190 ,,
Weight discharged - - - - 90 ,,
Nett (loaded) - - - - 100 ,,

Distance of centre line from stem - - - - 210 feet
Distance of centre of flotation from centre line - 10 feet
Distance of centre of flotation from stem - - 220 feet

WORKED EXAMPLES

Weight	From Stem	From C. of F.	Moment	To Trim Ship
120 tons (+)	60 feet	160 feet (For'd)	19200	by head
70 ,, (+)	300 ,,	80 ,, (Aft)	5600	,, stern
90 ,, (−)	150 ,,	70 ,, (For'd)	6300	,, ,,

$$\text{Moment to change trim} = 19200 - (5600 + 6300)$$
$$= 7300 \text{ foot-tons (by head)}$$

$$\text{Bodily sinkage} = \frac{\text{nett weight loaded}}{\text{T.P.I.}} = \frac{100}{50} = 2 \text{ inches}$$

$$\text{Change of trim} = \frac{\text{moment changing trim}}{\text{I.T.M.}} = \frac{7300}{1000}$$
$$= 7\tfrac{1}{4} \text{ ins. (by head)}$$

$$\text{Change of draft forward} = \frac{220}{420} \times 7\tfrac{1}{4} = 3\tfrac{3}{4} \text{ inches}$$

$$\text{Change of draft aft} = \frac{200}{420} \times 7\tfrac{1}{4} = 3\tfrac{1}{2} \text{ inches}$$

Original drafts	-	F. 23'	1"	A. 24'	5"	M. 23'	9"
Bodily sinkage	-	+	2	+	2		
		F. 23	3	A. 24	7		
Change due to trim		+	3¾	−	3½		
New drafts	-	F. 23'	6¾"	A. 24'	3½"	M. 23'	11"

Large Weights Loaded off Centre of Flotation.—An oil tanker, which is light, is found to be trimmed too much by the stern. In order to change the trim and also to increase the draft, a tank which has its centre of gravity 180 feet abaft the stem is filled with 1100 tons of water. The following details are found from the stability scales:—

Mean Draft	T.P.I.	I.T.M.	Centre of Flotation
13 feet	51·0	1250	9·6 feet abaft centre line
14 ,,	51·6	1290	9·8 ,, ,, ,, ,,
15 ,,	52·2	1330	10·0 ,, ,, ,, ,,

If the original drafts were 10 feet 2 inches forward and 15 feet 10 inches aft, find the new drafts. The ship is 500 feet long.

The original mean draft of 13 feet 0 inches gives a T.P.I. of 51·0

$$\text{Approximate sinkage} = \frac{\text{added weight}}{\text{T.P.I.}} = \frac{1100}{51}$$

$$= 21\tfrac{1}{2} \text{ inches, or 1 foot } 9\tfrac{1}{2} \text{ inches}$$

Approximate new mean draft = 13 feet 0 inches + 1 foot $9\tfrac{1}{2}$ inches
= 14 feet $9\tfrac{1}{2}$ inches

T.P.I. for 13 feet 0 inches = 51·0
T.P.I. for 14 feet $9\tfrac{1}{2}$ inches = 52·1 gives mean T.P.I. of 51·5

$$\text{Bodily sinkage} = \frac{\text{weight added}}{\text{mean T.P.I.}} = \frac{1100}{51 \cdot 5}$$

$$= 21\tfrac{1}{4} \text{ inches, or 1 foot } 9\tfrac{1}{4} \text{ inches}$$

New mean draft = 13 feet 0 inches + 1 foot $9\tfrac{1}{4}$ inches
= 14 feet $9\tfrac{1}{4}$ inches

At this new mean draft, the I.T.M. is 1320 foot-tons and the centre of flotation is 10 feet abaft the centre line.

Distance of centre line from stem	250 feet
Distance of centre of flotation from centre line	10 feet
Distance of centre of flotation from stem	260 feet
Distance of *C.G.* of tank from stem	180 feet
Distance of *C.G.* of tank from centre of flotation	80 feet

$$\text{Change of trim} = \frac{\text{moment changing trim}}{\text{I.T.M.}} = \frac{1100 \times 80}{1320} = 66\tfrac{3}{4} \text{ ins.}$$

$$\text{Change of draft forward} = \frac{260}{500} \times 66\tfrac{3}{4} = 34\tfrac{3}{4} \text{ ins., or 2 ft. } 10\tfrac{3}{4} \text{ ins.}$$

$$\text{Change of draft aft} = \frac{240}{500} \times 66\tfrac{3}{4} = 32 \text{ ins., or 2 ft. 8 ins.}$$

Original drafts	-	F. 10′	2″	A. 15′	10″	M. 13′	0″
Bodily sinkage	-	+ 1	$9\tfrac{1}{4}$	+ 1	$9\tfrac{1}{4}$		
		F. 11	$11\tfrac{1}{4}$	A. 17	$7\tfrac{1}{4}$	M. 14′	$9\tfrac{1}{4}″$
Change due to trim		+ 2	$10\tfrac{3}{4}$	− 2	8		
New drafts	- -	F. 14′	10″	A. 14	$11\tfrac{1}{4}$	M. 14′	$10\tfrac{1}{2}″$

(Note the large change in the mean draft caused by the change of trim, in this case.)

WORKED EXAMPLES

Loading a Weight to Produce a Desired Trim.—1. A ship has an I.T.M. of 1200 foot-tons and floats at drafts of 19 feet 8 inches forward and 21 feet 6 inches aft. How much water must be run into a tank, the centre of gravity of which is 150 feet forward of the centre of flotation, to bring the ship to a trim of 7 inches by the stern?

$$\text{Present trim } (t) \quad - \quad - \quad - \quad 22 \text{ inches by stern}$$
$$\text{Required trim } (t_1) \quad - \quad - \quad - \quad 7 \text{ inches by stern}$$
$$(t \sim t_1) \quad - \quad - \quad - \quad 15 \text{ inches by head}$$

$$w = \frac{\text{I.T.M.} (t \sim t_1)}{d} = \frac{1200 \times 15}{150} = 120 \text{ tons}$$

2. A ship which is loading cargo has 175 tons to come on board. Her centre of flotation is 4 feet abaft the centre line, her I.T.M. 1400 foot-tons and her draft 24 feet 7 inches forward and 24 feet 2 inches aft. How far from the centre line must the weight be placed to bring the ship to a trim of 12 inches by the stern?

$$\text{Present trim } (t) \quad - \quad - \quad - \quad 5 \text{ inches by head}$$
$$\text{Required trim } (t_1) \quad - \quad - \quad - \quad 12 \text{ inches by stern}$$
$$(t \sim t_1) \quad - \quad - \quad - \quad 17 \text{ inches by stern}$$

$$d = \frac{\text{I.T.M.} (t \sim t_1)}{w} = \frac{1400 \times 17}{175}$$

$$= 136 \text{ feet, abaft centre of flotation}$$

Distance of weight abaft centre of flotation - - 136 feet
Distance of centre of flotation abaft centre line - 4 feet
Distance of weight abaft centre line - - - - 140 feet

Loading to Keep the After Draft Constant.—A ship has to leave port with a draft not exceeding 21 feet 0 inches, in order to cross a bar. She is loaded until her drafts are 19 feet 10 inches forward and 21 feet 0 inches aft, when there are still 200 tons of cargo to come on board. The length of the ship is 420 feet, her T P.I. is 50, her I.T.M. is 1200, and the centre of flotation is 10 feet abaft the centre line. How far from the centre line must the remaining 200 tons be placed?

Distance of centre of flotation from centre line - 10 feet
Distance of centre line from aft - - - - - 210 feet
Distance of centre of flotation from aft - - - 200 feet

$$d = \frac{\text{I.T.M.} \times L}{\text{T.P.I.} \times l} = \frac{1200 \times 420}{50 \times 200}$$

$$= 50 \cdot 4 \text{ feet forward of centre of flotation}$$

Distance of weight forward of centre of flotation - 50·4 feet
Distance of centre of flotation abaft centre line - 10 feet
Distance of weight forward of centre line - - 40·4 feet

I

Increase of Draft Due to Bilging.—1. A box shaped vessel is 200 feet long, 35 feet wide and floats at a draft of 12 feet 0 inches. A compartment amidships is 50 feet long and has permeability of 40 per cent. What will be the new draft if this compartment is bilged?

Lost buoyancy $(v) = 50 \times 35 \times 12$ cubic feet.
Original waterplane area $(A) = 200 \times 35$ sq. ft.
Area lost in bilged compartment $(a) = 50 \times 35$ sq. ft.
Permeability $= \dfrac{40}{100} = 0.4$

$$X = \frac{vp}{A - ap} = \frac{(50 \times 35 \times 12) \times 0.4}{(200 \times 35) - (50 \times 35) \times 0.4}$$
$= 1.33$ feet, or 1 foot 4 inches.
New draft $=$ Old mean draft $+$ sinkage
$=$ 12 feet 0 ins. $+$ 1 foot 4 ins. $=$ 13 feet 4 ins.

2. A ship is 450 feet long, 60 feet beam and floats at a mean draft of 15 feet 0 inches. The coefficient of fineness of her waterplane, at this draft, is 0·740 and that of the midships section is 0·925. An empty compartment at the centre of flotation is parallel sided, 50 feet long and extends for the full breadth of the ship. Find the new mean draft if this compartment is bilged.

Since the compartment is parallel sided, its volume is equal to its length multiplied by the area of the midships section, below the waterline.

Area of midships section below the waterline $= 60 \times 15 \times 0.925$
Volume of compartment below the waterline $= 60 \times 15 \times 0.925 \times 50$
Original area of waterplane $=$ length $\times$ breadth $\times$ coefficient
$450 \times 60 \times 0.740$ square feet.
Area lost when compartment is bilged $= 60 \times 50$ square feet.

$$X = \frac{v}{A - a} = \frac{60 \times 15 \times 0.925 \times 50}{450 \times 60 \times 0.740 - 60 \times 50} = \frac{693.75}{283}$$
$=$ 2·45 feet, or 2 feet $5\frac{1}{2}$ inches
New mean draft $=$ Old mean draft $+$ sinkage $= 15'\ 0'' + 2'\ 5\frac{1}{2}''$
$= 17'\ 5\frac{1}{2}''$ (approximately)

This is approximate because we have made the assumption that the coefficient of fineness of the waterplane has not changed, whereas it may actually alter slightly. The above calculation would be accurate enough for practical purposes, however.

Drydocking.—A ship entered a dock with drafts of 10 feet 0 inches forward and 11 feet 6 inches aft. At this draft, her displacement was 4650 tons; *KG*, 24·3 feet; *KM*, 30·5 feet; I.T.M., 1240; and the centre of flotation was 240 feet from aft. Find:—

(1) The *GM* at the instant before the ship came flat on the blocks.

WORKED EXAMPLES

(2) The *GM* after she was flat on the blocks, so that her draft was 8 feet 9 inches and her displacement 3650 tons.

(1) $\quad t = 18$ inches.

$$\text{Old } GM = KM - KG = 30.5 - 24.3 = 6.2 \text{ feet}$$

$$P = \frac{\text{I.T.M.} \times t}{l} = \frac{1240 \times 18}{240} = 93 \text{ tons}$$

$$\text{New } GM = \text{Old } GM - \frac{P \times KM}{W} = 6.2 - \frac{93 \times 30.5}{4650}$$

$$= 6.2 - 0.6 = +5.6 \text{ feet}$$

(2) $\quad P = $ Old displacement $-$ new displacement

$$= 4650 - 3650 = 1000 \text{ tons}$$

$$\text{New } GM = \text{Old } GM - \frac{P \times KM}{W} = 6.2 - \frac{1000 \times 30.5}{4650}$$

$$= 6.2 - 6.6 = -0.4 \text{ feet}$$

PROBLEMS

Increase of Pressure with Depth.

1. A flat plate, 10 feet long and 3 feet wide, is placed horizontally at a depth of 17 feet below the sea surface. Find the pressure per square foot and the total pressure on the plate.

2. A sealed box is made of a metal which is capable of withstanding a pressure of 11 pounds per square inch. To what depth can the box be sunk before it will collapse?

3. Find the total pressure, in tons, on a keel-plate which has an area of 246 square feet and which is 31 feet below the sea surface.

4. Find the average pressure, in pounds per square inch, on the body of a diver who is working in 52 feet of water.

5. The "Swire Deep" has a depth of 5348 fathoms. What is the water pressure at the bottom, in tons per square inch?

6. A submarine is submerged to 30 fathoms. Find the average pressure, in tons per square foot, on her hull. Find also the total pressure on her hull, if it has an area of 9064 square feet.

Answers.—
1. 1088 lbs; 14·57 tons.
2. 24·75 feet.
3. 217·9 tons.
4. 23·1 lbs.
5. 6·37 tons.
6. 5·14 tons; 46614·9 tons.

Floating Bodies and Density.

7. A log weighs 4 tons and floats in water of density 1024. What volume of water does it displace?

8. A floating body displaces 21·45 cubic inches of water of density 1010. Find its weight in ounces.

9. A ship displaces 294148 cubic feet of water of density 1022. Find the density of the water in which she would displace 294512 cubic feet.

10. A log is 10 ft. × 3 ft. × 2 ft. and weighs 22·5 cwt. How much of it would be above the surface in water of density 1008?

11. A block of hardwood, 4 ft. × 2 ft. × 1 ft. weighs 513 lbs. Will it float or sink if it is placed in water of specific gravity 1·026?

Anwers.—
7. 140 cubic feet.
8. 12·538 ozs.
9. 1020·8.
10 20 cubic feet.
11. Block has the same density as the water—in theory it neither floats nor sinks.

PROBLEMS

The Effect of Density on Draft.

12. A box shaped barge floats at a draft of 11 feet 8 inches in water of density 1003. Find her draft in water of density 1020.

13. A ship has a fresh water allowance of 7 inches. To what depth could she submerge her loadline when loading in dock water of density 1011?

14. A ship has a fresh water allowance of $6\frac{3}{4}$ inches and a summer draft of 26 feet $8\frac{1}{2}$ inches. To what draft may she load in dock water of density 1007?

15. A box shaped vessel has a draft of 15 feet 0 inches in salt water. On entering a dock her draft becomes 15 feet 3 inches. Find the density of the dock water.

16. A ship has a fresh water allowance of $7\frac{1}{2}$ inches. By how much will she change her draft if she passes from water of density 1004 to water of density 1021?

17. A box shaped barge has a draft of 3 feet $6\frac{1}{2}$ inches in salt water, when she is fully loaded. To what draft could she load in water of density 1015?

18. A box shaped lighter draws 5 feet $1\frac{1}{4}$ inches in water of density 1004. Find her draft in water of density 1020.

19. To what depth can a ship submerge her load line in dock water of density 1012, if her fresh water allowance is $5\frac{1}{2}$ inches.

20. A ship enters port with a salt-water draft of 22 feet $3\frac{1}{2}$ inches. If her fresh water allowance is $5\frac{1}{4}$ inches, what will be her draft in a dock in which the specific gravity of the water is 1·009?

21. A box shaped vessel has a draft of 10 feet 8 inches in salt water. Find her draft in water of density 1000.

22. A box shaped lighter draws 12 feet $4\frac{1}{2}$ inches in water of specific gravity 1·010. What will be her draft in sea water?

23. By how much can a ship submerge her loadline in water of density 1011, if her fresh water allowance is $8\frac{1}{4}$ inches?

Answers.—

12. 11 feet $5\frac{1}{2}$ inches.
13. 3·9 inches.
14. 27 feet $1\frac{1}{4}$ inches
15. 1008·2.
16. 5·1 inches.
17. 3 feet 6·9 inches.
18. 5 feet 0·3 inches.
19. 2·9 inches.
20. 22 feet $6\frac{3}{4}$ inches.
21. 10 feet 11·2 inches.
22. 12 feet 2·3 inches.
23. 4·6 inches.

Areas.

24. Find the area of a square whose sides are 11 inches long.

25. Find the area of a square whose sides are 9·7 feet long.

26. A square has an area of 43 square feet. What is the length of its sides?

27. What is the area of a rectangle which has sides of 2·6 inches and 11·5 inches.

28. Find the area of a rectangle which has sides of 7·0 feet and 22·4 feet.

29. A box shaped ship is 172 feet long and 27 feet wide. Find the area of its waterplane when it is upright and on an even keel.

30. What would be the area of the waterplane of the ship in question 29 if she were on an even keel, but had a list of 20°?

31. A triangle has a vertical height of 6·2 inches and a base of 8·8 inches long. Find its area.

32. Find the area of a triangle having two of its sides 3·8 inches and 9·5 inches long, the angle between them being 36°.

33. A triangular plate has sides of 10·7 feet, 16·5 feet and 24·0 feet. What is its area?

34. Find the areas of the following triangles—
    (a) Base 22·5 feet. Perpendicular height 11·4 feet
    (b) ,, 30·2 inches   ,,   ,, 10·0 inches
    (c) ,, 3 ft 6 inches   ,,   ,, 2 ft. 3 inches

35. Find the areas of the following triangles.—
    (a) AB 26·0 inches BC 12·5 inches Angle B 36°
    (b) AB 5 ft. 0 inches BC 10 ft. 9 inches " B 58°
    (c) AB 1 ft. 3 inches BC 2 ft. 6 inches " B 27°

36. Find the areas of the triangles, having sides of the following lengths.—
    (a)   3·6 inches   4·4 inches   6·0 inches
    (b) 10·0 feet   15·5 feet   8·5 feet
    (c) 26 feet   38 feet   51 feet

37. Find the weight in hundredweights of a triangular steel plate, 1 inch thick, which has a vertical height of 15 feet 0 inches and a base of 18 feet 0 inches, if the specific gravity of the steel is 7·800.

38. Find the areas of the following trapezoids.—
    (a) Parallel sides, 12 inches and 21 inches. Perpendicular height 10 inches.
    (b) ,,   ,, 3 ft 6 in and 4 ft 2 in   ,,   ,, 1 ft 8 in
    (c) ,,   ,, 27·6 feet and 16·8 feet ,,   ,, 8·0 feet
    (d) ,,   ,, 11 inches and 38 inches ,,   ,, 21 inches
    (e) ,,   ,, 31·2 feet and 36·4 feet ,,   ,, 20 feet

39. A trapezoid has an area of 348 square feet and the two parallel sides have lengths of 10·4 feet and 14·6 feet respectively. What is the perpendicular distance between them?

40. Find the area and circumference of a circle of radius 2·62 feet.

41. A circle has a circumference of 32·8 inches. Find its area.

42. One circle has a radius of 33 inches, another a radius of 11 inches. Find the ratios between their areas and circumferences.

43. A circle has an area of 57·6 square feet. Find its circumference.

Answers.—

24. 121 square inches.
25. 94·09 square feet.
26. 6·36 feet.
27. 29·9 square inches.
28. 156·8 square feet.
29. 4644 square feet.
30. 4942·1 square feet.
31. 27·28 square inches.
32. 10·613 square inches.
33. 74·5 square feet,
34. (a) 128·25 square feet.
    (b) 151 square inches.
    (c) 567 square inches, or 3·9375 square feet.
35. (a) 95·52 square inches.
    (b) 22·79 square feet.
    (c) 102·15 square inches.
36. (a) 7·86 square inches.
    (b) 38·95 square feet.
    (c) 479·1 square feet.
37. 49·0 cwt.
38. (a) 165 square inches.
    (b) 920 square inches.
    (c) 177·6 square feet.
    (d) 514·5 square inches.
    (e) 676 square feet.
39. 27·84 feet.
40. 21·57 square feet; 16·47 feet.
41. 85·58 square inches.
42. 9/1, 3/1.
43. 26·91 feet.

PROBLEMS

Surface Areas and Volumes.

44. Find the surface area and volume of a cube, having edges 3 inches long.

45. A cube is made of metal which has a density of 7·290. Its edges are 2·4 inches long. Find its weight.

46. A cube-shaped tank has edges 10 feet 3 inches long. Find how much paint would be required for painting the outside, if one gallon covers 50 square feet.

47. Find the surface area and volume of a box-shaped tank which has sides of 2 feet, 6 feet and 17 feet.

48. Find the underwater volume of a box-shaped vessel of 350′×50′×10′ draft and her displacement, if she is floating in sea water. How much antifouling paint, covering 3000 square feet per hundredweight is needed to paint her up to the 10 feet draft?

49. A box-shaped lighter, 80 feet long and 20 feet wide, has a light draft of 2 feet 6 inches. How many tons of cargo must she load, when floating in salt water, to increase her draft to 6 feet 0 inches?

50. Find the weight of a log of wood, 32′×2′×4′, which has a specific gravity of 0·750.

51. A lighter is 100 feet long, 25 feet wide and weighs 145 tons. Find her draft in salt water.

52. A box-shaped lighter is 70 feet long, 20 feet wide and floats at a draft of 2 feet 6 inches in salt water. What is her weight?

53. Find the surface area of a rectangular tank, 30′×10′×5′.

54. How many pounds of paint would it take to cover the surface of a rectangular tank 20′×10′×8′, if one hundredweight of paint covers 3000 square feet?

55. Find the volume of a prismatic-shaped lighter if the area of each end is 35 square feet and the length 50 feet.

56. Find the volume of a wedge shaped tank, 12 feet long, if each of the triangular ends has sides of 3 feet and 4 feet long, with the angle between them, 30°. Find also how many gallons of fresh water the tank will hold.

57. A wooden wedge is 6 inches long and the triangular ends have a base of 3 inches and a perpendicular height of 5 inches. What is its weight, in ounces, if the specific gravity of the wood is 0·792?

58. A square log of wood floats on edge so that it has a triangular section under water. The draft is 2·0 feet, the width at the surface 3·5 feet and the length 20 feet. Find the displacement of the log in salt water.

59. Find the volume and surface area of a sphere of radius 2·1 inches.

60. Find the weight of a sphere of radius 3 inches and specific gravity 8·064.

61. What is the surface area of a sphere of a volume 268·2 cubic inches?

62. Find the relation between the radius of a sphere of surface area x square inches and that of a sphere of volume x cubic inches.

63. A sphere of radius 12 inches, weighs 14·00 cwt. in air. What will be its apparent weight when immersed in salt water?

64. A hollow sphere has an internal radius of 3 inches and an external radius of 6 inches. Find the volume of material in it.

65. Find the weight of a hollow sphere of internal radius 9 inches, external radius 12 inches and specific gravity 2·800.

66. One cubic foot of metal is made into a hollow sphere of external radius 10 inches. What is the internal radius?

MERCHANT SHIP STABILITY

67. A hollow sphere has an internal radius of 5 inches and an external radius of 6 inches. It is made from an alloy having a density of 2500. Find if it will float in salt water.

68. Find the volume and surface area of a cylinder, 7 feet long and having a radius of 18 inches.

69. A cylindrical boiler has a diameter of 10 feet, a length of 14 feet, and weighs 30 tons. Would it be possible, by sealing the openings in it, to float it ashore in an out of the way port?

70. How much paint would it require to cover the outside of a cylindrical tank, 20 feet long and 7 feet radius, if one hundredweight of paint covers 3000 square feet?

71. A hollow round section is 21 feet long and has internal and external radii of 9 inches and 15 inches respectively. Find the volume of material in it.

72. Find the weight, in tons, of a hollow mast which is 30 feet long and 24 inches outside diameter, made of steel 1 inch thick. Ignore the doubling at the joints and assume that the steel weighs 490 lbs. per cubic foot.

73. Find the volume of steel in a hollow round section, 6 inches long, 3 inches inside diameter and 4 inches outside diameter.

Answers—

44. 54 square inches, 27 cubic inches.
45. 58·32 ozs.
46. 12·6 gallons.
47. 296 square feet, 204 cubic feet.
48. 175000 cubic feet, 5000 tons, 8·5 cwt.
49. 160 tons.
50. 5·36 tons.
51. 2·03 feet, or 2 feet 0·4 inches.
52. 100 tons.
53. 1000 square feet.
54. 32·8 lbs.
55. 1750 cubic feet.
56. 36 cubic feet. 225 gallons.
57. 20·6 ozs.
58. 2·0 tons.
59. 38·81 cubic inches, 55·44 square inches.
60. 33·0 lbs.

61. 201·1 square inches.
62. $R = \sqrt{\dfrac{r^3}{3}}$ or $r = \sqrt[3]{3R^2}$
63. 11·61 cwt.
64. 792 cubic inches.
65. 424 lbs.
66. 8·37 inches.
67. It will sink, since it has positive weight under water.
68. 80·1 square feet, 49·5 cubic feet.
69. Yes. Weight of boiler is 30 tons. Weight of equal volume of salt water 31·4 tons.
70. 0·396 cwt., or 44·35 lbs.
71. 66 cubic feet.
72. 3·294 tons.
73. 33 cubic inches.

Simpson's Rules, Etc.

74. Use Simpson's First and Second Rules and the Trapezoidal Rule to find the area of a part of a waterplane which has the following ordinates spaced 20 feet apart. Find, also, the position of its centre of gravity:—

7·7, 12·5, 17·3. 21·8, 25·2, 26·5, 27·0 feet.

75. Find the area of the following part of a waterplane, using the Trapezoidal Rule:—

Ordinates, 4·4, 11·2, 15·7, 17·0, 17·8, 16·1, 12·8 feet.
Common interval 10 feet.

76. Find the area and position of the centre of gravity of a waterplane having the following half-ordinates and a common interval of 24 feet:—

0, 9·6, 15·6, 20·4, 24·0, 25·4, 24·0, 22·8, 17·6, 10·0, 0 feet.

PROBLEMS

77. Find the area and position of the centre of gravity of a waterplane having the following ordinates and a common interval of 6 feet:—
    0, 5·4, 8·2, 9·0, 8·6, 7·6, 5·4, 2·1, 0 feet.

78. Part of a waterplane has the following half-ordinates and a common interval of 12 feet:—
    3·3, 6·6, 11·1, 16·0, 20·8, 24·8, 26·2, 27·0, 26·8, 26·4 feet.
    Find the area of the part waterplane.

79. A prismatic shaped tank is 15 feet long. Its end is divided into the following ordinates, spaced 2 feet apart:—
    5·0, 4·5, 3·8, 2·0. feet Find the area of the end and the volume of the tank.

80. Find the area of a waterplane having the following ordinates and a common interval of 5 feet:—
    0·2, 3·6, 6·7, 8·9, 10·7, 12·0, 12·7, 12·0, 11·4, 8·8, 5·0, 0·3 feet.

81. Find the area of a bulkhead which has the following ordinates, spaced 2 feet apart:—
    3·0, 4·7, 7·4, 9·5, 11·1, 12·5, 13·6, 14·4 feet.

82. Three ordinates are spaced 12 feet apart and have lengths of 7·4, 11·7, and 17·5 feet. Find the areas between the first and second and second and third ordinates respectively. How does the total area so found compare with that found by Simpson's First Rule.

83. Find the area between two ordinates, 10 feet apart, having lengths of 10·3 and 15·0 feet, if the next ordinate has a length of 19·6 feet.

84. Find the coefficient of fineness of a waterplane which has the following half-ordinates, spaced 10 feet apart:—
    0·5, 4·0, 7·2, 9·1, 10·0, 9·8, 8·1, 5·1, 0 feet. The greatest breadth of the waterplane is 20 feet.

85. The midship section of a boat is 3 feet deep and is divided horizontally into the following equally spaced ordinates:—
    7·5, 7·2, 6·8, 6·0, 5·3, 3·3, 0·5 feet. Find the coefficient of fineness of the midship section.

86. A ship is divided up into a number of waterplanes, spaced 2 feet apart and having the following areas:—

    Keel,   -   -   1200 square feet.
    Waterplane   A,   10923   ,,   ,,
        ,,   B,   12429   ,,   ,,
        ,,   C,   13552   ,,   ,,
        ,,   D,   14395   ,,   ,,
        ,,   E,   14997   ,,   ,,
        ,,   F,   15488   ,,   ,,
        ,,   G,   15936   ,,   ,,

   D is the light waterplane and G the load waterplane. Find—
   (a) The light displacement.
   (b) The loaded displacement.
   (c) The block coefficient of fineness, assuming the length and breadth of the ship on waterplane G to be 400 feet and 54 feet, respectively.

87. The midship section of a ship has the following ordinates, spaced 3 feet apart, below her waterline:—
    54·0, 51·7, 51·4, 50·1, 48·7, 46·2, 42·1, 36·0, 26·1, 3·0 feet. Find its area. If the length of the ship is 420 feet and her displacement 11030 tons, find the prismatic coefficient of fineness.

Answers—

74. Simpson's First Rule gives 2419·3 square feet.
    Simpson's Second Rule gives 2421·0 square feet.
    The Trapezoidal Rule gives 2413·0 square feet.
    10·23 feet from mid-ordinate.
75. 864 square feet.
76. 8243·2 square feet.
    1·75 feet from mid-ordinate.
77. 281·6 square feet.
    2·46 feet from mid-ordinate.
78. 4188·6 square feet.
79. 23·9 square feet, 358·9 cubic feet.
80. 465 square feet.
81. 135·1 square feet.
82. 113·1 square feet, 173·7 square feet.
    Both total areas the same, 286·8 square feet.
83. 126·6 square feet.
84. 0·68
85. 0·73.
86. Light displacement, 2635·3 tons.
    Loaded displacement, 5245·0 tons.
    Block coefficient, 0·607.
87. 1149·2 square feet. 0·800.

Forces, Moments, Etc.

88. A man exerts a force of 50 lbs. on the end of a lever which is 12 feet long. Find the moment about the other end of the lever.

89. A weight of 3 tons is placed on a beam, so that its centre of gravity is 25 feet from the end. What is the moment about the end of the beam?

90. A bar is pivoted in the middle and a man pushes on it, in a clockwise direction at a distance of 7 feet from the middle, with a force of 60 lbs. Another man, on the other side also pushes in a clockwise direction with a force of 40 lbs. If the second man is 6 feet from the middle of the bar, find the moment about its centre.

91. If, in the above question, the second man turned and pushed with the same force in an anti-clockwise direction, what would the moment be?

92. A man presses down on the longer end of a bar with a force of 100 lbs. The bar is 15 feet long and is supported at a distance of 5 feet from its end. How much weight can the man lift on the shorter end?

93. Four men, working at a capstan, each push on a bar at a distance of 10 feet from the centre. If they push with forces of 40, 50, 55 and 60 lbs. respectively, find the moment to turn the capstan.

94. If a rope is wound around the capstan in the last question, and the radius from the centre of the capstan to the centre of the rope is 1 foot 6 inches, find the pull on the rope.

95. A wire, wound around a capstan, supports a weight of 8 cwt. The diameter of the capstan barrel is 2 feet. How much force must be exerted by each of 3 men, each at a distance of 8 feet from the centre, in order to lift the weight?

96. Two weights are placed on a beam, one of 2 tons being 36 feet from one end, the other of 3 tons and 20 feet from the same end. What is the moment about the end of the beam?

97. A weight of 150 lbs. is placed on a see-saw at a distance of 12 feet from the middle. What weight must be placed on the other side, at a distance of 10 feet from the middle, in order to balance the see-saw?

Answers—

88. 600 foot-lbs.
89. 75 foot-tons.
90. 660 foot-lbs.
91. 180 foot-lbs.
92. 200 lbs.
93. 2050 foot-lbs.
94. 1366·7 lbs.
95. 74·7 lbs.
96. 132 foot-tons.
97. 180 lbs.

PROBLEMS

Shift of G (general).

98. A plank weighs 62 lbs. What will be the shift of its centre of gravity if a weight of 38 lbs. is placed on it at a distance of 12 feet from its original centre of gravity?

99. A body weighs 2 tons and a weight of 12 cwt. is added to it at a distance of 4 feet from its centre of gravity. Find the shift of G.

100. A body, weighing 32 tons, has a weight of 8 tons removed from it. What is the shift of G if the centre of gravity of the weight removed is 15 feet from that of the body?

101. A beam carries a weight of 48 cwt. at a distance of 6 feet from one end and the centre of gravity of the whole mass is 20 feet from that end. If the weight of the beam alone is 84 cwt., what is the distance of the centre of gravity of the beam from the end mentioned?

102. A loaded truck weighs 6 tons. If a weight of 6 cwt. is shifted from one end to the other, through a distance of 20 feet, find the shift of the centre of gravity.

103. A boat weighs 23·6 cwt and when a man, weighing 1·4 cwt., sits in the bottom, the centre of gravity is 2·5 feet above the keel. What will be the new height of the boat's centre of gravity if the man stands up so as to raise his weight by 5 feet?

104. A see-saw has a number of weights placed on one end at a distance of 15 feet from the fulcrum (balancing point). The centre of gravity of the whole mass is 3 feet from the fulcrum and the total weight is 270 lbs. A number of the weights are moved for a distance of 30 feet along the see-saw to the other end, so that it balances. Find the amount of weight shifted.

105. A table top has a number of weights on it and the whole mass weighs 275 lbs. How far would it be necessary to shift a weight of 25 lbs. in order to cause the centre of gravity of the mass to shift 1 foot?

Answers—
98. 4·56 feet.
99. 0·923 feet.
100. 5·0 feet.
101. 28 feet.
102. 1 foot.
103. 2·78 feet.
104. 27 lbs.
105. 11 feet.

Moment of Inertia.

106. A rectangular surface is 12 feet long and 5 feet wide. Find its moment of inertia about:—
   (a) The transverse centre line.
   (b) The longitudinal centre line.

107. A box-shaped lighter is 120 feet long and 20 feet broad. Find the moments of inertia of its waterplane about its longitudinal and transverse centre lines.

108. Find the moments of inertia of a rectangle 6 feet long and 2 feet wide about its centre lines.

109. A barge of prismatic section has a rectangular waterplane, 48 feet long and 9 feet wide. Find its moments of inertia about the centre line in a transverse direction. Would the underwater form of the barge make any difference to the above, if the waterplane remains unchanged?

Answers—
106. (a) 125, (b) 720.
107 80,000, 2,880,000.
108. 4, 36.
109. 2916. No.

Shift of G in Ships.

110. A ship has a displacement of 2000 tons. Find the shift of her centre of gravity if a weight of 100 tons is shifted 40 feet across a hold.

111. A weight of 500 tons is loaded into a ship so that its centre of gravity is 10 feet from that of the ship. Find the shift of G if the ship's original displacement was 3000 tons.

112. A ship and her cargo displace 7200 tons. What will be the shift of the centre of gravity if a weight of 80 tons is removed from a point 100 feet from the original centre of gravity of the ship?

113. Find the effect of adding a weight of 80 tons at a distance of 120 feet from the centre of gravity of a ship, the original displacement of which was 7600 tons.

114. What will be the shift of G in a ship of 8000 tons displacement, if a weight of 40 tons is moved 50 feet horizontally across the deck?

115. A ship has a displacement of 11000 tons. Calculate the shift of G if a weight of 1000 tons is removed from a point 60 feet from the original centre of gravity.

116. A ship has a displacement of 3600 tons and a KG of 9·2 feet. A weight of 60 tons is raised from a hold into a 'tween deck, through a vertical distance of 24 feet. Find the new KG.

117. A weight of 25 tons is loaded into a ship at a distance of 20 feet above her centre of gravity. If her original KG was 14·7 feet and her new displacement, after the weight is on board, is 2200 tons, find the new KG.

What would be the KG if the weight had been added at a distance of 20 feet below the ship's centre of gravity, instead of above it?

118. A ship has a displacement of 2550 tons and a KG of 22 feet. What would be the KG after 950 tons of cargo had been loaded, with its centre of gravity 8 feet above the keel?

119. Find the shift of G and the new KG if a weight of 40 tons is discharged from a point 4 feet below the centre of gravity of a lighter. The lighter's original displacement and KG were 680 tons and 6·28 feet respectively.

120. A ship's displacement is 2800 tons and her KG 12·7 feet. What will be the new KG if a weight of 35 tons is lowered vertically downwards into her for a distance of 40 feet?

121. A weight of 9 tons is lifted from a hold by means of a derrick, the head of which is 50 feet above the original position of the centre of gravity of the weight. If the ship's displacement is 2700 tons, what will be the shift of G?

122. A ship has a KG of 15·0 feet and a displacement of 3000 tons. A weight of 20 tons is lifted from the lower hold and placed on deck by means of a derrick, the head of which is 75 feet above the keel. The centre of gravity of the weight was 5 feet above the keel when in the hold and 35 feet above the keel when on deck. Find—
    (a) The KG when the weight is hanging on the derrick.
    (b) The KG when the weight has been landed on deck.

123. 15 tons is lifted by a derrick, the head of which is 45 feet above the original position of the weight, in a ship of 1250 tons displacement and KG 10·4 feet. What will be the new KG when the weight is (a) 5 feet above the keel; (b) 35 feet above the keel?

124. A ship displaces 2415 tons and has a KG of 14·0 feet. A weight of 35 tons is lifted from the shore by a derrick, the head of which is 56 feet above the keel, and is placed in the hold, the final position of its centre of gravity being 9 feet above the keel. Find—
    (a) The KG when the weight is hanging on the derrick.
    (b) The KG when the weight is landed in the hold.

PROBLEMS 131

125. A double bottom tank when full, has its centre of gravity at a height of 2·4 feet above the keel and can hold 380 tons of water. The KG of the ship is 28·8 feet and her displacement 3700 tons when the tank is empty. What will be her KG when the tank is filled?

126. A tank holds 252 tons of water and its centre of gravity is 132 feet from that of the ship. If the ship's displacement is 3024 tons when the tank is full, what will be the shift of G caused by pumping it out?

127. 150 tons of oil are transferred from a fore peak tank to an after peak tank the distance between the centres of gravity being 410 feet. Find the shift of G due to this, if the ship's displacement is 7500 tons.

Answers—

110. 2·0 feet.
111. 1·4 feet.
112. 1·12 feet.
113. G will move 1·2 feet towards the centre of gravity of the weight.
114. 0·25 feet.
115. 6·0 feet.
116. 9·6 feet.
117. 14·9 feet;   14·5 feet.
118. 18·2 feet.
119. 0·25 feet;   6·53 feet.
120. 12·2 feet.
121. 0·17 feet, upwards
122. (a) 15·5 feet.
     (b) 15·2 feet.
123. (a) 10·9 feet.
     (b) The same.
124. (a) 14·6 feet.
     (b) 13·9 feet.
125. 26·3 feet.
126. 12·0 feet.
127. 8·2 feet, aft.

KG.

128. A ship displaces 2730 tons and has a KG of 18·0 feet. She then loads the following weights:—

540 tons, 15 feet above the keel.
370   ,,   26   ,,   ,,
110   ,,   31   ,,   ,,
850   ,,   14   ,,   ,,
620   ,,   18   ,,   ,,

Find her new KG.

129. A loaded lighter displaces 836 tons and has a KG of 5 feet. Find the new KG after the following weights have been discharged:—

160 tons, 8 feet above the keel.
 40   ,,   11   ,,   ,,
395   ,,   4   ,,   ,,

130. A ship leaves port with a displacement of 9060 tons and a KG of 14·3 feet. During the voyage she consumes the following fuel and stores:—

Oil fuel   - 260 tons, 2·7 feet above the keel.
Oil fuel   - 320   ,,   2·6   ,,   ,,
Stores   -   98   ,, 31·0   ,,   ,,
Fresh Water   87   ,, 32·5   ,,   ,,

What will be her KG on arrival at her port of destination?

MERCHANT SHIP STABILITY

131. The original displacement of a ship was 4285 tons and her KG was 8·11 feet. Find her new KG after she has loaded the following weights:—

    800 tons, 12 feet above the keel.
    440 ,, 25 ,, ,,
    110 ,, 19 ,, ,,
    630 ,, 11 ,, ,,

132. A ship has a KG of 21·2 feet and a displacement of 6020 tons. Find her KG after she has loaded and discharged the following weights:—

    Loaded - - 500 tons, 9 feet above the keel.
    ,, - - 850 ,, 15 ,, ,,
    ,, - - 220 ,, 27 ,, ,,
    Discharged - 300 ,, 17 ,, ,,
    ,, - 700 ,, 11 ,, ,,

133. Find the new KG of a lighter which has loaded and discharged the following weights:—

    Discharged - 140 tons, 8·1 feet above the keel.
    ,, - 270 ,, 4·7 ,, ,,
    Loaded - - 215 ,, 3·3 ,, ,,

The original displacement and KG were 646 tons and 6·5 feet respectively.

134. A ship arrives in port with a KG of 22·2 feet and a displacement of 6080 tons. Whilst in port, she discharges and loads the following weights:—

    Discharged - 1250 tons cargo, 15 feet above the keel.
    ,, - - 675 ,, ,, 12 ,, ,,
    ,, - - 420 ,, ,, 29 ,, ,,
    Burned - - 30 ,, oil 3 ,, ,,
    Loaded - - 980 ,, cargo 14 ,, ,,
    ,, - - 550 ,, ,, 21 ,, ,,
    ,, - - 700 ,, bunkers 3 ,, ,,
    ,, - - 70 ,, water 37 ,, ,,

She then sails on a voyage, during which she burns 840 tons of oil (3 feet above the keel) and uses 60 tons of water and stores (37 feet above the keel). Find the KG at the beginning and end of this voyage.

135. The light displacement of a ship is 2875 tons. She loads 390 tons at a height of 21 feet above the keel, and 710 tons at a height of 14 feet above the keel. If her KG was then found to be 17·4 feet, what was the light KG?

Answers—
128. 17·9 feet.
129. 3·65 feet.
130. 14·7 feet.
131. 17·1 feet.
132. 20·9 feet.
133. 5·5 feet.
134. 20·9 feet; 23·7 feet.
135. 17·8 feet.

Shift of B.

136. The volumes of the emerged and immersed wedges in a ship which is heeled, are each 55000 cubic feet and the distance between their centres of gravity is 36 feet. If the ship displaces 480,000 cubic feet of water, find the shift of her centre of buoyancy.

137. A ship, floating in salt water, has a displacement of 5500 tons. Find the shift of her centre of buoyancy when she heels, if the volume of the immersed wedge is 38,500 cubic feet and the distance between the centres of gravity of the wedges is 30 feet.

PROBLEMS

138. A box-shaped vessel is 270 feet long, 40 feet wide, and floats at a draft of 20 feet. Find the shift of B if the ship heels through an angle of 10° (take gg_1 as two-thirds of the ship's breadth).

139. A box-shaped lighter, 60 × 20, floating at a draft of 6 feet, lists through an angle of 30°. What was the original KB and the shift of B when she heels? (Assume gg_1 to be two-thirds of the breadth).

Answers—
136. 4·13 feet.
137. 6·0 feet.
138. 1·17 feet.
139. 3·0 feet: 3·21 feet.

The Inclining Experiment.

140. A weight of 25 tons is shifted transversely for a distance of 30 feet across the deck of a ship. A plumb line, which is suspended 14 feet above a horizontal batten shifts out along that batten for a distance of 1·0 feet. If the ship's displacement is 4950 tons, what is her GM, assuming that she was upright at the beginning?

141. When the inclining experiment is performed with a ship of 2304 tons displacement, a weight of 15 tons is moved 36 feet across the deck. The plumb line is suspended 24 feet above the batten and moves out 1 foot 6 inches when the ship heels. Find the GM.

142. A ship which has just been completed has a light KM (height of the metacentre) of 33·8 feet and a displacement of 3780 tons. A weight of 12 tons is moved across the deck for a distance of 35 feet and a plumb line, which is suspended 25 feet above a batten, moves out 3 inches. Find the ship's light KG.

143. Find the KG of a ship which has a KM of 24·2 feet and displaces 2400 tons. When the inclining experiment was performed, a weight of 10 tons was shifted 40 feet across the deck and caused a plumb line, 15 feet long, to move out 5 inches.

144. In an inclining experiment, a weight of 12½ tons was shifted 30 feet across the deck and caused a plumb line, 20 feet long, to move out 6 inches. A double bottom tank in the ship was full of water, which weighed 450 tons and had its centre of gravity 2·7 feet above the keel; otherwise the ship would have been in the light condition. If the displacement of the ship was 3750 tons and her KM 27·4 feet when the experiment was performed, find—

    (a) The KG of the ship at the time of the experiment.
    (b) Her light KG.

Answers—
140. 2·1 feet.
141. 3·8 feet.
142. 22·7 feet.
143. 18·2 feet.
144. (a) 23·4 feet.
    (b) 26·2 feet.

BM.

145. A box shaped ship is 350 feet long, 50 feet wide and floats at a draft of 15 feet. What is its BM?

146. Find the BM of a box-shaped lighter which has a beam of 18 feet and floats at a draft of 6 feet.

147. What is the height of the metacentre (KM) in a box-shaped vessel, 32 feet wide, when floating at a draft of 16 feet?

148. Find the KM of a box-shaped lighter which has a beam of 22 feet and floats at a draft of 3 feet 8 inches.

149. A ship displaces 3860 tons and the moment of inertia of her waterplane is 2756040. Find her KM, if the height of the centre of buoyancy is 11·7 feet above the keel.

150. What is the BM of a ship of 4160 tons, if the moment of inertia of her waterplane is 3564000?

151. Find the GM of a box-shaped lighter, 60 feet long, 18 feet wide, having a draft of 7 feet 6 inches and a KG of 5·2 feet.

152. The inclining experiment, when performed on a box-shaped ship of 21 feet beam and 8 feet 2 inches draft, showed the GM to be 2·4 feet. What is the KG?

153. An ordinary merchant ship has a beam of 54 feet and floats at a draft of 20 feet. Find her BM by approximate formula.

154. Use the approximate formula to find the BM of a merchant ship having a beam of 36 feet and draft 12 feet.

Answers—
145. 13·9 feet.
146. 4·5 feet.
147. 13·3 feet.
148. 12·8 feet.
149. 32·1 feet.

150. 24·5 feet.
151. 2·2 feet.
152. 6·2 feet.
153. 13·1 feet.
154. 9·72 feet.

Moment of Statical Stability.

155. Find the moment of statical stability of a ship of 3165 tons displacement and GM 2·7 feet, when she is heeled to an angle of 12°.

156. A ship of 1068 tons displacement has a GM of 3·9 feet. Find her moment of statical stability at an angle of heel of 6°.

157. What is the moment of statical stability of a ship which displaces 6752 tons and has a righting lever of 1·4 feet?

158. A ship of 5124 tons displacement has the following righting levers:—

Angle of heel - - 10° 20° 30° 40° 50° 60° 70°
Corresponding GZ - +0·4 +1·1 +1·6 +1·7 +1·3 +0·6 −0·3 feet

Calculate the moment of statical stability at each angle of heel and draw a curve of statical stability. Find from this:—
  (a) The moment of statical stability at 24° of heel.
  (b) The maximum moment of statical stability and the angle at which it occurs.
  (c) The range of stability.

159. A ship of 7200 tons displacement has a KB of 12·0 feet and a KG of 20·1 feet. At an angle of heel of 23°, the volume of the immersed wedge is 32,800 cubic feet and the horizontal shift of the centre of gravity of the wedge is 28 feet. Find the moment of statical stability and the length of the righting lever at this angle of heel.

160. A ship which is heeled to an angle of 57° immerses a wedge which has a volume of 70,000 cubic feet. The horizontal distance between the centres of gravity of the immersed and emerged wedges is 36·5 feet. The ship displaces 350,000 cubic feet of salt water and has a KG of 22·2 feet and a KB of 13·1 feet. What is the moment of statical stability, and is the ship in stable equilibrium?

PROBLEMS 135

161. A box-shaped ship is 350 feet long, 50 feet wide and floats at a draft of 12·0 feet. Her KG is 25·1 feet. Draw a figure to show a transverse section of the immersed and emerged wedges at an angle of heel of 25°, assuming that the deck edge does not become immersed nor the bilge emerged. From the drawing, find the volume of one of the wedges and the distance between the centres of gravity and thence find the ship's moment of statical stability.

Answers—
155. 1777 foot-tons.
156. 435·4 foot-tons.
157. 9452·8 foot-tons.
158. (a) 6850 foot-tons.
    (b) 36½°, 8900 foot-tons.
    (c) 67°.

159. 3452 foot-tons. 0·479 feet.
160. −3322 foot-tons; ship is unstable.
161. 87·6 foot-tons..

Angle of Loll.

162. A weight of 50 tons is shifted transversely across the deck of a ship for a distance of 42 feet. The ship's displacement and GM were 4350 tons and 1·4 feet, respectively, and she was upright before the weight was shifted. To what angle will she heel after the weight has been shifted?

163. A ship of 4800 tons displacement has a list of 8°, due to uneven loading of weights. If her GM is 0·8 feet, find how much weight must be shifted transversely across a 'tween deck, for a distance of 40 feet, in order to bring the ship to the upright.

164. A weight of 120 tons is loaded into a 'tween deck, so that it is 12 feet from the ship's centre line and at a vertical height of 18 feet above her centre of gravity. Before the weight was loaded, the ship was upright, had a GM of 1·4 feet and a displacement of 7080 tons. What is the effect of the weight?

165. A ship has a list of 12° to port, her KG being 12·6 feet and her displacement 5750 tons. A weight of 250 tons is to be loaded into the port and starboard wings of the 'tween deck at a height of 24·6 feet above the keel and a distance of 25 feet on either side of the centre line. If the KM, is 15·3 feet, how much weight must be placed in each wing to bring the ship upright?

166. 80 tons of grain shifts in a hold, 30 feet horizontally and 8 feet downwards. Before this happened, the ship was upright and had a GM of 1·2 feet, her displacement being 2320 tons. Find the angle of heel caused by the shift of the grain.

167. Find the angle to which a ship will loll, if her GM is −0·2 feet and her BM is 12·4 feet.

168. A ship displaces 2040 tons and has a GM of 0·3 feet. 120 tons of cargo are then loaded on deck at a vertical height of 12 feet above the ship's centre of gravity and the BM was then found to be 11·6 feet. What will happen?

169. To what angle will a ship loll if she has a BM of 19·8 feet and a GM of −0·6 feet?

Answers—
162. 19°.
163. 13·5 tons.
164. Ship heels 10¼°.
165. Port 59 tons; Starboard, 191 tons.

166. 34½°.
167. 10¼°.
168. The ship will heel to an angle of 14¾°.
169. 13¾°.

K

Free Surface Effect.

170. A seaman calculates his ship's GM to be 1·9 feet and her displacement in, salt water, 4640 tons. He has forgotten to allow for free surface of water in a rectangular tank 50 feet long and 40 feet wide, having no divisions in it. What is the ship's true GM when upright?

171. If the tank in the last question, had contained oil of specific gravity 0·875, what would then have been the ship's GM? Assume the ship to be floating in water of density 1025.

172. A ship of 6000 tons displacement has a KG of 11·1 feet and a KM of 12·0 feet, neglecting the effect of free surface, Free surface exists in an undivided rectangular tank, 40 feet long and 35 feet wide, which is partly filled with sea water. Find the actual GM when the ship is upright.

173. What would be the GM in the ship in the last question, if the tank were divided longitudinally at the centre line?

174. 100 tons of water are run into a rectangular tank, 35 feet long and 40 feet wide, in a ship of 5500 tons displacement, when the tank is found to be about three-quarters full. If the centre of gravity of this water is 1·5 feet above the ship's keel and the original KG of the ship was 16·2 feet, find the new KG when the ship is upright.

175. A box-shaped lighter is 100 feet long, 25 feet wide and floats at a draft of 3 feet 6 inches. Its KG is 2·5 feet. If 6 inches of water were allowed to run into the bottom, what would be the new GM when upright, if the new KM is 15·0 feet?

176. A ship has a displacement of 4880 tons and a KG of 19·3 feet when all her double bottom tanks are full. What would be the KG if 80 tons of water were pumped out of a rectangular tank, leaving it slack; the tank being 20 feet long and 45 feet wide, and the centre of gravity of the water removed being 15·5 feet below that of the ship?

177. A rectangular deep tank, 30 feet long, 40 feet wide and 20 feet deep, is divided at the centre line. When the tank is full, the ship has a displacement of 6080 tons and a KG of 18 feet. If the tank is pumped out until there are 6 feet of water left in it, what will be the new KG of the ship, assuming that the tank extends right down to the keel?

Answers—
170. 0·3 feet.
171. 0·5 feet.
172. 0·2 feet.
173. 0·7 feet.
174. 16·9 feet.
175. —0·2 feet.
176. 20·5 feet.
177. 18·6 feet.

BM_L.

178. A box-shaped ship has a length of 420 feet and floats at a draft of 24 feet What is her longitudinal BM_L?

179. Find the BM_L and GM_L of a box-shaped lighter, 90 feet long, 30 feet wide and floating at a draft of 6 feet, if her KG is 4·6 feet.

180. What is the KM_L of a homogeneous log, $30 \times 2 \times 2$ feet, which floats at a draft of 1 foot 6 inches?

181. A box-shaped lighter is 120 feet long and floats at a draft of 3 feet fore and aft. Find her BM_L and KM_L.

Answers—
178. 612·5 feet.
179. 112·5 feet; 110·9 feet.
180. 50·75 feet.
181. 400 feet; 401·5 feet.

PROBLEMS

T.P.I.

182. Find the tons per inch immersion of a box-shaped vessel, 210 feet long and 35 feet beam.

183. A ship is 450 feet long, 56 feet beam and floats at a draft of 18 feet 2 inches. If the coefficient of fineness of her waterplane at that draft is 0·763, find her T.P.I.

184. A box-shaped lighter is 84 feet long, 20 feet wide and floats on an even keel at a draft of 3 feet 2 inches. What is her T.P.I. and what will be her new draft after 30 tons of pig iron have been spread evenly over the bottom?

185. At a given draft, a ship of 360 feet length and 46 feet beam has a coefficient of fineness of the waterplane of 0·770. Find her T.P.I. at this draft.

186. A vessel's waterplane is measured up and its area found by Simpson's Rules. The ordinates, measured in feet, were 0, 14·6, 24·3, 31·8, 34·2, 33·1, 31·8, 17·7, 0·3, and the common interval was 20 feet. Find the T.P.I.

Answers—
182. 17·5.
183. 45·8.
184. 4·0; 3 feet 9½ inches.
185. 30·4.
186. 9·04.

I.T.M.

187. A ship is 420 feet long and displaces 4320 tons, her KG is 15·7 feet and her KM_L 431·5 feet. Find her I.T.M.

188. Find the inch trim moment of a ship, 372 feet long and displacement 3600 tons, which has a GM_L of 492·0 feet.

189. What is the I.T.M. of the lighter in question 179?

190. A box-shaped vessel is 250 feet long, 45 feet wide and floats at a draft of 15 feet 0 inches in sea water. KG is not known. Find her I.T.M.

191. Use an approximate formula to find the I.T.M. of a ship which has a beam of 54 feet and a T.P.I. of 39·60.

192. The area of a ship's waterplane is 9200 square feet and her beam is 40 feet. Find her I.T.M. by an approximate formula.

193. Find by approximate formula the I.T.M. of the ship in question 186, if her maximum beam is 34·2 feet.

194. What is the I.T.M. of a ship which has a T.P.I. of 54·11 and beam 62 feet?

Answers—
187. 356·4 foot-tons.
188. 396·8 foot-tons.
189. 47·5 foot-tons.
190. 558·0 foot-tons.
191. 895·6 foot-tons.
192. 370·3 foot-tons.
193. 73·7 foot-tons.
194. 1456·4 foot-tons.

Change of Draft Due to Change of Trim.

195. A ship has drafts of 12 feet 9 inches forward and 14 feet 4 inches aft, her centre of flotation being on the longitudinal centre line. A weight is shifted forward so that the trim changes by 1 foot 2 inches. What are the new drafts fore and aft?

196. Find the new drafts fore and aft if a weight is shifted aft in a ship, sufficiently to change the trim by 9 inches. The centre of flotation is on the centre line and the original drafts were 21 feet 10 inches forward and 21 feet 10½ inches aft.

197. The centre of flotation of a ship is 14 feet abaft her longitudinal centre line. Weights are shifted aft so as to change the trim by 16 inches. If the ship's length is 420 feet and her original drafts 19 feet 7 inches forward and 20 feet

MERCHANT SHIP STABILITY

0 inches aft, find the new drafts fore and aft and also the original and new mean drafts. How do you account for the difference in the mean drafts?

198. A ship is 360 feet long and floats on an even keel at drafts of 17 feet 10 inches fore and aft. Weights are shifted aft so as to change the trim by 11 inches. Find the new drafts, fore, aft and mean, if the ship's centre of flotation is 15 feet abaft amidships.

Answers—
195. F. 13 feet 4 inches   A. 13 feet 9 inches.
196. F. 21 feet 5½ inches   A. 22 feet 3 inches.
197. F. 18 feet 10½ inches   A. 20 feet 7½ inches.
     Mean draft—old 19 feet 9½ inches, new 19 feet 9 inches.
198. F. 17 feet 4 inches   A. 18 feet 3 inches   M. 17 feet 9½ inches.

Change of Trim Due to Shifting Weights.

199. A ship floats at drafts of 22 feet 7 inches forward and 23 feet 9 inches aft, her I.T.M. is 880 foot-tons and her centre of flotation is on the longitudinal centre line. Find the change of trim and the new drafts if a weight of 40 tons is shifted forward for a distance of 200 feet.

200. Find the change of trim and the new drafts fore and aft, if 120 tons of oil is transferred from the fore peak to the after peak tank in a ship which has an I.T.M. of 1200 foot-tons. The distance between the centres of gravity of the tanks is 480 feet, the ship's centre of flotation is at the longitudinal centre line, and the original drafts were 15 feet 6 inches forward and 14 feet 10 inches aft.

201. What will be the change of trim and the new drafts fore and aft if a weight of 90 tons is shifted aft for a distance of 300 feet in a ship having an I.T.M. of 1350 foot-tons? The length of the ship is 450 feet, her centre of flotation being 5 feet abaft the centre line, and her original drafts were 19 feet 9 inches forward and 20 feet 1 inch aft.

202. A ship is 480 feet long and her centre of flotation is 12 feet abaft the centre line. Her drafts are 21 feet 6 inches forward and 26 feet 1 inch aft and her I.T.M. is 1500 foot-tons. Find the change of trim and the new drafts if 300 tons of oil is transferred from No. 4 double bottom tank to No. 1 double bottom tank, a distance of 250 feet.

Answers—
199. 9 inches; F. 22 feet 11½ inches A. 23 feet 4½ inches.
200. 48 inches; F. 13 feet 6 inches   A. 16 feet 10 inches.
201. 20 inches; F. 18 feet 10¾ inches A. 20 feet 10¾ inches.
202. 50 inches; F. 23 feet 8¼ inches   A. 24 feet 1¼ inches   M. 23 feet 10¾ inches.

Effect on Draft of Weights Loaded or Discharged.

203. What is the effect of placing a weight of 140 tons over the centre of flotation in a ship having a T.P.I. of 40?

204. 300 tons of cargo is placed on board a ship so that its centre of gravity is directly over the ship's centre of flotation. The ship's T.P.I. is 45 and her original drafts were 20 feet 1 inch forward and 20 feet 11 inches aft. Find the new drafts.

205. A ship has a T.P.I. of 32 and drafts of 12 feet 8 inches forward and 13 feet 3 inches aft. Find the new drafts after 96 tons of cargo have been removed from a point directly over the centre of flotation.

206. Find the bodily rise of a ship which has a T.P.I. of 28, if a weight of 80 tons is removed from under the centre of flotation.

Answers—
203. The ship sinks 3½ inches bodily.
204. F. 20 feet 7¾ inches   A. 21 feet 5¾ inches.
205. F. 12 feet 11 inches   A. 13 feet 6 inches.
206. 3 inches

Moderate Weights Loaded off the centre of Flotation.

207. A ship is 450 feet long, has a T.P.I. of 50 and an I.T.M. of 1250 foot-tons. Her drafts are 15 feet 8 inches forward and 17 feet 2 inches aft. 250 tons of cargo are loaded at a distance of 150 feet from the stem. Find the new drafts, assuming the ship's centre of flotation to be on the longitudinal centre line.

208. The centre of flotation of a ship is at the longitudinal centre line, her length is 380 feet, her T.P.I. 38, and her I.T.M. is 840 foot-tons. A weight of 57 tons is removed from a point which is 130 feet abaft the stem. If her original drafts were 17 feet 2 inches forward and 17 feet 6 inches aft, what will her new drafts be?

209. A box-shaped lighter is 90 feet long, has a T.P.I. of 8 and an I.T.M. of 475 foot-tons. Her drafts are 3 feet 2 inches forward and aft. What would be the new drafts after a weight of 28 tons is added at a distance of 20 feet from the stern?

210. The following particulars are known about a ship:—
Length, 440 feet; T.P.I., 48; I.T.M., 990 foot-tons; centre of flotation, 230 feet abaft the stem; Drafts, forward 21 feet 2 inches, aft 21 feet 7 inches. Find her new drafts if 80 tons of cargo are loaded at a distance of 120 feet from aft.

211. A ship has drafts of 15 feet 9 inches forward and 18 feet 4 inches aft and in order to bring her more nearly to an even keel, 240 tons of water are run into No. 1 double bottom tank, the centre of gravity of which is 70 feet abaft the stem. The ship is 480 feet long, has a T.P.I. of 54 and an I.T.M. of 1440 foot-tons, whilst her centre of flotation is 6 feet abaft her centre line. Find the new drafts.

212. Find the new drafts after 120 tons of cargo has been discharged from a point which is 42 feet abaft the centre line of a ship. The ship is 360 feet long, has a T.P.I. of 40, an I.T.M. of 960 foot-tons, and her centre of flotation is 12 feet abaft the centre line. The original drafts were 21 feet 7 inches forward and 22 feet 5 inches aft.

213. A ship which is 420 feet long has a T.P.I. of 49 and an I.T.M. of 1030 foot-tons. Her centre of flotation is at the centre line and her drafts are 20 feet 7 inches forward and 21 feet 6 inches aft. What would be the new drafts if 140 tons of cargo is loaded at a distance of 100 feet from the stem and 56 tons at a distance of 300 feet from the stem?

214. A ship floats at drafts of 14 feet 1 inch forward and 15 feet 8 inches aft. Her length is 350 feet, T.P.I. 41, I.T.M. 980 foot-tons and her centre of flotation is 7 feet abaft amidships. Find the new drafts after the following weights have been loaded and discharged:—

Loaded, 55 tons, 142 feet abaft the stem.
Loaded, 100 tons, 220 feet abaft the stem.
Discharged, 73 tons, 292 feet abaft the stem.

215. A vessel is 280 feet long has her centre of flotation 5 feet abaft the centre line. Her T.P.I. is 20 and her I.T.M. is 400 foot-tons. 60 tons of cargo is discharged from a point 80 feet from the stem, and 40 tons is loaded at a distance of 200 feet from the stem. If the original drafts were 12 feet 8 inches forward and 12 feet 7 inches aft, find the new drafts.

Answers—

207. F. 16 feet $8\frac{1}{2}$ inches	A. 16 feet $11\frac{1}{2}$ inches	M. 16 feet 10 inches.
208. F. 16 feet $10\frac{1}{2}$ inches	A. 17 feet $6\frac{1}{2}$ inches	M. 17 feet $2\frac{1}{2}$ inches.
209. F. 3 feet $4\frac{3}{4}$ inches	A. 3 feet $6\frac{1}{4}$ inches	M. 3 feet $5\frac{1}{2}$ inches.
210. F. 21 feet 0 inches	A. 22 feet $0\frac{1}{4}$ inches	M. 21 feet 6 inches.
211. F. 17 feet $4\frac{1}{2}$ inches	A. 17 feet $6\frac{1}{4}$ inches	M. 17 feet $5\frac{1}{2}$ inches.
212. F. 21 feet 6 inches	A 22 feet $0\frac{1}{4}$ inches	M. 21 feet 9 inches.
213. F. 21 feet 4 inches	A. 21 feet 5 inches	M. 21 feet $4\frac{1}{2}$ inches.
214. F. 14 feet $6\frac{1}{2}$ inches	A. 15 feet 7 inches	M. 15 feet $0\frac{3}{4}$ inches.
215. F. 11 feet 11 inches	A. 13 feet $1\frac{1}{4}$ inches	M. 12 feet 6 inches.

MERCHANT SHIP STABILITY

Large Weights Loaded off the Centre of Flotation.

216. A ship is 480 feet long and floats at drafts of 16 feet 6 inches forward and 17 feet 6 inches aft. 600 tons of oil is then loaded into a deep tank, the centre of gravity of which is 20 feet forward of the ship's centre line. Find the new drafts, if the following information is found from the deadweight scales, and assuming the centre of flotation to be on the longitudinal centre line.

Draft 17 feet 0 inches; T.P.I. 52·0; I.T.M. 1232 foot-tons.
Draft 18 feet 0 inches; T.P.I. 52·6; I.T.M. 1268 foot-tons.

217. The following information is obtained from a ship's deadweight scale:—

Draft 20 feet; T.P.I. 40·2; I.T.M. 926 foot-tons.
,,   21 ,,   ,,   41·0; ,,   939 ,, Centre of flotation.
,,   22 ,,   ,,   41·8; ,,   952 ,, 10 feet abaft centre line

The ship is 400 feet long and floats at drafts of 20 feet 0 inches fore and aft. Find the new drafts if cargo is loaded into Numbers 2 and 5 holds, as follows:—

No. 2. - loaded 450 tons; centre of gravity 120 feet abaft the stem.
No. 5. - loaded 500 tons; centre of gravity 340 feet abaft the stem.

Answers—
216. F. 17 feet 10¼ inches   A. 18 feet 0¾ inches   M. 17 feet 11½ inches.
217. F. 20 feet 10 inches   A. 22 feet 11¾ inches M. 21 feet 11 inches.

Loading a Weight to Produce a Desired Trim.

218. A ship, which is completing her loading, has 120 tons of cargo to come on board. Her drafts are 23 feet 2 inches forward and 25 feet 8 inches aft and her I.T.M. is 1040 foot-tons. Where must the cargo mentioned be placed in order that the ship may leave port with a trim of one foot by the stern?

219. Find the weight of water which must be run into a double bottom tank in order to bring the ship on to an even keel, if the centre of gravity of the tank is 85 feet abaft the stem. The ship is 440 feet long, has an I.T.M. of 1200 foot-tons and her centre of flotation is 15 feet abaft the centre line. Her present drafts are 18 feet 8 inches forward and 21 feet 7 inches aft.

220. A ship has been in collision and her fore peak is flooded, causing her to trim 2 feet 0 inches by the head. In order to place her in a drydock, it is desired to bring her to a trim of 1 foot 0 inches by the stern. The after peak tank, which is empty can take 240 tons of water and its centre of gravity is 210 feet abaft the ship's centre of flotation. If the ship's I.T.M. is 1400 foot-tons, will it be possible to bring the ship to the desired trim by running up this tank, and, if so, what weight of water must be taken in?

221. The centre of flotation of a ship is 11 feet abaft her centre line, her I.T.M. is 960 foot-tons, and she floats on an even keel. 240 tons of cargo are to be loaded and it is desired to trim the ship 1 foot 6 inches by the stern. How far abaft the centre line must the weight be placed?

222. How far abaft the centre of flotation must a weight of 100 tons be loaded in order to change a ship's trim from 3 inches by the head to 12 inches by the stern if the I.T.M. is 1000 foot-tons?

218. 156 feet forward of the centre of flotation.
219. 280 tons.
220. Yes. Exactly 240 tons is required.
221. 83 feet abaft the centre line.
222. 150 feet.

PROBLEMS

Loading to Keep the After Draft Constant.

223. A ship is 420 feet long, has an I.T.M. of 1100 foot-tons, a T.P.I. of 44 and her centre of flotation is 10 feet abaft her centre line. How far forward of the centre of flotation must a weight be loaded if the after draft is to remain constant?

224. How far abaft the stem must a weight be loaded if the draft aft is not to change in a ship 460 feet long? The centre of flotation is 6 feet abaft the centre line the T.P.I. is 54 and the I.T.M. is 1320 foot-tons.

225. The centre of flotation of a ship is on her centre line and her length is 360 feet, whilst her T.P.I. is 40 and her I.T.M. is 960 foot-tons. Where, with relation to the centre line, must a weight of 140 tons be placed if the draft aft is not to change?

Answers—
223. 52·5 feet.
224. 186 feet.
225. 48 feet forward of the centre line.

Increase of Draft Due to Bilging.

226. A box-shaped lighter, 120 feet long, 30 feet wide and floating at a draft of 3 feet 0 inches, is divided into three equal compartments by two transverse bulkheads. If the centre compartment, which is empty, is holed below the waterline, find the new draft.

227. What would have been the draft, in the last question, if the compartment had been filled with cargo and had had a permeability of 40 per cent.?

228. A box-shaped vessel is 200 feet long, 40 feet beam and 19 feet deep. She floats at a draft of 15 feet 6 inches. What will happen if an empty compartment amidships, 40 feet long, is bilged?

229. A box shaped vessel, 250 feet long and 42 feet wide, floats at a draft of 20 feet 6 inches. A compartment amidships, which has a permeability of 60%, is 40 feet long. Find the new draft if this compartment becomes bilged.

230. A ship is 400 feet long, 54 feet beam and floats at a draft of 14 feet 0 inches. She is parallel-sided for a length of 100 feet amidships and at her draft the coefficient of fineness of the midships section is 0·924, whilst that of the waterplane is 0·750. Find the new draft if an empty compartment amidships, 60 feet long, is bilged.

231. A ship, which is parallel-sided amidships, is 350 feet long, 45 feet beam, and has a mean draft of 15 feet 6 inches, The coefficient of fineness of the midships section is 0·915 and that of the waterplane is 0·700. What will be the new mean draft if a compartment at the centre of flotation, 50 feet long and extending for the full breadth of the ship, is bilged, assuming that it has a permeability of 60%?

Answers—
226. 4 feet 6 inches.
227. 3 feet 5½ inches.
228. The vessel sinks.
229. 22 feet 0¼ inches.
230. 17 feet 2¾ inches (approximately).
231. 17 feet 6 inches. (approximately).

Stability Curves.

Use the curves given in the back of this book for solving the following problems Nos. 232 to 246.

232. Find all possible information from the displacement curves for the following drafts—(a) 11 feet 0 inches; (b) 15 feet 6 inches; (c) 17 feet 1 inch; (d) 20 feet 3 inches; (e) 24 feet 8 inches.

233. Find the ship's fresh water allowance, assuming the summer draft to be 25 feet. Use the formula $\dfrac{\Delta}{40T}$.

234. What will be the moment of statical stability of the ship at a mean draft of 17 feet 10 inches and at an angle of heel of 10°? Assume KG to be 21·9 feet.

235. The ship floats at a mean draft of 17 feet 2 inches and has a KG of 22·7 feet. Find her new GM after a weight of 100 tons is shifted vertically downwards in the hold for a distance of 35 feet.

236. The mean draft is 21 feet 3 inches and the KG 22·0 feet. Find the new mean draft and metacentric height if a weight of 250 tons is loaded at a height of 30 feet above the keel.

237. The ship arrives in port with a KG of 22·0 feet and a mean draft of 19 feet 0 inches. She then loads and discharges the following cargo:—

Discharged	-	750 tons,	at a height of	12·5 feet	above the keel.
Discharged	-	140 ,,	,,	31·0 ,,	,,
Loaded -	-	170 ,,	,,	20·0 ,,	,,
Loaded -	-	480 ,,	,,	15·5 ,,	,,

Find the GM and mean draft on leaving port.

238. The ship floats at drafts of 19 feet 8 inches forward and 18 feet 4 inches aft In order to trim her by the stern, 100 tons of oil is transferred from the fore peak tank to the after peak tank, the centre of gravity of this oil moving through a distance of 350 feet. If the length of the ship is 400 feet, find the new drafts.

239. 140 tons of cargo are loaded at a distance of 355 feet from the stem, the ship being 400 feet long. If the original drafts were 14 feet 2 inches forward and 14 feet 6 inches aft, find the new drafts.

240. A voyage is to be made in ballast and a deep tank, which is 45 feet abaft the centre line, is filled with 650 tons of water. What are the new drafts, if the original ones were 10 feet 6 inches forward and 10 feet 8 inches aft.

241. The ship is 400 feet long, 54 feet beam and floats at a mean draft of 12 feet 0 inches. An empty compartment at the centre of flotation is parallel sided, extends for the full width of the ship and is 55 feet long. What will the ship's mean draft become, approximately, if the compartment is bilged?

242. The drafts are 19 feet 6 inches forward and 17 feet 2 inches aft and the KG of the ship is 20·9 feet. 450 tons of cargo are discharged from a height of 10 feet above the keel and 180 feet abaft the stem. 600 tons are loaded at a height of 17 feet above the keel and 340 feet abaft the stem. Find the new drafts and GM, if the ship is 400 feet long.

243. A ship arrives in port with a mean draft of 10 feet 4 inches and a KG of 25·0 feet. She then loads the following:—

700 tons of oil fuel,	centre of gravity	2·0 feet above the keel.
5060 tons of lumber	,, ,,	20·0 ,, ,,
650 tons of deck cargo	,, ,,	45·0 ,, ,,

She then sails, and on the voyage to the next port she burns 780 tons of oil, the centre of gravity of which is estimated to be 2·0 feet above the keel. Use the curves to find her GM on leaving port and also her condition at the end of the voyage.

244. A ship, which is completing her loading, has a mean draft of 22 feet 4 inches and her KG is 22·0 feet. She has 500 tons of cargo to come on board. It is estimated that, during the coming voyage, she will burn 640 tons of coal from a height of 12 feet above the keel and will consume 80 tons of water and stores from a height of 26 feet above the keel. At what height above the keel must the remaining 500 tons of cargo be placed on board in order that the ship may arrive at her next port with a metacentric height of one foot?

245. In the last question, if the drafts were 21 feet 6 inches forward and 23 feet 2 inches aft, find where the 500 tons must be placed longitudinally for the ship to sail with a trim of 1 foot by the stern.

PROBLEMS

246. The ship, which is 400 feet long, makes the following voyages:—

(a) She arrives in port with drafts of 14 feet 2 inches forward and 14 feet 6 inches aft. KG, 23·0 feet. She then loads the following cargo:—

500	tons,	20	feet	above the keel,	40	feet	abaft the stem.
800	,,	12	,,	,,	150	,,	,,	
950	,,	16	,,	,,	300	,,	,,	
400	,,	25	,,	,,	340	,,	,,	

Find her KG, GM and drafts on sailing.

(b) During the voyage to the next port she consumes:—

250 tons oil fuel, 2·2 feet above the keel, 166 feet abaft the stem.
60 tons water, 30·0 feet above the keel, 276 feet abaft the stem.

Find her KG, GM and drafts on arrival in port.

(c) In this next port, she loads 650 tons of cargo, with its centre of gravity 25 feet above the keel and 200 feet abaft the stem. Another parcel of 150 tons of cargo remains to be loaded, and it is decided to place it in the 'tween deck with its centre of gravity 35 feet above the keel. In order to cross a bar the after draft must not be increased. Find where this last 150 tons must be placed, also the ship's drafts, KG and GM on sailing.

Answers—

232.

	(a)	(b)	(c)	(d)	(e)
Displacement	3900	5920	6650	8170	10330
KB	6·2 ft.	8·7 ft.	9·5 ft.	11·3 ft.	13·6 ft.
KM	27·9 ft.	24·2 ft.	23·5 ft.	23·0 ft.	23·4 ft.
KM_L	990 ft.	700 ft.	645 ft.	558 ft.	468 ft.
I.T.M.	754	852	879	930	980
T.P.I.	36·3	38·6	39·2	40·3	41·4
C. Flotation abaft amidships	2·8 ft.	5·8 ft.	6·9 ft.	8·8 ft.	10·6 ft.
C. Buoyancy abaft amidships	3·2 ft.	4·6 ft.	5·1 ft.	6·1 ft.	7·2 ft.
Midships Section coefficient	0·905	0·934	0·940	0·949	0·959
Waterplane coefficient	0·705	0·752	0·765	0·785	0·807
Prismatic	0·632	0·663	0·671	0·687	0·709
Block	0·573	0·620	0·630	0·654	0·680

233. 6·3 inches.
234. 1702 foot-tons.
235. 1·6 feet.
236. 21 feet 9¼ inches; 0·9 feet.
237. 18 feet 6 inches; 0·9 feet.
238. F. 18 feet 0 inches A. 19 feet 10½ inches. M. 18 feet 11¼ inches.
239. F. 13 feet 4¾ inches A. 15 feet 10 inches. M. 14 feet 7½ inches.
240. F. 10 feet 6 inches A. 13 feet 7 inches. M. 12 feet 0½ inches.
241. 14 feet 6½ inches (approximately).
242. F. 15 feet 5 inches A. 21 feet 6¼ inches. M 18 feet 5½ inches; GM 1·9 feet.

243. GM leaving, 1·1 feet; GM arriving —0·8 feet; ship will have a list of 21¼° arriving.
244. 10·4 feet above keel.
245. 15½ feet forward of the centre of flotation.
246. (a) F. 19 feet 5½ inches. A. 20 feet 5¼ inches. M. 19 feet 11½ inches. KG, 20·9 feet; GM, 2·1 feet
(b) F. 18 feet 6 inches. A. 20 feet 0¾ inches. M. 19 feet 3½ inches, KG, 21·5 feet; GM 1·6 feet.
(c) F. 20 feet 9 inches. A. 21 feet 1¾ inches M. 20 feet 11¼ inches. KG, 22·0 feet; GM, 1·0 feet. Load weight 161 feet abaft stem.

Deadweight Scale

Use the deadweight scale given in the back of this book for solving the following problems, Nos. 247 to 260.

247. Find all possible information from the deadweight scale, for the following drafts—(a) 11 feet 6 inches; (b) 16 feet 0 inches; (c) 18 feet 3 inches; (d) 20 feet 10 inches; (e) 23 feet 2 inches.

248. The ship for which the scale is given has only the following weights on board:—

Fuel oil,	420 tons, centre of gravity	1·7 feet above the keel.
Fresh water	80 ,,	,,	1·8 ,,	,,
Stores, etc.	60 ,,	,,	32 ,,	,,
Water ballast	600 ,,	,,	12 ,,	,,

Find the ship's mean draft and GM, if her light displacement is known to be 3458 tons.

249. What is the deadweight and GM of the ship at a draft of 17 feet 4 inches?

250. Find the ship's moment of statical stability at a mean draft of 18 feet 9 inches and an angle of heel of 12°, if the light displacement is 3458 tons and the KG is 22·6 feet.

251. At a draft of 18 feet 0 inches, the ship's displacement is 7088 tons and her KG is 23·0 feet. What will happen if a deck cargo is loaded at a height of 34 feet above the keel, so that the mean draft becomes 18 feet 6 inches?

252. The ship floats at drafts of 19 feet 3 inches forward and 19 feet 1 inch aft 120 tons of oil is transferred from No. 1 tank to No. 5 tank, through a distance of 240 feet. Find the new drafts assuming that the centre of flotation is on the ship's centre line.

253. In the last question, it was later found that the centre of flotation was 8 feet abaft the centre line and not on it, as assumed previously. If the length of the ship is 400 feet, what should the calculated drafts have been?

254. The ship has a mean draft of 23 feet 7 inches. If she loads 712 tons of cargo at the centre of flotation, what will be her new mean draft?

255. At the beginning of a voyage, the drafts are 23 feet 7 inches forward and 24 feet 3 inches aft and the GM is 1·2 feet. During the voyage the ship burns 325 tons of oil from a height of 2·0 feet above the keel and a distance of 110 feet abaft the stem; also 36 tons of water and stores from 28 feet above the keel and 200 feet abaft the stem. It is estimated that during the voyage, a deck cargo of lumber takes up water and increases its weight by 120 tons, the centre of gravity of this cargo being 36 feet above the keel and evenly distributed about the centre of flotation. The ship is 400 feet long, has a light displacement of 3458 tons and the centre of flotation is estimated to be 8 feet abaft the centre line. Find the drafts and GM at the end of the voyage.

256. The ship is completing her loading and has 350 tons of cargo still to come on board. Her drafts are 22 feet 2 inches forward and 22 feet 6 inches aft and her GM is 1·8 feet. It is estimated that during the coming voyage she will burn 217 tons of oil from a height of 2·0 feet above the keel and consume 30 tons of water and stores from a height of 25 feet above the keel. If the light displacement is 3458 tons, at what height above the keel should the remaining 350 tons of cargo be placed in order that the ship may end the voyage with a GM of 1·0 feet?

257. Suppose that, in the last question, the ship had had a list of 8° to port, due to uneven distribution of the weights in her, when the 350 tons remained to be loaded. If this weight were to be placed in the wings, 25 feet on either side of the centre line, how much should have been loaded into each wing in order to bring the ship upright?

258. The ship has nearly completed her loading, and when there are 250 tons of cargo to come on board, her drafts are 20 feet 9 inches forward and 22 feet 1 inch aft. In order to cross a bar, the maximum draft aft must not exceed 22 feet 0 inches. Where must this remaining cargo be placed in order that the ship may sail with this draft? Her length is 400 feet and the centre of flotation is assumed to be at the centre line.

PROBLEMS 145

259. On arrival at a loading port, the ship has drafts of 10 feet 3 inches forward and 16 feet 5 inches aft. She then loads the following cargo:—

No. 1 hold, 570 tons, 50 feet abaft the stem.
No. 2 ,, 950 ,, 120 ,, ,,
No. 3 ,, 300 ,, 180 ,, ,,
No. 4 ,, 680 ,, 290 ,, ,,
No. 5 ,, 250 ,, 350 ,, ,,

The ship is 400 feet long, has a light displacement of 3458 tons, and the centre of flotation on completion of loading is 10 feet abaft the centre line. Find the drafts on sailing.

260. In the last question, it is desired to bring the ship to a trim of 1 foot 0 inches by the stern before sailing. The after peak tank will hold 270 tons of water and its centre of gravity is 390 feet abaft the stem. Can the desired trim be obtained by filling this tank, and, if so, how much water must be run into it?

Answers—

247.

	(a)	(b)	(c)	(d)	(e)
Deadweight	430	2670	3750	5000	6125
T.P.I.	36·25	38·8	39·7	40·5	41·1
I.T.M.	760	860	900	935	970
KM	27·95 ft.	23·95 ft.	23·15 ft.	23·07 ft.	23·15 ft.
KB	6·20 ft.	8·93 ft.	10·18 ft.	11·60 ft.	12·85 ft.

248. Mean draft 12 feet 8 inches. *GM* 6·5 feet.
249. 3300 tons; 13·7 feet.
250. 774 foot-tons.
251. *GM* becomes −0·3 feet. Ship lolls to 12¼°.
252. F. 17 feet 11¼ inches. A. 20 feet 4¾ inches. M. 19 feet 2 inches.
253. F. 17 feet 10½ inches A. 20 feet 4 inches M. 19 feet 1¼ inches.
254. 25 feet 0½ inches.
255. F. 21 feet 8 inches. A. 25 feet 1¼ inches. M. 23 feet 4¾ inches; *GM* 0·4 feet.
256. 32·2 feet above the keel.
257. Port wing, 137½ tons. Starboard wing, 212½ tons.
258. 53·2 feet forward of centre of flotation or 146·8 feet abaft stem.
259. F. 20 feet 9¼ inches. A. 18 feet 2 inches. M. 19 feet 5½ inches.
260. Yes! 219·9 tons is necessary.

Metacentric Diagram.

261. Using the *KB* and *KM* given in the deadweight scale at the back of this book, construct a metacentric diagram for drafts of between 15 feet 0 inches and 25 feet 0 inches. From this, find the ship's *KB*, *KM* and *BM* for drafts of (a) 16 feet 3 inches (b) 20 feet 7 inches (c) 22 feet 2 inches.

262. Calculate the *KB* and *BM* for a box-shaped lighter, 100 feet long and 20 feet beam, for every foot of draft from 2 feet to 10 feet. Then construct a metacentric diagram and from this find the *KB*, *KM* and *BM* for drafts of (a) 4 feet 10 inches and (b) 8 feet 6 inches.

Answers —

261. (a) KB 9·1 ft. KM 23·8 ft. BM 14·7 ft.
     (b) KB 11·5 ft. KM 23·0 ft. BM 11·5 ft.
     (c) KB 12·3 ft. KM 23·1 ft. BM 10·8 ft.
262. (a) KB 2·4 ft. KM 9·3 ft. BM 6·9 ft.
     (b) KB 4·3 ft. KM 8·2 ft. BM 3·9 ft.

Drydocking.

263. A ship enters a drydock with drafts of 9 feet 5 inches forward and 10 feet 11 inches aft. Her displacement is 3000 tons; KG, 24·0 feet; GM, 6·0 feet; I.T.M., 729; and the centre of flotation is 180 feet from aft. What will be her GM at the instant before she settles flat on the blocks fore and aft?

264. In the case of the ship in the last question: what would be her GM when she was flat on the blocks and the water level had fallen to 9 feet 0 inches fore and aft, her displacement then being 2500 tons?

265. The ship is trimmed 1 foot 10 inches by the stern when she enters a dock Her displacement is 4600 tons; KG, 22·8 feet; KM, 34·1 feet; I.T.M., 1150; and the centre of flotation is 220 feet from aft. Find the GM at the instant before the ship comes flat on the blocks, fore and aft.

266. A box-shaped ship is 300 feet long, 40 feet wide and floats at drafts of 8 feet 0 inches fore and aft. Her KG is 18·0 feet. Find her new GM when she is flat on the blocks in drydock and the water level has fallen so that drafts are 7 feet 0 inches fore and aft.

267. A box-shaped vessel enters a drydock with drafts of 6 feet 4 inches forward and 8 feet 5 inches aft. Her length is 250 feet, beam 35 feet, KG 16·6 feet and I.T.M. 650. Find her GM at the instant before she comes flat on the blocks fore and aft. What will happen in this case?

Answers.—
263. + 5·27 feet.
264. + 1·0 feet.
265. + 10·45 feet.
266. + 0·1 feet.
267. − 0·3 feet. Ship becomes unstable and may fall over whilst in dock.

Cross Curves.

Use the cross curves given in Figure 76 for solving the following problems. Nos. 268 to 270.

268. Find the righting levers for:—

    (a) Heel 30°, Displacement 9000 tons, KG 23·0 feet
    (b) ,, 60°, ,, 6700 ,, ,, 22·0 ,,
    (c) ,, 45°, ,, 7800 ,, ,, 23·4 ,,
    (d) ,, 15°, ,, 8100 ,, ,, 22·2 ,,

269. Draw a curve of statical stability, shewing righting levers, for a displacement of 5000 tons and KG 23·0 feet. From this, find the range of stability and approximate GM.

270. Draw a curve of statical stability for a displacement of 8500 tons and KG 22·5 feet. Find the angle of vanishing stability and approximate GM.

Answers.—
268. (a) 1·18 feet.   (c) 2·22 feet.
    (b) 1·03 feet.   (d) 0·29 feet.
269. Approx. GM, 1·5 feet. Range 85°.
270. Approx. GM, 0·7 feet. Angle 69°.

ABBREVIATIONS.

a	-	Waterplane area in bilged compartment.
A	-	Area of waterplane.
b	-	Breadth of the ship.
B	-	Centre of buoyancy.
d	-	Distance (of shift of weights, etc.)
D	-	Depth, or draft.
F	-	Centre of flotation.
g	-	Centre of gravity of weight or wedge.
G	-	Centre of gravity of ship.
GM	-	Transverse metacentric height.
GM_L	-	Longitudinal metacentric height.
GZ	-	Righting lever.
h	-	Common interval (Simpson's rules, etc.).
hh_1	-	Horizontal displacement of the centres of gravity of wedges.
i	-	Moment of inertia of free surface.
I	-	Transverse moment of inertia of a waterplane.
I_L	-	Longitudinal moment of inertia of a waterplane.
ITM	-	Inch trim moment.
K	-	Denotes the keel.
KB	-	Height of the centre of buoyancy above the keel.
KM	-	Height of the transverse metacentre above the keel.
KM_L	-	Height of the longitudinal metacentre above the keel.
l	-	Length.
L	-	Length.
M	-	Transverse metacentre.
M_L	-	Longitudinal metacentre.
p	-	Permeability of a compartment.
t	-	Trim.
T	-	T.P.I.
TPI	-	Tons per inch immersion.
v	-	Volume of immersed or emerged wedge, or volume of buoyancy lost through bilging a compartment.
V	-	Volume of displacement of a ship.
w	-	Weight shifted, added, etc.
W	-	Displacement of a ship.
φ	-	Angle of heel.
δ	-	Density.
$\triangle$	-	Displacement at summer draft.

FORMULAE.

Angle of Loll.

$$\text{Due to weight out of centre line} - \cot \varphi = \frac{W \times GM}{w \times d}$$

$$\text{Due to negative } GM - \tan \varphi = \sqrt{\frac{2GM}{BM}}$$

Areas of Common Figures.

Circle	Area =	πr^2
Rectangle	,, =	ab
Square	,, =	a^2
Trapezoid	,, =	$\dfrac{h}{2}(a+b)$
Triangle	,, =	$\dfrac{bh}{2}$
,,	,, =	$\dfrac{ab \times \sin \varphi}{2}$
,,	,, =	$\sqrt{s(s-a)(s-b)(s-c)}$

Areas of Waterplanes, etc.

Five-eight rule	Area =	$\dfrac{h}{12}(5x+8y-z)$
Simpson's first rule	,, =	$\dfrac{h}{3}(t+4u+2v+4w+2x+4y+z)$
Simpson's second rule	,, =	$\dfrac{3}{8}h(t+3u+3v+2w+3x+3y+z)$
Trapezoidal rule	,, =	$h\left(\dfrac{u+z}{2}+v+w+x+y\right)$

B—Shift of B.

$$BB_1 = \frac{v \times gg_1}{V}$$

BM.

For all shapes	$BM =$	$\dfrac{I}{V}$
For box shapes only	$BM =$	$\dfrac{b^2}{12D}$
Approximate, for ship shapes	$BM =$	$\dfrac{ab^2}{D}$

ABBREVIATIONS

BM_L.

For all shapes — — — $BM_L = \dfrac{I_L}{V}$

For box shapes — — — $BM_L \ \dfrac{l^2}{12D}$

Circumference of a Circle $= 2\pi r$

Density and Draft.

For box shapes — — $\dfrac{\text{New draft}}{\text{Old draft}} = \dfrac{\text{Old density}}{\text{New density}}$

For ship shapes — — Sinkage $= \dfrac{F(1025 - \delta)}{25}$

For ship shapes — — Sinkage $= \dfrac{W(\delta - \delta_1)}{\delta_1 \times \text{T.P.I.}}$

Fresh water allowance — — — $= \dfrac{\triangle}{40T}$

Draft.

Loading to keep constant aft — $d = \dfrac{\text{I.T.M.} \times L}{\text{T.P.I.} \times l}$

Drydocking.

New $GM =$ Old $GM - \dfrac{P \times KM}{W}$

Where $P =$ Old displacement $-$ new displacement

Or $P = \dfrac{\text{I.T.M.} \times t}{l}$ (approx.)

Dynamical Stability.

(Moseley's formula)—

Dynamical stability $= W\left\{\dfrac{v(gh + g_1h_1)}{V} - BG \times \text{Versine } \varphi\right\}$

Free Surface of Liquids.

Rise of G, due to free surface of any shape — $GG_1 = \dfrac{i}{V}$

Rise of G, due to rectangular free surface — $GG_1 = \dfrac{lb^3}{12V}$

G — Shift of G.

$GG_1 = \dfrac{w \times d}{W}$

GM.

By Inclining Experiment — — $GM = \dfrac{w \times d}{W} \times \dfrac{CF}{FL}$

GZ.

By the Wall Sided Formula $\quad GZ = \sin \varphi \, (GM + \tfrac{1}{2} BM \times \tan^2 \varphi)$

Inch Trim Moment.

For all shapes — — — — $I.T.M. = \dfrac{W \times GM_L}{12L}$

Approximate, for ship shapes — $I.T.M. = \dfrac{30 \cdot 84 \; T^2}{b}$

Approximate, for ship shapes — $I.T.M. = 0 \cdot 000175 \dfrac{A^2}{b}$

Moment of Inertia.

Transversely, for rectangular waterplanes — — $I = \dfrac{lb^3}{12}$

Longitudinally, for rectangular waterplanes — — $I = \dfrac{bl^3}{12}$

Pressure.

At depth D, in salt water — — — $= 64D$ lbs, per sq. ft.
On area A, at depth D, in salt water — $= 64AD$ lbs.

Sinkage.

Due to bilging an empty compartment — $X = \dfrac{v}{A-a}$

Due to bilging a compartment with cargo $\quad X = \dfrac{v\,p}{A-a\,p}$

Due to added weights — — Bodily sinkage $= \dfrac{w}{T.P.I.}$

Statical Stability.

At small angles - Moment of statical stability $= W \times GM \times \sin \varphi$
At any angle   - Moment of statical stability $= W \times GZ$
Attwood's Formula - Moment of S.S. $=$
$$W \left\{ \dfrac{v \times hh_1}{V} - BG \times \sin \varphi \right\}$$

Surface Areas.

Box shape — — — — Area $= 2\,(al + bl + ab)$
Cube — — — — — Area $= 6a^2$
Cylinder — — — — Area $= 2\pi r\,(r + l)$
Sphere — — — — — Area $= 4\pi r^2$

ABBREVIATIONS

Tons per Inch Immersion.

$$\text{T.P.I.} = \frac{A}{420}$$

Trim.

$$\text{Change of trim} = \frac{\text{moment changing trim}}{\text{I.T.M.}}$$

$$\text{Change of trim} = \frac{w \times d}{\text{I.T.M.}}$$

$$\text{Loading to produce desired trim} \quad - \quad d = \frac{\text{I.T.M.} (t \sim t_1)}{w}$$

$$\text{Loading to produce desired trim} \quad - \quad w = \frac{\text{I.T.M.} (t \sim t_1)}{d}$$

Volumes.

Box shape	Volume =	abl
Cube	Volume =	a^3
Cylinder	Volume =	$\pi r^2 l$
Hollow round section	Volume =	$\pi l (R + r)(R - r)$
Hollow sphere	Volume =	$\frac{4\pi}{3}(R^3 - r^3)$
Sphere	Volume =	$\frac{4\pi r^3}{3}$
Wedge, or prism	Volume =	Al

Wetted Surface.

$$\text{Area} = L \{1.7d + (C \times b)\}$$

DEFINITIONS.

Angle of Vanishing Stability.—The angle at which a ship's stability becomes 0: numerically the same as the range of stability.

Centre of Buoyancy.—The geometrical centre of the underwater part of the ship.

Centre of Flotation.—The point about which the ship heels and trims. The centre of gravity of the waterplane.

Centre of Gravity.—The centre of all the weight in a body. The point about which the body would balance.

Deadweight.—The weight of all cargo, stores, bunkers, etc. in a ship.

Displacement.—The actual weight of the ship and all aboard her at any time.

Draft.—The depth of the bottom of the keel below the surface of the water. Measured forward and aft.

Dynamical Stability.—The amount of work done in inclining a ship to any given angle of heel.

Equilibrium.—The state of balance of a body.

Force.—Any push or pull exerted on a body.

Freeboard.—The distance from the deck line to the water.

Height of the Metacentre.—The height of the metacentre above the keel.

Inch Trim Moment.—The moment to change the ship's trim by one inch.

Inertia.—The resistance of a body to motion or to change of motion.

Initial Stability.—The statical stability of a ship at a small angle of heel. Indicated by GM.

Isochronous Rolling.—The name given to the rolling of a ship when the period of each roll is exactly the same.

KG.—The height of the centre of gravity above the keel.

Law of Archimedes.—A body immersed in a liquid appears to suffer a loss in weight equal to the weight of liquid which it displaces. From this law we conclude that a floating body displaces its own weight of water.

Light Displacement.—The displacement of a ship when she is floating at her designed light draft. The weight of the hull, machinery, spare parts and water in the boilers.

DEFINITIONS

Loaded Displacement.—The displacement of a ship when she is floating at her designed summer draft. The light displacement plus the deadweight.

Longitudinal Metacentric Height.—The height of the longitudinal metacentre above the centre of gravity.

Mean Draft.—The mean of the ship's drafts fore and aft.

Metacentre.—The point at which the vertical line through the centre of buoyancy, at a small angle of heel, cuts the ship's centre line. It is only considered to exist for angles of heel of up to about 15°.

Metacentric Height.—The height of the transverse metacentre above the centre of gravity.

Moment.—The attempt of a force to turn a body. It is usually measured by the product of the force and the length of lever.

Moment of Statical Stability.—The moment which will try to return a ship to the upright when she is inclined.

Period of a Ship.—The time taken by a ship to roll from one side to the other and back again.

Period of Waves.—The interval between the passages of any two consecutive wave crests.

Prismatic Bodies.—The term "Prismatic" is used in stability to indicate a body which has a constant cross-section throughout its length. For example in the case of a box-shaped vessel which is on an even keel fore and aft, but heeled, the immersed and emerged wedges are prismatic.

The volume of a prismatic body is the area of its cross-section multiplied by its length.

Range of Stability.—The angular range over which a ship will have positive statical stability. The angle to which the ship could heel before she would tend to capsize.

Reserve Buoyancy.—The volume of a ship's hull between the waterplane and the freeboard deck.

Righting Lever.—The perpendicular distance between the centre of gravity and the vertical line through the centre of buoyancy. The lever on the ends of which the weight of the ship acts to return her to the upright when she is heeled.

Stiff Ship.—A ship which has a large moment of statical stability. One having a large metacentric height, or righting lever.

Synchronism.—Said to occur when the ship's period of roll is the same as that of the waves.

Tender Ship.—A ship which has a small moment of statical stability. One having a small metacentric height, or righting lever.

Tonnages.—Measures of certain spaces in a ship, expressed in terms of 100 cubic feet to the "ton".

Tons per Inch Immersion.—The weight which must be added to a ship in order to cause her to sink one inch bodily.

Trim.—The difference of the drafts forward and aft. The longitudinal equivalent of heel.

INDEX.

A
	PAGE
Abbreviations	147
Added, weights, effect on G	24, 30
Added weights, effect on draft and trim	74
Angle of loll	55, 107
Angle of vanishing stability	99, 152
Approximate formula for I.T.M.	80
Archimedes' Law	2
Areas of common shapes, etc.	9
Areas of waterplanes	10, 105
Attwood's Formula	53

B
B	35, 48, 71, 107
BM	50, 52, 108
BM_L	77, 112
Bale measurement	5
Ballast, ships in	61
Bilging, effect of	76, 85, 120
Bilge keels	89
Block coefficient of fineness	15
Bodies, moment of inertia of	26
Box shapes, B of	35
Box shapes, BM of	50, 108
Box shapes, G of	22
Box shapes, surface areas and volumes	10
Breadth	4
Bulkhead subdivision	94
Bulkheads, longitudinal	93
Bulkheads, pressure on	95
Buoyancy, reserve	93

C
Calculation of angle of loll	55, 109
Calculation of areas and volumes	9
Calculation of areas of waterplanes	10, 105
Calculation of BM	50, 52, 108
Calculation of BM_L	77, 112
Calculation of change of draft	80, 82, 92, 113
Calculation of change of trim	81, 114
Calculation of draft and trim	80, 82, 113
Calculation of draft	6, 92, 104
Calculation of dynamical stability	68
Calculation of effect of density	6, 92, 104
Calculation of free surface effect	56
Calculation of GM	48, 91, 104, 120
Calculation of GM_L	77, 112
Calculation of GZ	53, 54
Calculation of I.T.M.	79, 80, 113
Calculation of increase of draft	85, 120
Calculation of KG	31, 107
Calculation of KM	77
Calculation of KM_L	48, 108
Calculation of moments	20, 106
Calculation of moments of inertia	26
Calculation of moment of statical stability	53, 109
Calculation of pressure on bulkheads	95
Calculation of pressure with depth	1, 104
Calculation of shift of B	36, 107
Calculation of shift of G	24, 30, 107
Calculation of statical stability	53, 109

	PAGE
Calculation of T.P.I.	78, 112
Calculation of volumes of ship shapes	14
Causes of instability	62
Centre line, moment of inertia about	28
Centre of buoyancy	35, 48, 71, 107
Centre of flotation	35, 71
Centre of gravity	21, 30, 44, 71
Centre of gravity, shift of	24, 30, 107
Change of draft with change of trim	72, 80, 113
Change of mean draft	72, 113, 117
Circle, area and circumference	9
Circle, centre of gravity of	22
Coefficients of fineness	15
Combinations of moments	20
Common interval	11
"Conditions"	96
Continuous longitudinal bulkheads	93
Crank ships	46, 62
Critical period	90
Cross Curves	100, 146
Cube, surface area and volume	9
Cures for heavy rolling	89
Cures for instability or tenderness	62
Curve of floodable lengths	96
Curves of displacement	96
Curves of statical stability	44, 67, 99
Cylinder, surface area and volume	10

D
Deadweight	5
Deadweight scale	98
Decks	5
Deck line	7
Deck cargoes	64
Deep tanks	33, 61, 65
Definitions	152
Density	1
Density effects of	4, 6, 47, 57, 92, 104
Depth of ships	4
Depth, effect on pressure	1
Derivation of fresh water allowance	93
Derricks and weights lifted	33
Desired trim, to produce	75, 83, 119
Dimensions	4
Displacement	5
Displacement, coefficient of	16
Displacement curves	96
Divided tanks and free surface	47, 58
Double bottom tanks	33, 61
Draft	6, 92, 104
Draft, effect of change of trim	72, 80, 113
Draft, effect of density	6, 92, 104
Draft, effect of weights	74, 75, 114
Draft, increase due to bilging	76, 120
Draft, to keep constant aft	75, 84, 119
Drydocking	90, 120
Dynamical stability	67

E
Emerged wedge	35
Emptying tanks, free surface effect	59, 112
Equilibrium	29, 39, 42

155

F

	PAGE
Factors affecting statical stability	44
F	35, 71
Filling of tanks	56, 61, 62
Fineness, coefficients of	15
Five-eight rule	14
Floating bodies	4
Floodable lengths	94
Forces	18
Formation of waves	86
Form of ship, effect on stability	44
Formulae—summary	148
Freeboard	6, 44, 62
Freeboard deck	5
Free surface of liquids	46, 56, 65, 111
Fresh water allowance	6, 93

G

G	30, 44, 71
GM	41, 48, 60, 65, 99, 104, 111
GM_L	42, 71, 77, 112
CZ	41, 43, 54
Grain measurement	5
Gross tonnage	5
Grounding	92

H

Half-ordinates	10
Heavy rolling, cures for	89
Height of B	35
Height of G	30
Height of the metacentre	41
Hollow round sections	10
Hollow sphere	10
Hydrostatic curves	96

I

Inclining experiment	48, 108
Increase of draught due to bilging	76, 85, 120
Increase of draught due to trim	72, 113
Increase of draught due to weights loaded	72, 74, 112, 114
Immersed wedge	35
Inch trim moment	71, 79, 113
Inertia	26
Inertia, moment of	26, 46, 50
Information supplied to ships	96
Initial stability	43
Instability	62, 90
Isochronous rolling	87
Interval, common	10

J

Jettisoning cargo	62

K

KB	35, 48
KG	30
KM	41
KM_L	77

L

Large weights loaded	82, 117
Law of Archimedes	2
Length	4
Light KG	30

	PAGE
Liquids, free surface of	46, 56, 65, 111
List	46, 55, 109
Loading a weight to produce a desired Draft Aft	84
Loading to produce desired trim	75, 83, 119
Loading to keep constant draft	75, 84, 119
Loadlines	7
Loll	46, 55, 109
Longitudinal BM	77, 112
Longitudinal bulkheads	93
Longitudinal effect of weights shifted	73, 81
Longitudinal metacentre	42, 71, 77
Longitudinal metacentric height	42, 71, 77, 112
Longitudinal position of B	35, 71
Longitudinal position of G	22, 30, 71
Longitudinal stability	71, 77
Lumber load lines	8

M

M	41, 50, 108
M_L	42, 71, 77, 112
Margin line	94
Mean draft, effect of trim	72
Measurement, grain and bale	5
Metacentre	41, 50, 108
Metacentric diagram	98
Metacentric height	41, 48, 60, 65, 108, 111
Midships section coefficient	15
Miscellaneous matters	90
Moderate weights loaded	74, 82, 115
Moment	19, 106
Moment of inertia	26, 46, 50
Moment of statical stability	43, 53, 109
Moment to change trim one inch	71, 79, 113
Moseley's formula	69
Motion of waves	86
Multipliers	13

N

Negative GM	41, 44, 55, 62
Neutral equilibrium	29, 42
Nett tonnage	5
Non-continuous longitudinal bulkheads	94

O

Oil tankers	66
Ordinates	11, 14

P

Parallelogram of forces	19
Partial longitudinal bulkheads	94
Period of ships	87
Period of waves	87
Permeability	76
Placing of weights	60
Plimsoll mark	7
Position of centre of gravity	21, 31
Positive GM	40
Practical tranverse stability	60
Pressing up tanks	95
Pressure, increase with depth	1
Pressure on bulkheads	95
Pressure on tank-tops	95
Prisms	10
Prismatic coefficient of fineness	16
Prismatic wedges, G of	24

INDEX

	PAGE
Pro-metacentre	41
Problems on angles of loll	166
Problems on areas and volumes	123
Problems on areas of waterplanes	126
Problems on BM	133
Problems on BM_L	136
Problems on change of draft	137
Problems on change of trim	138
Problems on change of draft and trim	139
Problems on the deadweight scale	143
Problems on draft	123
Problems on drydocking	146
Problems on effect of density	122, 123
Problems on free surface effect	136
Problems on GM	133
Problems on GM_L	136
Problems on I.T M.	137
Problems on increase of draft	141
Problems on KG	131
Problems on KM	133
Problems on KM_L	134
Problems on metacentric diagrams	145
Problems on moments	128
Problems on moment of inertia	129
Problems on moment of statical stability	134
Problems on pressure with depths	122
Problems on shift of B	132
Problems on shift of G	129, 130
Problems on stability curves	141
Problems on T.P.I.	137
Problems on volumes of ship shapes	127

R

Radius of gyration	26
Range of stability	43, 64, 99, 153
Real centre of gravity	32
Rectangles	9, 22, 28
Rectangular free surfaces	57
Removed weights	25, 31, 75
Reserve buoyancy	93
Resistance to rolling	88
Resultant force	18
Righting lever	41, 43, 54
Rise of G due to free surface	46, 56, 65, 111
Risks in drydocking	90
Rolling	61, 65, 90

S

Scales	98
Sharp-ended waterplanes	14
Sheer	94
Shifting weights, effect on G	25, 30, 107
Shifting weights, longitudinal effect	73, 81, 114
Shift of B	36, 107
Shift of G	24, 30, 107
Ship dimensions	4
Ship sections, area of	10
Ship shapes, centre of buoyancy of	35
Ship shapes, BM of	52, 108
Ship shapes, centre of gravity of	30
Ships in ballast	61
Ships, period of	87
Ship tonnages	5
Simpson's First Rule	12
Simpson's Second Rule	13
Simpson's Multipliers	13

	PAGE
Sinkage due to bilging	76, 85, 120
Slack tanks	46, 56, 66, 111
Sounding pipes	95
Specific gravity	1
Spheres	10
Squares	9
Stability curves and scales	96
Stable equilibrium	29, 42
Statical stability	43, 48, 53, 60, 99, 109
Statutory freeboard	6
Stiff ships	46, 61
Summary	147
Surface areas	9
Synchronism	87

T

Tanks	33, 46, 56, 61, 65
Tender ships	46, 62, 95
Timber deck cargoes	64
Timber load lines	8
Tipping centre	71
Tonnage deck	5
Tonnages	5
Tons per inch immersion	72, 78, 113
Transverse bulkheads	94
Transverse stability	35, 39, 43, 48, 60, 67
Trapezium	9, 22
Trapezoid	9
Trapezoidal Rule	11
Triangles	9, 22
Trim	71
Trim, effect of density	92
Trim, loading to produce desired	75, 83, 119
Trochoidal theory	86

U

Under deck tonnage	5
Unresisted rolling	88
Unstable equilibrium	29, 42
Unstable ships	42, 62
Unsuitable numbers of ordinates	14

V

Virtual centre of gravity	32
Volumes	9, 14
Vanishing stability, angle of	99, 152

W

Wall sided formula	54
Water	1
Water ballast	61
Water in pipes	95
Waterplane coefficient of fineness	15
Waterplanes	10, 22, 28, 105
Watertight longitudinal bulkheads	93
Wave formation	86
Wedges	9, 24
Wedges, immersed and emerged	35
Weights loaded	30, 46, 55, 74, 82, 107, 114
Weights removed	30, 46, 55, 74, 82, 107, 114
Weights shifted	30, 46, 55, 74, 82, 107, 114
Wetted surface	16
Winging-out weights	61
Work	67
Worked examples	104

DEADWEIGHT SCALE

DEADWEIGHT TONS	DRAFT FEET	TPI	LTM	KM	KB

LIGHT KG = 23.18 FEET

DEADWEIGHT TONS	DRAFT FEET	TPI	LTM	KM	KB
7000	25		755	23.43	13.80
	10	41.35		29.48 / 23.32	9.4 / 13.51
	24	39.00	975	28.25 / 23.24	9.25 / 13.26
	11	41.14	750	27.85 / 23.18	9.50 / 13.00
	23	39.58		27.22 / 23.13	9.57 / 12.74
6000	12	40.92	725	26.94 / 23.08	9.17 / 12.47
1000	22	39.12		26.20 / 23.05	7.01 / 12.20
	13	40.67	800	25.17 / 23.03	7.28 / 12.03
	21	39.88		25.35 / 23.01	7.55 / 11.68
5000	14	40.39	852	24.83 / 23.00	7.81 / 11.49
2000	20	38.17	925	24.45 / 23.10	8.08 / 11.12
	15	40.10		24.40 / 23.02	8.31 / 10.85
	19	38.65	850	24.18 / 23.05	8.55 / 10.57
	16	39.78		23.85 / 23.11	8.83 / 10.30
3000	18	39.01	900	23.70	9.21
	17	39.40	875	23.52	9.48